Most affect.

Anner.

The Sun Always Breaks Through

The Sun Always Breaks Through

Autobiography

Anneke Evans

Quellin Press

Date of Publication:
May 2000

Published by:
Quellin Press

© Copyright 2000 Anneke Evans

Printed by:
ProPrint
Riverside Cottage
Great North Road
Stibbington
Peterborough PE8 6LR

ISBN: 0 9538178 0 6

A CIP record for this book is available from the British Library

CONTENTS

Introduction   1
Preface   2

Part One: Belgium
Chapter 1: My Dawn   4
Chapter 2: War!   72
Chapter 3: The Resistance   81
Chapter 4: Liberation   123
Chapter 5: Lieutenant Evans   130
Chapter 6: Titch   147
Chapter 7: 'War' Bride!   168

Part Two: England   171
Chapter 8: Adaptation: A New Life   176
Chapter 9: Journalism   199
Chapter 10: House Owners Again   213
Chapter 11: Spilly's Happiness   228
Chapter 12: Helping Nature   231
Chapter 13: Covering A Royal Visit   234
Chapter 14: Part Time Courier   239
Chapter 15: Farewell Titch   246
Chapter 16: Holiday Myths   247
Chapter 17: The Butcher Experiment   254
Chapter 18: My First Mini   259
Chapter 19: End Of A Brave Jew   265
Chapter 20: BBC Pebble Mill Advisory Council   267
Chapter 21: As Time Goes By . . .   272
Chapter 22: The Umbilical Cord Severed   278
Chapter 23: National Exhibition Centre   294
Chapter 24: 'Custer's Last Stand'?   298
Chapter 25: America   301
Chapter 26: My Dusk   310
Appendix   319
Letter from Colonel Louette   324

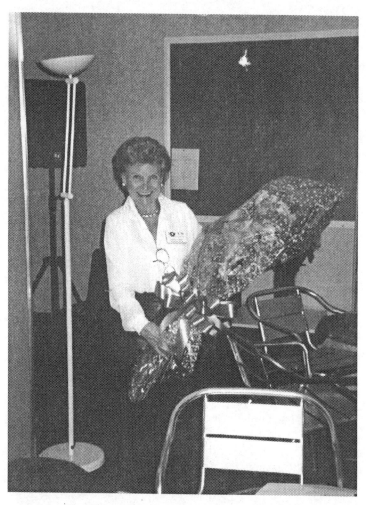

Anneke Evans in 1999, with the bouquet presented to her by Mary Walker at the National Exhibition Centre, Birmingham to mark her 77th birthday and 23 years working there as an interpreter at international exhibitions.

INTRODUCTION

Was born Antwerp, Belgium 27.2.1922
Married 21.12.1948
Settled in England 4.1.1949

Just as I used to listen to my Grandma as a child, fascinated by her stories of 'the good old days' and WW1 events etc, so I found myself narrating my own stories to my many friends in Belgium as well as in England where I spent most of my life.

This life was never left on automatic pilot which is quite obvious from my autobiography, which I found time to write only in the Autumn of my life.

I accomplished this first in Flemish and the result was published by a Publisher in Ypres in the Armistice month of November 1998.

I translated it into English and hope that many of you will read it as from now . . .

My heartfelt thanks to all my friends for their unwavering faith in me and their longstanding friendship and devotion.

My love to Judy Maguire, my Director and dear friend of the Judy Gould Agency, who also saved my sanity the year of my darling husband's death.

To the Directors and Staff of the Organising Bodies at the various International Exhibitions at the NEC I was able to serve, and last but not least to dear Mary Walker, most efficient organiser, kindest and most generous of souls, who introduced me to my hardworking and devoted consultant, John Gammons.

Anneke, Solihull 1999

PREFACE

It was with profound trepidation that I practically tiptoed into the Foyer of the Palace Hotel in Brussels. The year 1943 was gradually coming to its end. The German sentry carefully perused my letter of introduction, more of a summons really, and told me to accompany him to the handsomely appointed room where the Court Martial was to be held and which, in normal times, would have served as the restaurant.

My heart was beating like a steam hammer and I was scarcely aware of the repetitious clank of the soldier's boots on the floor, spasmodically interrupted by the odd stretch of carpeting which, by virtue of its wear and tear, had escaped from the 'art-collecting' zeal of the occupying enemy. We climbed the wide stairs to the first floor. (Long afterwards I could neither recall the decor in the form of wall coverings, panelling, chandeliers, nor the multitude of prints, all of which under normal circumstances I would have been able to vividly describe). I felt like a zombie and must have acted as one as the sentry kept looking back at me.

All of a sudden we came to an abrupt halt in front of an ornately carved doorway flanked by two armed soldiers who scarcely gave us a look. After a sharp rap, the door was flung wide open and I entered somewhat hesitantly. My mouth became cork-dry, I could hardly control my shivering and my skin was suddenly covered in goose pimples. I was, however, politely led to the 'witness box'. The members of the Tribunal were seated behind a long table and were obviously older officers of very high rank; their uniformed breasts richly adorned with multi-coloured ribbons; the lapels of their jackets embroidered with silver or gold filigree. This was indeed the panoply of military power!

Two SS Officers, clad entirely in black, were the only interruption amongst the general 'feldgrau'. Their Iron Crosses dangled from red-white-black silk ribbon around their necks. They looked formidable. I became faintly aware of a hubbub of voices, the rustling of papers and my thoughts, already caught in a maelstrom of horror visions, furtively recalled the immediate past. Would this be the end of my relative freedom? Would I be able to save the life of a Belgian, a fellow-man, (See page 119) and because of my testimony tip the balance to the inexorable demise of another, albeit an enemy? Although by then the latter was already a foregone conclusion in this, even in accordance with military procedures so impressive a trial, I would afterwards not exactly keep thumping my breast in mea-culpa. In my conscience, however, I remained ill at ease throughout the ensuing years of my life and wish I could have avoided this irreversible deed; this slur on my Christian inspired and, otherwise, unimpaired existence!

As with a drowning person, my brain filmed the episodes which formed my past and so I feel I should start my story from the very beginning, from the foetus as it were, to the child with the influences that ultimately decided the character and gave form to the adult.

PART 1: BELGIUM

Chapter One

My Dawn

Had my cradle been deposited twenty metres further forward, it would have been submerged in the water of the River Scheldt flowing past Antwerp.

As I greedily sucked at my Glaxo bottle (according to the doctor, my ma's breasts were 'fleshy' rather than the mini-dairy normally associated with childbearing) my little ears already filled with the diverse but familiar noises abounding in most pre-war ports. And as I grew up I inhaled the different smells emanating from the river, a mish-mash of the strangest aromas arising from the holds of the ships and the discharged goods arriving from all parts of the world.

It was during a cold February day 'Spilly' was liberated from her burden. This being an essentially Flemish colloquialism for giving birth. I often asked myself why this specific expression was ever chosen. In fact, as I was warmly ensconced in her womb I caused no trouble to the carrier except for the occasional kick just to let her know I meant it.

It was this 'liberation', however, so very primitive in contrast to the norm these days which caused her the cruellest physical pains as I was literally pulled into the world by means of 'instruments'. Three times these slipped from the slimy babyhead and I shot like a catapult back up into that warm cocoon. No wonder that I hate the winter! When at last I slithered outside for good and my backside received the customary slaps, I opened my throat full throttle and it has since been progressively more difficult to shut me up!

Like every mother, Spilly had dreamt of a child like a doll, in her case with blonde curly hair, big blue eyes and a mouth like a rosebud. Poor wretch!

The instruments had knocked me about so much that the little heap of human misery pushed into her arms sported deep splits in the forehead and at the ears, had a face like a skinned rabbit full of wrinkles due to constant crying for I was all too soon very hungry, and with little eyes such as normally adorned the heads of dead fish lying on the marble slabs of the fishmonger's.

Admittedly, the mouth was small but the sound trumpeting out of it resembled that of a baritone with a chest infection, what the French call a 'bass crevé'. As far as the blonde curly locks were concerned, suffice it to say, my scalp was in competition with my buttocks . . .

Had this birth taken place in a hospital instead of on the wooden top of her own kitchen table, Spilly would have flatly refused me, thinking someone had made a mistake.

Years later, as we both laughed at funny memories and experiences she joked, in her own juicy vernacular, that she first thought they had thrown the baby away and kept the afterbirth . . . During my early years, when I eagerly questioned her as to whether I, as the ugly duckling, would grow into a beautiful swan, her laconic answer left me with little illusion: 'No child, you'll never be beautiful but . . . you're very friendly!'

The evening prior to my birth Spilly danced through half the night as though her appointment with the midwife was more or less abstract. Our little flat - nowadays it is called an apartment - was situated on the third floor of 5 Quay Ortelius, right opposite Hangar No. 26 where the ships of The Canadian Pacific Railway Shipping Co regularly docked, followed by many others of English nationality - for the most part cargo carrying ships, although some were also equipped with passenger accommodation.

Listening to the tales of the older generations, the Port of Antwerp became internationally known and increasingly popular soon after the First World War.

Today we refer to annual statistics but during my early youth it seemed as though a never ending number of ships of all nationalities came steaming along to berth at Antwerp and I grew up amongst the familiar sight of white, yellow and black faces, not to mention strange garb. The babble of foreign languages reverberated in my ears and I assimilated it all together with the daily happenings during my young formative years.

I still remember vividly the hundreds of immigrants embarking via the ships of The Red Star Line to a new future on the opposite side of the globe in America or Canada. They were for the greater part Poles or Russians, the women dressed in sombre, long and old-fashioned clothing with a shawl covering their hair, the majority of the older men bearded and with dark and deep-set eyes, continuously and furtively looking around them.

I did not fully understand then but now looking back I realise that I sometimes detected hope in those eyes yet mostly consternation, wistfulness, the majority being fugitive Jews, victims of the merciless pogroms occurring with monotonous regularity from the depths of the Russian steppes over the Balkan countries to Germany and beyond . . .

The café, The Scheldt, was the name of the pub situated at street-level of our building. Its English name (in Flemish it would have been De Schelde) was prominently displayed in white embossed print on the top of one of its windows and the clientèle consisted exclusively of British ships' officers as The Scheldt had acquired a pleasant notoriety with the British Shipping Companies.

The pub blossomed like a rose between thorns, surrounded as it was by some 'cabardouches', the expression in the

Antwerpian slang for those establishments where, politely expressed, one was not too particular about the morals of the serving wenches. These, however, thrived more in the adjacent and notorious alleys that adorn the dock areas of most international ports.

The family Jacobs

Ma and Pa Jacobs in the Autumn of their lives

The Scheldt offered a 'home from home' to the sort of seafarer longing for a tasty imported English beer, without being interrupted by the attentions of ladies of doubtful mien. There he could even obtain his favourite brand of whisky of real Scottish origin, poured from 'under the bar counter', for avoiding the payment of a duty on spirits levied to pubs and drinking clubs was *the* sport par excellence as far as the Antwerpian landlord was concerned! Even the occasional bottle of champagne was cracked (no less than Moêt & Chandon, Veuve Clicquot or Piper Heidsieck) for celebration purposes even if it was simply the fact that the sailor stood on dry land. 'Ma Jacobs' was the landlady, a distinguished looking woman with a beautiful crop of naturally wavy hair which many years later resembled spun silver. She was assisted by her daughter, Lucy, and a 'decent' barmaid. In fact, as soon as any bar personnel were recruited it was made abundantly clear that 'marching' was not tolerated even after serving hours. Marching being the expression in those circles for the oldest profession in the world. Ma Jacobs also had two sons, the elder married, the youngest in the Army for his National Service. Pa Jacobs enjoyed a high position as recruiting officer for dock workers at the port.

Little me, as usual, in Ma Jacobs' arms.

When it became obvious, after a certain time, that Spilly, the tenant of the 'third floor flat with attic' could be listed under the category of 'decent ladies', and lived a somewhat lonely life as the wife of a seafaring man absent for intervals of up to two months, she was encouraged by Ma Jacobs to assist behind the bar.

It was during that particular period that the three of us become known as 'Spil' or thereabouts. The British friends thought our surname 'Spillemaeckers' was too much of a mouthful and baptised our Ma 'Spilly' and Pa, after he made their acquaintance when ashore from one of his sea voyages, as 'Spil'. I became 'Spilleke' which name was soon to be adopted by my school friends. Years later, for some unexplained reason, my intimate friends in Belgium called *me* Spilly. Just to demonstrate how one can juggle with names, my very good friend in Antwerp, Margie, calls me Titch as did the Army officers I later befriended after the liberation of Antwerp. My birth certificate features as my Christian name Angelica (you know, like the green candied stuff but don't let that fool anyone!). My husband-to-be later called me Anne as he too found Angelica too long, saying that by the time he had pronounced it the urgency would be gone . . . and when he subsequently learnt that everything small in Flemish acquires a 'ke' at the end, promptly called me Anneke . . . which I am called to this day by all my English friends. So, what's in a name?

In the Nineteen Twenties, before the world depression set in, the Port of Antwerp resembled a veritable hive with coming and going and constant noise. Flat, open and heavy freight wagons pulled by tractors, loaded to the hilt with long iron or steel laths, flat or U-formed, and bars of various diameters, clattered day in, day out, over the rough cobblestones; their iron wheels spitting fire whenever they hit an uneven cobblestone. Come summer, come winter, the drivers sat on an open saddle-throne, bedecked in dark blue thick reefer jackets and caps. How their intestinal condition must have looked under X-rays after years of service at the port is mind-boggling!

One of the most painful memories of my early years was undoubtedly the death of a magnificent Borzoi, a Russian greyhound. He was the pride of his owner who, together with his brother, kept a garage in one of the more infamous adjoining alleys especially known for their multiple 'window box' façades displaying ladies of easy virtue in various modes of undress. The two brothers regularly ferried captains, first officers, ships' doctors, chief and second engineers and chief pursers 'to and fro' from the Scheldt to their ship that, although not having berthed a long way off, nevertheless was too distant for them to cover on foot, even when not exactly tight as a newt, they were just happily tipsy. You know how it is when a seaman thoroughly enjoys himself, his buttocks seem to adhere to the bar stool! Adrian was inseparable from his dog whom he lovingly and meticulously groomed. The dog's shiny pelt, in shades of light beige with a hint of chocolate brown, portrayed the excellent health of the animal. One day, when going for their regular walk, while Adrian had the dog on a leash, a strange dog started playfully darting around the Borzoi. All of a sudden the latter pulled himself free from his leash and ran after the other four footer whom, in the meantime, had stormed across the main road and dived under a heavily laden iron wagon, reappearing on the other side of it. Adrian's dog followed suit. Unfortunately his paws were too high and could not bend down sufficiently low and the heavy wagon broke his spine. By the time that we horrified spectators had run across the road, the dog was already dying on the lap of his master who, in the meantime, had rushed across like an arrow out of a bow and knelt by his canine friend. The look in the eyes of man and animal I shall never forget, nor the first time that I saw a mature man cry like a child.

Apart from the heavy flat carts and wagons filled to the brim with bales of cotton, logs and vats, sacks of all sorts of dried animal feed or chemical products, the trams clanged by in a continuous tumult from dawn to late night; a veritable cauldron of sound to which our ears nevertheless had become immune.

It was not just the tractors that were pulling the heavy stuff. Who could possibly forget the famous heavy work-horses with their regular, almost angry, clip-clop step on the rough cobblestones and the sparks that sprang from under their horseshoes when the iron nails hit the granite of the street stone. Their long manes fluttered like spun silver in the wind or had been neatly tied with colourful ribbons. Their sweaty hide shone like a mirror and the brewers' carts of the Wielemans Brewery, the only suppliers of Belgian beer to The Scheldt and also pulled by two such heavy horses, could never pass this pub, delivering or not. Sure enough a small bundle of humanity was seen stamping her foot until Spilly brought some sugar, an apple or a carrot for Pete or Jock and these two quadrupeds were all too soon aware from where the wind blew . . . !

As far as I'm concerned that was also the epoch of the 'heavy' docker who, armed with muscles like garden hoses, biceps like ante-natal breasts and the appropriate iron hook in a fist like a steam hammer, disembowelled the ships' holds from their cargo and carried the heavy sacks on his back, either to the appointed storage space or loading wagon, the nape of his neck and shoulders covered by an empty jute sack. To me he was the 'Beau Geste' of the Antwerpian Port. They were known as 'the men of the basseng'; this being a bastardised version of the French word Bassin (dock) and they were the salt of the earth, with a sense of humour and racy expressions, only surviving today in the vocabulary of the older, dyed-in-the-wool Antwerpian or to give him his nickname 'Sinjoor' (an adaptation of the Spanish Señor dating back to the Spanish occupation of the Netherlands during the Middle Ages).

Spil, as Chief Engineer during one of his many voyages to the Belgian Congo

In my childhood I had easy access to the Port even during loading or discharging of the ships, partly because I lived opposite the berthing quays and also by virtue of there not being any necessity those days for vigilant control. Mainly though through Spil, my Pa. He was regularly employed as Chief Engineer on one or other 'Congo-boat' for the well-known Shipping Company Agence (and Compagnie) Maritime Belge with headquarters in Antwerp's centre and he regularly sailed between this Port, the Belgian Congo (now Zaire) and West African Ports, sometimes even to South America. Whenever his ship docked I hurried along, for in his cabin I could invariably find something typically African for me, not always practical I must confess.

Once he brought me a young ant-eater but kept it in the pocket of his uniform. 'Just feel what I have for you, my child' he said while his eyes shone mischievously behind his glasses. 'Child' put her hand into the pocket indicated, felt something hairy and soft, nearly wet her pants in terror and . . . . . squeezed the little animal to death in panic. Another time he brought me a chameleon, one of Mother Nature's most eccentric creations of the lizard kind. Whatever it was placed upon, be it pink or yellow, it gradually took on the colour of the object on which it rested. Indeed one of the most interesting and efficient camouflages in the jungle. After a few days of amusement, it was presented to the Antwerp Zoo; followed, after a further voyage, by 'Little Josephine'. This was a young chimpanzee, a darling of a monkey that I found in a cardboard box in the cabin near Spil's bunk. It rocked constantly to and fro, pointed at times a crooked little finger forward as though there was something to show and uttered the same, monotonous sound, a short 'ou' with a kind of semi-cough, difficult to emulate. I was immediately besotted with her; she with Spil but . . . Spilly found Josephineke's body odour a little strong for a tap-room so . . . off she moved to the Zoo.

After the animals came the beans and seeds of one or other exotic African plant which usually found their way to the son of one of my teachers who specialised in African fauna and flora. My most cherished memories of Spil's voyages were undoubtedly the best of Congolese fruits, then unknown in our part of Europe, nowadays imported from Africa as well as Mexico and other parts of the globe where the sun unceasingly kisses the earth. Where other children nibbled at apples, I enjoyed mangoes, an oval fruit in warm hues of yellow to orange/pink, with a taste rather difficult to describe; a cross between a ripe melon and a banana . . . no first prize for contradictions!

This easy access to the various berthing quays inspired in me, from the earliest years, a love for all ports and my veneration and respect for the dock worker of that time. To see them bent under sacks of sugar and coal weighing 100kg of saltpetre which filled the air with a strange smell, coupled with less pleasant aromas like lugano (the fertiliser from bird droppings imported from South America and later discharged only in the Port of Rotterdam), filled my little heart and still forming brain with awe.

As in all ports, small docking areas were jotted about with stone steps leading from the river to the quay where rowing boats occasionally delivered crews from the dredgers. The water around such places swarmed with flotsam, pieces of old wood, fruit skins, etc, slowly wriggling in the tide and small oil slicks which formed a strange smelling mass in the corners. In my childlike imagination it was all so adventurous; so undeniably foreign, and, yet, so familiar. The dredgers formed another aspect of the daily Scheldt scene. The endless monotony of the metal scoops, deeply clawing the mud out of the riverbed was almost soporific providing, of course, one was far enough distanced not to be deafened by the mechanical clatter. These colossi were impressive in every way as the scoops with their contents rose out of the Scheldtwater like the dark grey ski-chairs propelling their human loads to the top of the Alps in the snow-covered mountains. Resembling automated mini-motor bodies, these scoops disposed of their mud loads in their deep holds on the way down.

Whilst complying with his tasks abroad during his voyages and even in the ports of destination, not a drop of alcohol passed Spil's lips.

The black Congolese stokers, forming the majority of his crew in the engine room, held him in high respect for 'the Chief' never stood for manhandling any of them, something at times sadly overlooked by the other white officers. Whenever they had a problem, the Chief would mostly find a solution. If they did something wrong, he would patiently show them or explain. In the Port of Antwerp for that matter, they had the facility of their own Seamen's Home and Club in an antique building situated opposite The Steen, one of Antwerp's oldest castles on the edge of the river and very much part of the city's history and folklore.

Unmistakable large white lettering on top of this building proclaimed the Club's existence and could be seen from afar especially during the last stages of a voyage up-river: 'NDAKO YA BISO' (In Congolese, House for Seamen). Antwerpian sailors and dockers soon rechristened it in their own crude idiom 'Kakken en Pissen' - the translation of which seems unnecessary.

The moment Spil's soles touched Antwerpian dry land however, we seldom saw him sober! Unfortunately he could be categorised as a 'political drinker', argumentative, sometimes aggressive; never as far as I was concerned though. I was the apple of his eye and he . . . sometimes the cloud

15

above my little head. All too often there were times I woke up in the night to the sound of angry voices penetrating the walls of my bedroom on the third floor, under the attic, when Spil and Spilly were engaged in a flaming row. I would sleepily creep downstairs as children hate arguments between their parents. When they caught sight of my alarmed face, the familial storm abated but I remained until Spil retired.

Looking back on that period, strengthened by the understanding that maturity brings, I suppose that Spil was jealous of those well-mannered, friendly Britons who frequented The Scheldt as their welcoming base practically day and night and whom Spilly regaled with her songs. She had a beautiful soprano voice albeit untrained and knew many English and Irish ballads. She also sometimes accepted an invitation to dance to the tunes of our 'electric-music rolls' piano or when one of the more gifted customers among them played it himself. My parents could never go out together during his ashore periods as Spilly could not be missed.

With the cunning of a child's detection sense, I had 'discovered' Pa's habitual haunts and if he failed to put in an appearance in time to take me to the pictures as promised - those days the last of the 'silent' films were still in evidence - I fetched him out of these with the greatest of ease. I would simply put my head inside the doorway and Spil came docilely away although I sometimes regrettably came to the conclusion that his state of inebriation shattered any hope of a visit to the cinema.

I was an early cinema enthusiast. It was the end of the 'silent' film era and my scrapbook was full of the photos of the then famous Hollywood stars, most of them now resting on the stage of eternity. In winter, returning from a performance, we would run home as fast as we could to warm our numbed feet, for those days the only heating in the theatres came from our own breath! I always kept my hand in

Spil's pocket and, although he did not possess a sixth sense, nevertheless I clearly remember his prediction turned into fact today: 'Perhaps one day we will be able to see films in our own living room, cosily installed near the fire,' he said.

At the corner of Zirk and Lange Doornikstreets, one of the private houses was inhabited by an old couple royally supplementing their income by secretly serving gin. With her own quick wit, Spilly had baptised the establishment 'Chez the old farts' and I hated having to find Spil at those premises for it was above all the Dutch gin which created in him a kind of rebellion hostile to his generally good-natured character and caused that lamentable self-pity of the drunk. The fact remains that the Excise and Tax officers were never remotely aware of the lucrative side earnings of the old dears!

For me and my playmates of the neighbourhood, the street was our playground and our terrain covered the Ortelius and Koolkaai, St Paulusplaats and St Pietersvliet, all in the very heart of the Quays area which runs along the entire length of the River Scheldt from North to South. The Customs House, one of the most outstanding buildings of Old Antwerp, now demolished by the 'modern school' of planners and replaced by the umpteenth example of unimaginative architecture (best to be compared to Prince Charles' 'carbuncle' description) lent its granite steps for our throne whilst during rainy weather we sheltered under the overhanging part of its sculptured façade.

We romped in the street during the holidays and in the summer after school hours until dusk. We played hopscotch on the pavement on the squares formed with white chalk. Above all, though, I loved trotting along, mostly on my scooter, along the quays, returning via the streets and alleys beyond, getting to know the most intimate spots of that old part of the Port with its unexpected twists and turns; its breathtaking sculptures and religious statuettes neatly built against the corners of some of the houses be they large or small. We called these scooters 'trotinettes' and the then up-to-date version was one with a fairly wide pedestal board on which to rest the foot and balloon tyres. One could place a shopping bag on the pedestal part as well as one's foot and I would pedal to my heart's content. I wish from the bottom of my heart that I had one now - wouldn't it make shopping so much more comfortable qua parking? Spil had saved special tokens from tobacco packets as in those days on the continent the majority of men rolled their own cigarettes. As some of his friends and colleagues smoked the same brand, they all contributed and so we arrived at the required number of tokens and, with the addition of a small cash amount, we were able to acquire this longed for toy.

On rainy days I was allowed to bring my friends to play in the large private entrance to the apartments above the pub. The door gave easy access to the kitchen beyond where Spilly's mother reigned supreme. She always had a large cooking pot full of 'hutsepot', a thick broth with chunks of meat and about five different vegetables from an old Flemish recipe, or beef stews made with beer, cauldrons of home-made soups, simmering all day on the Küppersbusch, a large kitchen range of German manufacture, fired by anthracite, which never went out during the winter months.

You see, in the meantime, something had changed in our lifestyle. Ma Jacobs had decided to sell The Scheldt pub and to open an establishment at the Oude Leuwenrui nearby and which was to be known, sumptuously, as 'a Brasserie'. Talk about 'a step up the society ladder'! (Actually it was there that her daughter Lucy met her intended whom she married, a British Chief Engineer on the Fyffe banana boats. Later on, during the first days of war, she emigrated to England).

It was obvious that the best buyer for Ma Jacobs's business was Spilly. However, those days there was an acute shortage of the readies . . . In spite of this, Ma Jacobs decided to give her a chance and Spilly, after much deliberation, decided to buy it lock, stock and barrel 'on the never never' as it was then called. Two years later, bearing in mind she saw little of her bed as the place became more famous, she was able to settle the debt in full!

Those large cauldrons and cooking pots full to the brim with food giving off the most tantalising aromas as they simmered on the Küppersbusch, formed the basis of Spilly's diplomacy. Indeed, to the customers, Grandma's kitchen was the eternal Grotto of Santa. When hungry they made their way to what they had discovered in the meantime as a veritable culinary Nirvana, presented to them free of charge with the compliments of the management . . . throwing out a sprat to catch a mackerel! Naturally, as long as they remained in situ, they ordered drinks! In any case, the old Flemish burgher's cuisine was a real revelation for the British and Canadian visitors as its success was due to dishes carefully cooked with the emphasis on taste. No wonder there was never a demand for bottles of the many piquant sauces which were always in evidence on the tables of their own homes and restaurants.

When I was four years old I was taken to nursery school, about three minutes walk from our home, in order to give my grandmother some respite during school time in the execution of her numerous tasks. She too had moved in the meantime and now lived on the second floor of our building. I took sandwiches or little rolls which were placed in a special metal and gaily painted container hanging by a silken cord from my neck. Even today I can remember the metallic smell when I opened the tin, as well as the taste of the marvellous soup we were daily served for lunch except Fridays when it was porridge made with buttermilk. These soups were based on broiler chicken stock or vegetable broth with minced beef. The cook thickened these with rice. I will never forget those marvellous soups nor the porridge . . . Later on, Spilly would prepare buttermilk porridge with pearled barley and sweeten it with black treacle, which combination seems to have vanished from our culinary plateau. What I wouldn't give now for a plate of this ambrosia!

My grandma was a religious person and it seemed to follow that I, like her own daughter, would be raised in the Christian faith. I was baptised in the famous St Paul's Church and in later years attended both Sunday Mass and Sunday School on its premises. Came the day for enrolment at the secondary school, the doorstep to serious education. Spilly decided on a well known Antwerpian catholic school run by nun teachers. As a child she herself had attended the lessons at a 'Nun's School' (as they were referred to by the populace) in Merksem, one of Antwerp's suburbs. Due to certain circumstances prevailing at the time, she had to leave at a fairly early age but one of the advantages those days of a catholic school was the excellent tutorial of the French language which motivated her in her decision where I was concerned. Although Flemish born, we were never fanatically so and, thinking of the future in a bi-lingual country, she looked a little further than the tip of her nose.

Unfortunately she sadly reckoned without one's 'Christian' host! Because she ran a public house, Mother Superior declined to accept me into the lap of her establishment. It did not seem to matter one iota how Spilly pleaded, even going as far as to give carte blanche for impromptu control visits from their school authorities and producing a certificate of good conduct with regard to herself and the propriety of her business, personally signed by the Commissioner of Police of our District no less. The daughter of a pub landlady was not suitable for Mère Supérieure's establishment.

After this episode, Spilly never set foot into a church except for the occasional wedding or funeral service of friends; this out of respect for the families. And so I landed at one of the leading Girls Schools for Official Education situated in the Eikenstraat. The term 'official education' meant that no religion was taught and pupils of any religious belief were accepted. The school was listed as fee-paying in so far as we bought our own school books and requisites as well as the required outfits for physical education (gymnastics, etc) and cookery. Our teachers, all females, were exceptionally dedicated, a prerequisite on recruitment. Moreover, their distinguished behaviour created an atmosphere of respect. Qua clothes and hair care, they were always impeccable and they spoke civilised Dutch; the equivalent of what the British called the King's English . . .

We were free to indulge in our own vernacular at home or with one another but in the class the emphasis fell on the 'civilised' language. Discipline was indeed very strict and, paradoxically, this was precisely why we so respected the teachers. As a matter of fact discipline formed the basis of our general education. From the beginning we were taught to respect parents and the old, and although, as is inherent in young children, we often poked fun at our teachers after school, this fundamental training remained chiselled into my character as well as their unforgettable names. They weaned us on deontology, so to speak. Our daily breaks took place at 10am and 3pm in our extensive and pleasant playground. The school janitor served coffee and sold bars of chocolate which formed a welcome bridge between breakfast and lunch during the winter months. Sometimes I returned home for the lunch time break between noon and 2pm; other times I stayed in the school dining room eating my sandwiches, surveyed by the teacher in charge.

During the summer of 1933, Antwerp's then longest transport tunnel was completed and inaugurated and thousands of school children from Great Antwerp marched through it from the Left Bank of the Scheldt called St Anne, to its entrance on the Right Bank, from then onwards called the Grote Tunnelplaats; singing enthusiastically as only school children can when liberated from a normal school day. The tunnel walls reverberated from the sound of the specially composed Tunnel song and the older familiar tunes taught since our early years. One of the songs referred to the proud spire of Antwerp's main cathedral dedicated to Our Lady and our wide flowing River Scheldt. We soon and disrespectfully altered the wording, 'Our Proud Spire, The Wide Scheldt Flood' into 'Our Lopsided Spire' and 'the dried out ditch' . . . Kids!

The zenith of each school year, however, was prize giving day held at the Grand Civic Festival Hall situated in the Meir, Antwerp's main shopping street. One looked upon a sea of shining children's faces, multi-coloured summer dresses which transformed the hall as if by magic into a flower meadow. There followed the calling of your name and your prizes; normally three children's books according to the age of the recipient. We collected them from the platform where the Councillor for Education handed them to us individually with a few words of praise or encouragement. Beaming faces of the parents, the hum of voices and then, led by the conductor, the orchestra played one of his own compositions whilst we sang our hearts out in a long rehearsed choir. Many a parental tear secretly slid down the cheeks!

On the 12th May 1935 our beloved Royal Couple, Leopold III and Queen Astrid visited Antwerp. It was in the port that a few years previous the then Swedish Princess entered Belgium as the official fiancée of the young Crown Prince. She returned this time as Queen to say thank you for the overwhelming welcome received by the Antwerpians during her former arrival. Again thousands of school children lined the pavements of the streets covered by the visit, dressed in their Sunday best and waving miniature Belgian flags. I, too, was there and from far off we heard the swelling noise of the cheering exploding from thousands of young throats as the Royal Couple approached. My heart was beating with emotion, for our Royals represented the symbol of our national roots and they figured almost God-like in my imagination. All of a sudden my school friends on each side began shouting 'Leve de Koning, leve de Loningin' and 'Vive le roi, vive la reine' (Long live the King, Long live the Queen) - we were after all bilingual - I could hardly see them, as two sturdy soldier's legs partially obliterated my view. My emotion seemed to glue my epiglottis and, completely bewildered, all I squeezed out was 'I too, I too'. Since then, every time I see a photo of the Belgian Royals, I just say 'I too'.

It was during our seventh and eighth school years that we received biology lessons, called sex education today. Ours were packed in a wrapping of tact with the emphasis on procreation and presented in such a manner that mention of the genitals of man and woman were added almost in hurried afterthought. The teacher, at that time our own form mistress, dealt with motherhood in such a romantic way that we clung to what she said and I followed her lessons with damp eyes and full of rapture. Strange that, in adulthood, I never became baby-oriented. This same teacher taught us the 'Netherlands' language (there is a subtle difference between this and Dutch) and often meted out punishment for me, in the form of verbs in all their conjugations, as she did not believe in writing umpteen times 'I must not talk in class' etc. As I was an incorrigible chatterbox and laughter inducer, I regularly went home with the punishment to five of these verbs. Perhaps that is the reason why, even now, I seldom make grammatical mistakes in my mother tongue . . . ! In any case, in later years, it all proved most useful, especially as in addition I was blessed with a flair for essays.

We had a marvellous teacher for cooking lessons during our last two years when we were 13 and 14 and my love of haute cuisine in its Flemish form (which culinary experts often say knocks the French for six!) found its origin indubitably during these years. Later, when on holiday in Antwerp, I often met them, by now retired teachers, and was able to express my gratitude for their patience and excellent instruction. From year one in that school we learned to read and the classroom walls were covered with large prints of people, objects and animals which I can still rattle off in the sequence they were placed. I soon developed into an early and avid reader.

The curriculum at the school was extensive and the standard of education on leaving at the age of 14 exceptionally good, with French as our second language and a fair grasp of English. In addition there seemed to be a healthy absence of class distinction although there was a cross section of daughters from the professional classes, commercial and Bank employees, shop keepers and pub landlords. The broad minded teachers allocated the seats so that some of the Jewish girls sat next to a Gentile. The former were usually absent on Friday afternoons but, in spite of the fact that their religion, and to some of us their cuisine and customs, represented an unknown factor, there never existed any form of friction between us. We just did not pay any more attention - in the nicest sense of the word - to their periodical absence, than to my daily late morning appearances after catechismus lessons and Mass at St Paul's Church prior to my Confirmation. Spilly had promised this to her mother but unfortunately my Grandma died at the age of 64 before this celebration took place.

Those days it was customary to lay out a corpse, washed, combed and dressed, in the open coffin. Friends and relatives would visit to pay their last respects although it was not a wake such as is the habit in Ireland. The modern concept now is much more hygienic and certainly less traumatic for the bereaved. Grandma too was thus 'laid out' with hands folded as in prayer on the chest. Before the lid was nailed, I too was led to behold her peaceful countenance for the last time and I shook like an aspen leaf in fear. Moreover, on my way to my own bedroom and for three consecutive nights, I had to pass hers; there was no light on the landings and I nearly died a thousand deaths! What is the mystery that possesses one with such fear for a being that, in death, could not possibly cause one any harm and that, in life, loved one so?

For as long as I can remember and in time-honoured tradition, we went on an annual 'pilgrimage' on the 1st November (All Saints Day) to pay our respects to our beloved deceased buried at the Schoonselhof, Antwerp's main cemetery. Not only was it always bitterly cold, often freezing (after half an hour on the tram my feet were like blocks of ice) but the heart breaking grief manifesting itself at grandma's and the adjacent graves was too much for my compassionate little heart. Surrounded by a carpet of virgin white chrysanths placed on the gravestones, with the odd yellow or mauve ones dotted here and there forming a pattern which, under different circumstances would have been festive, my Mama sobbed her heart out. Stupid child that I was, it embarrassed me. It is only now that I realise the full burden of her sorrow, now that she too has gone forever . . .

In our fourth year at school a new pupil joined the class. Yvonne was the daughter of a well known funeral director situated in one of the old parts of Antwerp near the Groenplaats, a famous square full of beautiful trees, benches for visitors to rest, a kiosk for the regular Band performances and the statue of Rubens, Antwerp's world famous painter-son. On the same premises her mother kept a fishmongers and upstairs in the kitchen she fried fish for sale every Friday. There was scarce ventilation in that little old house and it was obvious that the clothes of Yvonne were saturated for the better part with the smell of the fried delicacy. It went against my better nature that my school friends secretly laughed about it, and I consequently and categorically took her under my wing, respectfully requesting the teacher to place her next to me on the school bench. I rarely strayed from her side until this periodic fishy aroma became part and parcel of everyday life. I hasten to add that she wasn't exactly tongue-tied herself. Two years later we happened to have a form teacher, robustly built, butch almost, with flat feet, a spinster, who all too often showed her dislike for the two of us. It was not only my late arrival each morning, due to the catechism lessons prior to my confirmation, but my open admiration for everything British or evolving around Great Britain; this obviously having been discussed amongst the teaching staff following reports on my fair knowledge of the English language from our English mistress. Our form teacher, for reasons of her own, was anti-British and years later we learned that she was arrested during the immediate post-war period for pro-Nazi activities. One day, and not for the first time I must add, she asked us to bring along a present in aid of a tombola for one of her charities. Upon questioning, one pupil would promise a book, others toys, chocolate, etc. 'And you, Yvonne?' our least popular Miss asked, and this shortly after she had beleaguered my friend with yet another tirade about the fishy smell, 'What are you going to bring along?' Without looking up from her book, sharp as a knife, Yvonne's reply sliced the air 'A fish in a coffin, Miss.' For a minute there was silence then the entire class exploded into fits of laughter. Miss's cheeks turned as red as a cockscomb.

I remained friends with Yvonne throughout our teens into adulthood. I temporarily lost touch with her in our later teens but renewed the friendship during the war years when she got married. We remained close during those fateful years, after the liberation of Antwerp, whilst I waited for my fiancé, after my marriage and consequent departure for England, during my holidays spent in our 'City of the Scheldt', until she died in 1984. The news of her demise came as a thundercloud especially as, during the last years, these close ties had cemented even more the bond to what became more of a sister relationship. She gave birth to six children, three boys and three girls, all different characters. The three girls in turn later stayed with us in Albion to improve their knowledge of the English language. During their stay they were spoilt rotten by their English 'Uncle' as he too always had a soft spot for Yvonne and her brood. After her marriage Yvonne proved to be a hardworking, extremely shrewd, honest and much liked business woman and became well known on the Left Bank where she and her husband Albert opened various restaurants.

During my engagement period I spent many a weekend with her and at extremely busy times, especially in the summer months, helped her out in the business. The love I nurtured for Yvonne, I transferred to her offspring and I am very fortunate in the reciprocation thereof. Friendships that are formed during the early youth years and stimulated throughout one's life remain the most sturdy of pillars. They put into the shade some of the subsequent acquaintanceships which fleetingly occur in life but are like ships passing in the night.

*

I was four the first time I was operated on for appendicitis and 12 for peritonitis. Our GP-Surgeon happened to be a treasure of a man dedicated to his calling, father of two sons and dying to have a little girl, a wish that was never granted. No wonder he idolised me, having attended to me throughout the usual children's ailments and personally performing both operations. These took place at the St Camille Private Nursing Home and each time I was very much cosseted by the nursing nuns especially where the menus were concerned. While Dr Van Looveren sat on the edge of my bed during his first of many regular post-operative visits and dived into my grapes or sucked my boiled sweets, we discussed my first meal after the last operation. Something very special, perhaps even exotic, was the expected request but they certainly hadn't bargained for . . . a pickled herring followed by a pancake! Fact is that, where most females have a sweet tooth, I prefer sucking sweet and sour gherkins . . .

As far as the last operation is concerned, only a hair's breadth prevented me from ever writing this book. When my initial stomach cramps started, Spilly called on a local GP as Dr Van Looveren was attending a conference abroad which would take several days. This GP prescribed a 'lemonade purgatif' which duly made me vomit, as sweet medicines always acted as an emetic for me. According to this 'expert' I had a slight attack of the cholics. As my condition visibly exacerbated and during painful cramp attacks, a cord-like thickness appeared under the skin in the centre of my tummy, which the said GP again insisted was due to the cholics, Spilly became panicky. At dawn the following day I was vacantly staring out, not even reacting to the cramps now alarmingly following each other at ever shorter intervals. My eyes had sunk deep into their sockets, my little ears stood out from my head and I looked as grey as a corpse. At the end of her tether, Spilly rang Dr Van Looveren, to be told he had by chance returned that same night. He was still in bed but after hearing Spilly's report, he threw his mackintosh over his pyjamas and arrived not long after in his Minerva car. He took one look, saw the bulge formed on my tummy after each cramp attack, wrapped me in a blanket and took me home where he X-rayed me at once. Orders to prepare the operating theatre and reserve a room for me were given and less than an hour afterwards I was under his skilful scalpel, as we heard afterwards, only just in time! Acute peritonitis.

I remained his patient until I left Antwerp and even now I can clearly recall that efficient, conscientious and caring man, true to his Oath, always dressed in a dove-grey suit, and hope his doctor-sons have lived up to his image!

After my convalescence, he prescribed a daily morning diet of fresh cream as proper breakfasting never was my forte. I fetched the cream from our local patisserie baker and that man baked the best 'coffee-cakes' in the whole of the city with my preference going to his longish, narrow and folded currant ones with the most gorgeous home-made apricot jam. Coffee cakes in Belgium could best be compared with what we, in England, call Danish pastries and were made with real butter.

My poor grandmother's patience was put to the test every morning in her efforts to induce me to take the prescribed cream, help me get ready for school, in short, I was one helluva nuisance as she often reproached me. In retrospect, psychologically I tried to attract Spilly's attention as I did not see all that much of her after school due to her being so very busy in the business. If I went too far, however, I was on the receiving end of a few well-aimed slaps around the ears both from Grandma and Spilly as the hands of these dear ladies 'hung on a silken thread' as they say in Antwerp. During one of the morning Masses prior to my Confirmation and after having once more refused to take the cream or any sustenance I duly fainted and was carried home by the worried nuns.

I must admit I was never very religious but nevertheless full of admiration for our main Notre Dame Cathedral and the beautiful St Paul's Church in my own parish, with its multiple, breathtaking paintings of Rubens and Van Dyck and other Flemish painters of their time, the magnificently sculpted pulpit, panelling, the altars with their gold candelabra. (It seems inconceivable that throughout the centuries, whilst the populace lived in such extreme poverty, the churches and cathedrals kept adding to their opulence and were seen to be doing precious little to alleviate the living conditions of their parishioners!) Very often I would enter St Paul's Church to visit the marble statues which depicted the three Crosses on Mount Calvary and Jesus after having been taken down from the cross, lying resting in His Mother's arms. These statues created in a courtyard at the side have now been replaced. Walking through into the Church garden, I would come upon a small grotto with an image of the Holy Mother, dressed in her habitual blue cloak (hence the fact that in Belgium baby girls are always dressed in blue, boys in pink). It was a quiet spot for the occasional visit and a prayer for a successful exam . . .

*

For as long as I can remember street fairs regularly took place in the more densely populated areas of Antwerp and mainly in one of its oldest parts called 'Schipperskwartier',. the seaman's own quarters, be it a native or visiting. These fairs were, and still are, called 'Braderijen', best translated as 'roasteries', as in the Middle Ages they were always epitomised by the roasting on spits of beeves. The St Paul's Square, Kei- and Korte Manstreets became transformed into a hive of activity and the air filled with the buzz of many languages as on this palette of foreign businesses, everybody partook in the festivities.

Amongst the 'cabardouchkes' (local pubs of ill repute) the decent locales nestled serenely side by side with Spanish wine-bars (called Bodegas in the more chic establishments near the Central Station, the nucleus of entertainment) and a Chinese eatery emanating strange spicy smells which tickled the taste buds. There were the 'kapeneions' or Greek barbershops, the cheaper stalls selling chips and other eateries which by no stretch of the imagination could one call restaurants and where Spanish, Greeks and Turks as well as Scandinavians came to fill empty bellies and where sometimes knives were drawn during some argument or another, mainly because of inanities such as which race represented the strongest 'macho' image and could triumph in stamina where sexual prowess is concerned. The majority of the ethical population, however, were owners of modest grocer shops, tobacconists, butchers or bakeries. A centrally situated glaziers did a roaring trade due to the regular smashing to smithereens of everything connected with this mineral during repeated misunderstandings in one pub or another. I specially remember its predominant stink of putty, whenever I passed it. One of the larger, well-stocked groceries was called 'In the Beehive', and situated next door to the police station on St Paul's Square. The grocer had two daughters, both blessed with musical talent. Irene taught piano and her sister was engaged as a singer at the Flemish Opera. Both held diplomas from the Academy of Music, a famous institution in Antwerp, and twice weekly I visited Irene for my lessons. At the beginning I was filled with enthusiasm but the continuously monotonous, albeit essential exercises, became so boring I soon hated attending. At the end of each lesson Irene would play for me a lovely Spanish composition 'as a reward for my efforts' and which strangely excited me. I still consider 'Espana' by Chabrier one of my favourites. However, it became 'piano lessons with tears' and later, as my studies at the Eikenstraat School escalated to a demanding peak in homework and, moreover, I had become aware of the sacrifice forced upon Spilly in order to pay for these lessons, I was able to persuade her to dispense with them. Her reproof that I would rue it in later years became indeed the bitter truth!

During the said street fairs, hastily installed counters on wooden supports outside the little shops held goods on special offer, for the main part what the Antwerpians called 'old shop assistants', ie items proven to be virtually unsaleable. Many shopkeepers, as is wont during carnivals, would dress up in various outfits which added to and considerably enhanced the cosmopolitan cauldron. Intriguingly colourful items of little note exhibited by the Chinese, red Turkish fezzes, the odd Greek evzone (that manly skirt which an old Greek had taken out of the mothballs for the occasion and which evidently had known better times), the sparkling costume jewellery sported by the ladies of easy virtue with their skirts so short they were akin to curtain pelmets, and who, precisely because of their attire, attracted the loitering seamen, shiftily disappearing whenever the navy blue of a police uniform was spotted. *Those* were the colourful street fairs of my early youth in the Antwerpian Schipperskwartier.

Added to this kaleidoscopic palette, the tinkling of piano keys drifted from the mini-pubs. The occasional accordion squeezer accompanied by raucous song added to the rumpus. The violinist played his part and simply stood there, in the street, sawing away as though there was no tomorrow. As the influence of American jazz was already much in evidence in Western Europe, jazz orchestras, captured for eternity on wax discs (or so they were led to believe), instrumented their irresistible sound from the acme of musical inventions, namely the gramophone, which formed part of the sparsely furnished 'kotjes'; the nearest translation for the abode of the port whores being 'little cages'. All this encouraged many visitors and passers-by to dance in the streets.

There were vendors selling hot sauerkraut with frankfurters, or small baked potatoes and sprats, kept warm in a sort of metal mini-oven secured by means of a broad leather strap over their shoulder. Delicacies indeed after all that activity. They took advantage of the fair by getting rid of their first food supplies prior to their evening visits to daily customers, going from pub to pub throughout the winter months, and The Scheldt too was one of their more lucrative outlets.

We had the regular visit of a family from south Italian origin, gypsies by all account. They made a colourful group. The father played the accordion, one daughter danced, the other played the violin and the mother, very much the matriarch in her splendid Romany outfit, guarded the spoils pushed into an old cap of unmistakable European origin and, in our establishment, always bulging with British notes! After their performance, they would go from table to table, in addition selling peanuts coated in a roasted sugary mixture.

One day the group entered minus the matriarch, and in broken Flemish speckled with Italian the daughter told us Mum had gone to the eternal gypsy caravan in the sky . . . The old Dad was obviously emotional and his rheumy eyes looked vacantly into space. Spilly translated the story for the British ships' officers in the full to bursting pub and when they finally left, their decrepit cap was filled with currency.

While one of these fairs was in full swing, Spilly was approached by a neighbour wondering if she had given me permission to parade in the surrounding streets wearing her blue fox and her jewels. Spilly's feet hardly touched the ground and there I was, blissfully enjoying the atmosphere, dressed in her best silk dress, the seam sweeping the street cobbles, her blue fox draped over my shoulders for all the world like a 'dame du monde' (I was just 11!), her two large diamond rings glittering in the dying ember of an evening sun; on my feet her crocodile shoes, remarkably as comfortable on the high heels as in my slippers. That 'silken thread' seemed more supple than ever and my feet as well hardly touched the ground as I fled home!

During my first school years I was accompanied daily by an older school friend cum chaperone whose family lived around the corner of The Scheldt. In spite of the fact that I could hardly ever manage to eat any breakfast, each time I entered their home to wait for my friend, the water would run out of my mouth as I inhaled the tantalising aroma of fried ham and eggs and fresh coffee which seemed to impregnate the whole place. Now, all these years later, I cannot prepare this dish without recalling those days.

A few years afterwards I was allowed to go and return from school on my own, for those days, even in that vast world port, the streets were free of lechers, muggers and child molesters. Furthermore, Spilly had drummed it into me from my earliest years never to go anywhere with men not under any circumstances, not even when I knew them, unless she personally gave permission.

The only unpleasant experience I had was, when playing with my friends near the imposing entrance to the offices of a shipping firm a few houses along from our home, I noticed a man exposing his genitals and starting to masturbate. Whilst in my innocence it did not mean any actual harm to me I nevertheless instinctively condemned it as wrong in that public place. I called my friends and together we ran to tell

Spilly. By the time she had reached the spot the man had gone. He was lucky. Spilly could be a wild cat not to be touched without thick gloves!

I was more than surprised when I once saw her tackle a drunken Scandinavian who stumbled in demanding a beer, generally acting in an intimidating way and proceeding to smash a beer glass. Spilly rushed from behind the bar, grabbed him by the pants and back (she could not reach his neck as she was only 5ft!) and literally threw him outside. By the time he got up she was ready with one of those knife sharpeners in the form of a sabre, fashionable those days, and normally hidden under the bar counter. The man stumbled onwards mouthing gruesome Viking curses, at least that's what they sounded like!

It stands to reason that a child keen on learning and with a playing area like the Antwerp Schipperskwartier would soon be aware that the Burggracht, the Guldenberg, Gorterstreet, etc were not just visited for their artistic style of architecture. I occasionally caught the word 'boekwijven' which is the common folklore name for whores (translate it to 'bookwives' as in the early 19th century they could only execute their trade if they passed regular health checks, the results of which were scribbled in a special book). Being in the habit of continually asking questions, it was tactfully explained to me that these ladies conducted a profession as old as creation. With my normal childlike curiosity, I would often walk through these alleys and streets as these heavily made-up women, scantily clothed, sitting like merchandise in their windows (the 'use by' date had long since expired for some!) were like a fair booth to me. The 'act of love' was explained rather superficially to me and in my early juvenile, more romantically orientated consciousness, I had difficulty juxtaposing this fact with the vast number of men furtively entering those premises supposedly because of their being in love with the same creature. I had heard a bell toll but could not find the clapper . . .

Oh, those days of the picturesque, brimming with life, Antwerpian Schipperskwartier, the Burggracht, the 'Poesje' (puppet theatre, even then known for their political satire), the Vleeshuis (a museum of weaponry and antiques dating from the Middle Ages) which could be approached via wide, cobblestoned steps leading from the main Van Dijckkaai; the old houses with their façades built in the Middle Ages, the miniature shops, the pavements leading to them every Friday religiously scrubbed by their owners so you never saw dog excrement anywhere! I could never erase my love for that old City with its historical past!

Mentioning excrement, the Municipal Cleaning Department annually emptied the cesspits then existing in most houses. On the stipulated date a large enclosed Panzer-like vehicle would arrive; duly elevated to 'the shitwaggon' by the populace. Thick, black rubber pipes of about 15/20cm in diameter were coupled up by metal sections into one long hose with small inspection windows placed at regular intervals. This pipe was then placed on the floor from the front door to the cesspit at the back of the house. Although everything was sealed to almost perfection, a fairly healthy, fertilising smell would pervade during the operation. The 'chaps of the shit farm' as these knights of the Antwerp hygiene hordes were called in the vernacular, were afterwards treated to a tip or a glass of the necessary 'medicine' and/or tasty titbit left by the lady of the house. Woe betide the mean or forgetful client . . . traces of human excrement, caused by negligent dismantling of the sections, would be found in abundance from cesspit to front door . . . Some of the suburbs and large country houses would be visited regularly by farmers for the emptying of cesspits. A long ladle would be lowered in the pit and many a farmer would lightly dip the point of his finger in this to taste the quality. After all, they only paid according to strength of content . . . but I have since learnt this was a folklore joke!

From babyhood onwards I was totally spoilt by Ma and Pa Jacobs. They could not have been dearer to me had they been real grandparents and I loved them 'till they died when Pa was 78, Ma 82. We had baptised her 'the old tough 'un'. They too were never bereft of tragedy. Their daughter, Lucy, became insane after her menopause, the oldest son lost a leg in middle age and the younger son never returned from the infamous Buchenwald concentration camp after he was arrested by the Gestapo as a member of the White Brigade 'Fidelio', the Resistance Movement Group to which he had been recruited by my father.

I was besotted with them and as Ma lavished so much love on me I was forever climbing on her lap. Even now, when I close my eyes and concentrate, I can smell her pleasant body odour.

After they moved from the Brasserie near The Scheldt and their daughter's marriage, they opened a Cinema in Deurne, a suburb of Antwerp. As a young teenager I spent many weekends with them and saw the most famous, colourful talkies and Broadway musicals of the pre-war period. During the day I would borrow the scooter of her small grandson, Gordon, and treadle to the Rivieren park not far from the cinema. The wonderful aroma of trees, shrubs and nature in general formed such a maximal contrast with the smells of the Port.

Whenever aunt Lucy came to visit, however, the weekends were a constant fight for either the scooter or any toy I wished to play with, as Gordon was one of these 'enfants terribles' with only one desire - to take whatever the other child wanted. I am very pleased to say, however, that he grew up to be a delightful man, a credit to his British birthright. In fact in

1991 he was granted an OBE. His adoring grandma would have been so proud!

*

Man is born with his own genes, inherited from father and mother, to which are added character traits sometimes recognised in aunts and uncles. The raw materials, influences and inborn strength, coupled with life's experiences, can be orchestrated to a definite unity. From experience in the world around me, I am convinced that the actual upbringing in one's own family, the right reading material from the early years, and, to a certain important extent, basic instruction in the Christian belief, will ultimately knead the 'raw clay' into a useful integrity. It is not important that in later life many stray from their religious rigidity; the principles, the seeds were planted and the difference between good and evil stays with them, in or out of the Church!

My parents were not exactly ideal philosophers. Spilly, of necessity, had to leave school when she was only 10 years old. Spil was educated mainly at the orphanage where he passed his exams for entry into the Antwerp Nautical College. He subsequently obtained his diplomas, first as Third, then Second and finally as Chief Engineer - the latter after his marriage - after intensive studying and many sacrifices. Like most seamen, his practical experience was attained on board the ships he joined. The discipline in the orphanage was strict but not harsh and, as it was of such importance in those days, much attention was given to proper behaviour at all times and particularly during functions. During one of his voyages, Spil was congratulated by his Captain when, as deft as a surgeon, he filleted his fried plaice in a minimum of time, without spilling any of it over the rim of his plate, and never hesitated as to which cutlery to use and in which order. Good table manners were no sinecure for socially more elevated people according to the orphanage management.

From my earliest years, my parents inculcated in me moral standards, respect for my elders and consequently oneself, self-discipline so very difficult to accept by the energetic, lively child and which, with my sometimes irascible character, came to the fore rather slowly. Also a sense of duty and responsibility without which a civilised society cannot possibly remain preserved.

They were madly in love when they got married at the age of 17 (Spilly) and 21 (Spil) respectively. As far as Spil was concerned, in addition, this meant his release from the orphanage. After the death of his parents, as he was the youngest of six children, four boys, two girls, and there being a great time lapse between him and the previous child, the two oldest, both sisters, in turn would look after him. In growing up though, Spil was full of life and a daredevil getting into all sorts of unimportant but annoying affrays. When both sisters became pregnant, one after the other, he was too much of a burden so Spil landed in the orphanage.

Spil and Spilly, my parents, on their wedding day.

With Spil on the day
of my confirmation.

Spilly and me calling for
Daddy as his ship
passes the Quay

The young couple rented a small attic room in an old house at the Vlasmarkt, a densely populated area. They slept 'pailliasse parterre' (mattress on the floor donated by Spilly's mother). She also had a small second-hand wardrobe delivered and empty orange crates formed dining table and chairs. Both were blessed with an exceptionally soft heart and, in spite of their poverty, were impulsive givers. I often heard it said in later years that Spil would pull the shirt from his back for whoever had a need of it and Spilly too wasn't slow in following suit.

During the prosperous years at The Scheldt, each year around St Nicholas time (the 5th of December on the Continent as against Father Christmas in Great Britain) she not only took my toys of the previous year, still in excellent condition, to our local orphanage, but purchased new ones from one of our main toy shops. Many a British ship's officer bought toys for his own children, prior to Christmas, and equally contributed most generously to the orphanage funds.

Treating animals well was an important part of my upbringing as I grew up with either a cat and/or dog. Most of these were foundlings and they landed into an animal heaven in our home. Once I brought the umpteenth dirty, very long haired dog home and baptised him, as with most of his predecessors 'Boule' . . . don't ask my why! The metamorphosis after his first bath was astonishing, revealing a beautiful animal with shining white curly hair. Shortly afterwards it became obvious Boule was expecting and Spil, at the time perchance ashore, realised how difficult this would be in a busy pub like ours. As nobody seemed keen on adopting the poor creature and with the responsibilities of its pregnancy, Spil had no option but to take Boule to the equivalent of the RSPCA clinic near Antwerp to have her humanely put to sleep . . . After school I looked everywhere for my dog, accustomed as she was to practically fetch me from its portals, and when she proved untraceable I went on a voluntary hunger strike, shedding tears like a waterfall. Two days later Spil couldn't stand it any longer. Back to the home where he found to his profound regret that Boule had been put to sleep just a few hours earlier. It took some time before I forgave my dad, but not that long, he was my idol.

One of my most cherished birthday presents when I reached the age of 11 was undoubtedly a proper bicycle, a black shining Velox with gold lettering, a 'stand' at the rear wheel for parking, a folding soft shopping bag placed over the baggage rack and a dynamo-lamp on the wheel. We were inseparable and I ventured everywhere with it during any spare time I could get. My school friends annually went on holidays with their parents, but my holiday paradise stretched between St Anne on the Left Bank of the Scheldt with its miniature beach, swimming pool and restaurants, or, to the north of the Port, the new 'Noordkasteel', an artificially created mere and leisure centre, mostly with swimming facilities in much cleaner water than the even then sometimes murky Scheldt, but now sadly dispensed with in order to make room for the container terminals.

Two fairly old paddle ferries regularly took passengers to the Left Bank of 'St Anneke' (as it was known by Antwerpians) and these were aptly christened 'St Annekesboten'. The smell of tar and oil emanating from the thick ropes, the muffled thuds of the horses' hooves on the wooden jetty as they pulled their burden, the tanned crew, the lapping noises of the Scheldt water against the bows of the ferry, that unmistakable disinfectant smell consistent with ships' cabins, that alone already created a sense of adventure!

My friend Yvonne's father, the funeral director, had acquired a small plot at St Anneke on which he had built a wooden hut, grandiosely called a 'bungalow'. As children are wont to do, we romped there during the holidays like free spirits for, apart from our chaperone - usually Yvonne's older, married sister, her mother or, sometimes even her father during the weekends - there was not a soul in sight on that seemingly endless space. As far as the eye could detect, there was but sand and meadow. If, by chance, we had missed the ferry, we would make the crossing via the regular motorboats which took less time but weren't anywhere near as romantic as that tested St Anneke's boat on which I dreamed of voyages to faraway ports with intriguing names - Rio de Janeiro, Panama, Tangiers, New York . . .

Back home at dusk, all aglow from grandma's 'hot water and soap' scrub, in my clean nightie, I was allowed to drape myself over the windowsill of her apartment which by then took up the third floor (where Spilly had lived and I was born). An unforgettable spectacle would unfold before my eager eyes: the sun unrepentantly disappearing beyond the horizon, shrouding the sky in a sea of deep yellow and red-orange, the tips of the clouds cloaked in a golden glow, the funnels and ships' cranes of the moored vessels at the Scheldt's borders sharply contrasting with the shimmering background which seemed to embrace infinity. Sometimes in the close evening air, a vague smell of tar would hover over the river, like an invisible haze almost ashamed to completely land on the water yet very much in evidence. Those days we could still see extensive stretches of virginal land uninterrupted by bricks or mortar. And later, when the 'Noordkasteel' (North Castle) was officially opened, *'the Sinjoren'* found a second source of relaxation. (This nickname dates back to the Middle Ages when the Spanish invaders concentrated on Antwerp as their main West European port and Centre for Trade and the Arts and its tradesmen/leaders became rich and dressed in all the finery of that epoch so that they resembled the noble Señors of Spain. The Flemish population subsequently spelled it their way 'Sinjoren'.) Indeed, St Anneke had, in the meantime, lost some of is appeal due to its obvious small size as it was overpopulated, especially at weekends. Moreover, the Noordkasteel with its much cleaner water for undisturbed swimming, its green dykes and so easily approached by bike or regular bus service, offered the picnic aficionados cheap and ideal shelter. Refreshments, however, were of a more primitive nature as, apart from a few barrack like huts, where cold drinks were served, there existed but one small restaurant. Somehow inexplicably it never developed into a modern leisure centre.

Between the swimming expanse and the lane leading to the main road, a high and long grassy dyke had been built as protection against the wind. The top of this dyke formed a very pleasant walking area. Steps were provided at the entrance to it but not at the end and unless one was prepared to descend from the dangerously steep side, the only alternative was to return to Point A.

One day I cycled to the Noordkasteel's new site, put my bike on my shoulders and mounted the steps of the dyke where I cycled up and down and felt free as the wind. Until .. . a gendarme on duty stopped me, as this space was for pedestrians only . . . I philosophically placed my bike on the top of the dyke, went to stand underneath and carefully pulled my transport downwards over the grass. Once on safe ground I removed the grass form between wheels and saddle, sternly observed by the gendarme, looked up at him and . . . cocked a snoot . . . ah, cheeky youth!

*

From the moment I could read I buried my nose constantly in everything printed. At first mostly children's books, then weeklies to which Spilly regularly subscribed and then the daily Nieuwe Gazet, one of Antwerp's leading daily newspapers. Spil was ' a blue one' (in Belgium there were three political parties: the liberals - colour blue, the socialists - colour red, and the Catholics yellow) and I grew up with the liberalism of my surroundings and the liberalism of our political beliefs. Both my parents were broadminded and I was encouraged, from an early age, to openly ask questions, irrespective of their origin, the replies rendered as candidly as possible. Spilly never believed in the 'you are too young to know' syndrome and, during the early thirties, the young generation did not mature as early as is the case now. It so happened that during an extremely busy late afternoon in the business, after finishing my homework and warmly installed behind the anthracite stove, I spotted in the Nieuwe Gazet something I had not previously met in my vocabulary.

'Mummy, I'm reading in the paper that a foetus was found in a street, what's that?' Spilly, momentarily taken aback, was really too busy to give a detailed explanation and, in order to wriggle out of it temporarily with the intention of telling me afterwards, replied offhand 'A Congolese fruit'. Unfortunately afterwards she forgot all about it. Came the day for the geography lesson at school. 'Which fruits does the Belgian Congo provide?' asked our teacher. After the usual obvious answers, I put my hand up. 'Foetuses, Miss' Miss thought she had misunderstood. 'How do you spell it?' she asked. 'F o e t u s e s' I replied, proud to spell it properly. After a little hesitation from Miss, 'No, I don't think so'. 'Oh yes, my Mum told me and she knows from Dad because he regularly visits the Congo'! Shortly afterwards Spilly was summoned to the Headmistress. They both had a hearty laugh about it when she explained, but from that moment on she never fended me off with an airy excuse.

When Spil was ashore, he would sometime dabble in a little cooking. He taught us scrumptious dishes, learned from the ship's cook to whom international cuisine had a certain allure. His more down to earth dishes were not to be scoffed at either. His stew of lamb cutlets with butter swedes and potatoes was a finger licking experience a Scot would have given his sporran for. Sometimes he would use butter beans instead of potatoes. The fact that he added to these dishes, as well as to stewed rabbit, 'Leuvens' beer (one of the many Belgian beers at present unfortunately discontinued), was an ingenious inspiration. Left over cooked mussels, their own juices forming the sauce with lots of celery, onions and parsley, he would transform into a tasty curry. If he was ashore and free during my birthdays, my school pals were treated to waffles or pancakes which he personally baked all afternoon. He varied his pancakes by adding sultanas or apple slices; sometimes home-made jam; the batter was either made with self-raising flour or yeast. There were few delights he would not try and I think some of his genes were undoubtedly passed on to little me as I too will try anything in the culinary field . . . not always with total success!

One day the unexpected happened - Spilly fell ill. Our GP diagnosed not only blood poisoning but also what we called 'The Rose'. Her face swelled to such an extent that her eyes almost disappeared in their sockets and she looked inhuman. Furthermore the illness was contagious and, as school holidays had just started, the doctor advised her to ban all personal contact. Spilly's oldest friend, domiciled at Borgerhout, an immediate suburb of Antwerp, took me at once into the bosom of her family. She had two sons, the eldest Frank, three years older than I, and the younger Fons, my father's godchild, just about two years older than I. I was twelve. An only child can be a lonely one and so I adored from the onset my new friends who I had hitherto only met sporadically. We romped all day long and these were indisputably the happiest weeks I spent as a child. Frank, furthermore was my first love, and acted as my protector. The day I had to return home veritable floodgates opened . . .

About a year afterwards at dusk, the two brothers were riding their bikes round and round the adjoining streets. Their father called them as it was getting darker. 'Once more around the block', Fonske yelled, and they raced as though the devil snapped at their heels, turning the corner for their last run. In the meantime, a neighbour had parked his Minerva car in front of his house. On top of the bonnet a steel mascot stood resplendent as was fashionable on prestigious cars. Fonske, head bent over the handlebars of his bike, as racing cyclists do during a sprint, did not see the black car in the twilight; in any case did not expect it to be there, and collided with it at full speed. The mascot severed his neck artery. By the time his brother, having jumped from his bike, had reached him and in

spite of the immediate assistance of a nearby doctor, he died
on the spot, just 15 years old . . .

*

Towards the end of the twenties, Belgium too succumbed
to the economical crisis that enveloped the greater part of the
civilised world. The 'Wall Street crash' was behind the
suicide of a number of bankers jumping to their death from
skyscrapers in New York, bankrupt and at the end of their
tether. Firms and factories, dotted across the whole of Europe,
closed their gates overnight. Ships were taken out of
circulation and laid up; these events forming the headline
news of the world press. Spilly's profits had always been of
such a lucrative nature that she was able to deposit Spil's
complete monthly salary in the bank with the addition of a
substantial sum from her own earned income even after
household expenses had been generously provided for. Those
days the value of the £ hovered just over B.Frs.200 as against
+ - 60 nowadays, and as an occasional exchange agent, she
also made a good profit in that field. She banked her savings
with a private bank situated in the centre of Antwerp and her
account approached 1 million Belgian Francs. Moreover she
worked like a Trojan, sometimes day and night, for as one
ship left, another would arrive. It naturally stood to reason that
the Income Tax Department undauntingly followed her
improving circumstances. Heavy income tax demands
followed each other at regular intervals and Spilly regularly
complied.

The Compagnie Maritime Belge, Spil's employers, were
not able to avoid the world crisis and they were forced to take
some of their ships out of circulation. Spil was one of the
victims. Then, one infamous night, the Director of Spilly's
bank absconded with all the funds and whatever of value he
could grab and, although some of the smaller savers later

47

enjoyed a certain compensatory repayment, Spilly lost all her savings so assiduously earned. When the next income tax demand, of an exceptionally high amount, slipped through the letterbox, she could not settle it. There was no longer any ready cash, no salary from Spil, no significant British or Canadian ships calling at Antwerp anymore as the economical crisis had struck at the heart of the merchant navies in those countries as well. She was forced to sell her rings and let nobody tell you that, made into jewellery, diamonds are an investment! The blue fox went the same way, even her expensive clothes. It was all in vain. Our sad story landed on deaf ears where the tax people were concerned. The bailiff honoured us with his visit and from one week into the next our situation changed drastically from 'comfortably off' to 'poor as church mice'. The entire pub installation was confiscated as well as the furniture. In accordance with the law, only two beds were left and, as the bailiff in question proved to be a kind man, he let me keep my small wardrobe and Spilly hers and a kitchen cabinet as well. My grandmother luckily never experienced this sad event. She had died of hardening of the arteries a few months previously. I think she was one of the first people to have been treated successfully in Antwerp for cancer of the cervix, just a year before, by one Dr Casman, a leading consultant, in his private clinic.

Shortly afterwards Spil found employment with Beliard & Creighton, Ship Repairers, in their dry-docks but his heart was at sea . . . It so happened I was in my growing period, only temporarily I am sorry to say, as I stopped at 4ft 11ins and instead of the usual dresses, coats and shoes from Antwerp's leading children's fashion houses, Spilly had to sacrifice a few of her remaining dresses to be adapted and styled for me but which I thought marvellous. In one of the apartments of the house next door, there happened to live a dressmaker of English nationality. After the death of her Belgian husband,

48

she lived a lonely existence and found solace in speaking her mother tongue with Spilly. In addition, she was saving up for her return home and welcomed the dress alterations we put her way. From Spilly's dresses she designed and sewed my first fashionable garb deviating from the hitherto childish outfits supposedly 'suitable' for my age. She lived above the barber's shop whose owner was a Jew emigrated from Poland. To underline the complexity of some children's minds: the barber had a little son, Maurice, who just wouldn't eat at home. Spilly made friends with him and encouraged him to take his daily lunches with us. Whether it was the Flemish 'burgher's cuisine' or the company, little Maurice waded through the menu of soup, meat and vegetables and fruit. I heartily disliked the little chap simply because Spilly found time to busy herself with him . . .

After the bailiff departed with our household effects, the barber came to offer his financial assistance, albeit on a small scale. Spilly charmingly refused but his attitude had made a profound and touching impression calling to mind that he, himself, having arrived almost penniless a few years before, would still have found it difficult to make ends meet. Later, during the war years, we heard the family had been transported by the Nazis and after the Liberation, when the horror of the camps was made public, we presumed they had perished as we never saw or heard from them again!

Two other regular playmates were sons of a Jewish couple, he being a watchmaker/jeweller with a shop the size of a stamp situated underneath the Congolese Seamen's Mission at the Van Dijckkaai. Mr Zucker had been driven out of his birthplace, the Ukraine, by the infamous pogroms and, after a long lasting sea voyage followed by a harrowing travel overland full of hardships, had finally landed in Antwerp. The Jewish Community assisted financially when opening his business. He was undoubtedly the softest and most kind-hearted man I ever met and I learned to love him as a special uncle. He' had always dreamed of having a daughter and spoiled me with delicacies from the Jewish cuisine with delicious cakes and pastries crumbling with pure butter. The complete family consisted of Mr and Mrs Zucker and their two sons, his mother-in-law, sister and brother-in-law. After we moved from the Orteluiskaai, we only met them from time to time and when, again during the war, they suddenly disappeared, we were hoping that they had gone underground or found refuge elsewhere. As they never contacted us, Spil, by then a member of the Resistance, was unable to assist. We later found out that they were one of the first Jews to be snatched from their home during the night by the Nazi hangmen. However, the brother-in-law, by chance absent during the razzia, was able to disappear underground. Having arrived in Buchenwald concentration camp at the end of a degrading voyage by rail in cattle trucks, of which so much has been unforgettably written, Zucker witnessed his wife, sister, mother-in-law and youngest son being driven to the gas chambers. As his identity card mentioned his profession, he was appointed as the official watch repairer of the camp. He not only repaired but also assembled new watches and clocks from old material for the guards, their families and the inhabitants of the surrounding villages. His older son was allowed to stay with him as his assistant for in later years he worked with gold and fashioned jewellery, unbeknown to him but almost certainly provided from the melted gold extracted from the teeth of the wretched Jewish prisoners . . .

Towards the end of the war, however, the camp SS-men, one fateful day, burst into his primitive workshop and literally pulled his son away from his clinging embrace. Zucker begged for them to leave the boy, crying that he would even share his meagre ration with his child. To no avail, the gas chamber was the boy's fate and Zucker returned to Antwerp after the Liberation as the sole survivor of the family. Again, sustained by the Jewish Community, he consequently opened a shop and sold watches and jewellery in the Pelikaanstraat, opposite the Central Station galleries, where his brother-in-law later joined him in partnership.

*

Although Belgium was within easy reach of her neighbouring countries, paradoxically, few people travelled abroad; the Belgian seaside towns and the Ardennes in the South offered vacations to those of a more ambitious nature. In fact, only the black sheep of the family were sent abroad. It was, therefore, most adventurous that we were able, during the last year of our schooling, to visit Paris accompanied by some of our teachers. What a happening! The highlight of my school years. Imagine, so far Paris, almost a neighbour, represented but a name on the European map.

The train seats were hard as nails - third class for us, young botties - and the journey took the best part of three hours. We stayed at a third class hotel, with little sleep as there seemed to be constant marching up and down during the whole of the night and much noise coming from the water closets and pipes as France was not exactly famous for its plumbing!

We visited the main historical attractions and sagedly downed the end product of the French cuisine, famous only in the exorbitantly priced hotels and restaurants. We unobtrusively dropped the inedible peas, manoeuvring them under the table . . . one could have catapulted a rider off his horse with them! This and a few visits to the countryside in the surrounding provinces were the sum total of my youthful travels.

A few months after the forced closing of The Scheldt café, one hot summer's afternoon Spilly opened the doors for ventilation during a thorough cleaning of the deserted space. Three men, undeniably dock workers, stepped inside and looked around in surprise. They were extremely thirsty and disappointed not to find a cooling glass of beer at the ready. Spilly realised they had a heavy shift behind them and fetched a few bottles of English beer from some crates she still had left in the cellar. 'Here boys, have one on me, when it's gone the cooking is done' she said quoting a Flemish proverb. 'Missus, have you got an ironing board?' asked one of them. Spilly, surprised, said 'Yes, why?' 'Well, open it up, get us a few crates of beer, we'll return tomorrow and to hell with the tax people!' as in the meantime Spilly had explained the reason why the place was devoid of furniture, etc.

No need to guess, Spilly was not used to that kind of customer especially as the songs they were rendering after having had one over the odds, plus the jokes they told in their juicy Antwerpian dialect, did not exactly form the acme of 'prudish decency'. They boasted hearts of gold though, brought some of their pals along, behaved impeccably and re-baptised the establishment 'The Pub without Bar', held behind prudently closed doors of course. I still recall one of the songs. I secretly listened to it on several occasions. It was the version of O Sole Mio, and with apologies to the lyricist, this is it:

'Oh my sweet b . . . s, dear
The Cross ships call here (this Cross was a logo printed on the funnels of a Belgian Shipping Company)
A strong cheese or three,
and a lot of salami,
on bread of Help Yourself (a popular bakery those days)
I then broke wind
but gave no hint'

As clandestine pub landlady, Spilly slightly profited from this clientèle but had no intention of continuing the trade in that establishment.

Through one of his shipmates, Spil was recruited into a 'Tunclub' at a café situated at the Vrijdagmarkt, one of Antwerp's more colourful little squares. A tun represented a piece of furniture in thick solid wood akin to a heavy table but with its top slanting downwards at an angle and in which numbered holes had been bored at regular intervals. Round iron discs of approximately 1cm thickness would be thrown into these holes from a certain distance by each competitor. The number of successful drops were counted at the end of the round and the winner was the contestant with the highest total.

In view of his advanced age, the landlord of this pub, after many years in business, had decided to sell out. He offered it to Spil and after weighing up the odds, and not without debating arguments on Spilly's part, an agreement was reached and we moved.

As far as I was concerned this offered a new adventurous horizon. That typical and popular Antwerpian little square with its folklore past, where twice weekly second-hand furniture and household goods were sold, either privately or confiscated by bailiffs, swarming with people, not to mention the public games during Antwerp Fair . . . heavenly!

An old building contained our private residence consisting of a dark kitchen behind the pub, an entresol bedroom destined for my grandfather who, after the demise of Grandma, had come to live with us; on the first floor two bedrooms, the front one looking out onto the street for my parents, the rear one for myself.

Life from a vantage point not hitherto experienced started at once. Twice a week, Mie the Fishwife, would arrive pushing a large barrow-cum-cart full of fresh fish and, during the season ditto mussels. From my Dad I learned to eat these raw, after she had opened them for us at her cart, and we squeezed a lot of fresh lemon juice and pepper from the peppermill over the white crustaceans, still sweet smelling of the sea, and ate them with fresh baked bread. In general, Spilly cooked these to the known Antwerpian recipe which is indubitably the most famous one in Flemish culinary art. Mie was adept as a champ opening the mussels which Spilly would take out of the shells, rinse under a cold water tap, leave to drain, then dry in a clean kitchen towel, sprinkle with flour and fry in butter in a pan, turning them occasionally until golden brown, this being yet another way of preparation. I still sometimes indulge in this 'deadly sin for the heart' but only if I can find a volunteer to open the mussels as this is for the initiated.

The two main auctioneers at the Vrijdagmarkt, and for many years known from far afield, were De Keuster and Sels; the latter's son still in business today. Their patrician-style houses had storage facilities both at street level and in their cellars. The Square boasted a magnificent building in one corner, housing the Plantin & Moretus Museum where in the Middle Ages, the first book was bound and where a variety of antique presses, bookbinding requisites and old books were, and still are exhibited, and was surrounded by smaller pubs. Just one shop, known for its range of anthracite stoves and kitchen ranges occupied one of the other corners. A small statue of the Virgin Mary which adorned a great number of houses in old Antwerp, reigned in colourful splendour against its façade. On one of the walls of my living room now hangs a coloured drawing by the hand of the famous Flemish artist Hebbelinck depicting part of the square with this particular house and statue, the Notre Dame spire protruding over the roofs of the houses in the adjoining alley. After the liberation of Antwerp in 1944, a flying bomb practically demolished most of the houses of the Vrijdagmarkt and although the square was rebuilt the 'Stoves shop' disappeared to make room for yet another pub. Judging by the number of drinking establishments confronting the public, Antwerpians must have made a pact with Bacchus.

The houses in irreplaceable period-style were never restored to their former glory, a question of 'modernisation'!

Trade in second-hand furniture proved very lucrative as the most beautiful private houses of the Vrijdagmarkt were undoubtedly those of the auctioneer families. Mr and Mrs De Keuster were both fairly tall, white haired and most expensively dressed. In fact, there existed an obvious competition between them and the Sels family. Mrs Sels and her daughter personified elegance, clad always in haute-couture which, in the immediate pre-war days, even then cost the earth and the Sels women seemed to regularly leave behind a cloud of French perfume so thick you could cut it up and sell it for bath-cubes (to borrow an expression from my late friend Jean Rook of the Daily Express). Whenever they wore a new outfit, Mrs De Keuster soon followed suit in similar elegance. As Spilly laconically commented 'When one cow lows the other raises her tail' . . . which is the Flemish sarcastic equivalent of 'Keeping up with the Jones's'.

Our new establishment was much frequented during the market days, held each Wednesday and Friday (hence the name of the square - Vrijdagmarkt, Friday market). Other days we were inundated with disc table and card players on a regular basis and, mainly during the summer months, tourists visiting the Plantin Museum. The British especially seemed keen and many were surprised to hear a child not only showing them the way to this building but inviting them, in fluent English, to come and partake in a cool English beer after their visit, in Spilly's pub.

In a pub such as ours it stood to reason that the regulars were of varied mien. One of them was a man built like a tree.

We called him The Shuffler, understandably as he was about 6ft 7in with hands like rowing oars and feet like paddle boats, with a shuffling gait rather than actually walking, and we never found out where he bought his footwear! The Shuffler came as a regular card player and was in the habit of chewing tobacco. The previous pub-owner had provided a metal spittoon for that purpose, strategically placed at the corner of the bar, just where the giant had a habit of sitting whilst playing cards so that he more or less was able to spit in it straight over his shoulder, which he had perfected. When Spilly, prior to the opening of the place, came upon this strange utensil during her scrubbing and polishing, she thought it was an ornament and eagerly proceeded to put 'spit and polish' into this, if you'll pardon the pun. Until Spil put her in the right direction . . . with a throw doing justice to an Olympic discus champion, the spittoon landed in the gutter outside and The Shuffler was courteously, albeit positively, requested in future to either swallow his tobacco juice or to spit it outside. This received not a little animosity. He was no match, however, for the fury that shone in the eyes of that 5ft piece of skirt as he afterwards succinctly put it!

What a character that man really was though. He carried small cupboards under the arm as though they were out of a doll's house. In one hand he would sometimes hold two dining room chairs, in the other a fair sized kitchen table. He did not earn according to his performance but nevertheless seemed to have found it sufficient for his daily brew intake. We never found out details about his background but it was generally presumed he was a bachelor and lived with his mother.

During the Annual Fair held in Antwerp in August, pub landlords of the Vrijdagmarkt would create an outdoor terrace in front of their pubs and Spilly allowed me to temporarily act as a barmaid, mainly serving the customers outside, and which

I enthusiastically indulged in as the punters were a happy lot and I got numerous tips. At the age of 13, this represented my first earnings. Since then I have learnt that in the pursuance of a lucrative existence, I only succeed after hard work!

Part of the week long Fair involved public games: running in sacks, trying to hit eggs suspended from strings, picking apples out of a water barrel with one's teeth and with the hands tied behind one's back, etc and neighbours as well as customers would take part. These were daily events which ultimately led to the highlight of the celebrations, a walking marathon around the square. Contestants would march dressed in white shorts and singlet for a stipulated time, the victor being the one who managed the greatest number of laps. It stood to reason The Shuffler won 'feet' down each year for he took one step when the others needed three. The first time I witnessed this competition, I experienced an education revelation. When I saw The Shuffler approaching, his head slightly bent like that of a turtle out of its shell, his elbows pushing the arms forward like paddles of a windmill to give himself more impetus, my eyes almost cleared their sockets! I promptly asked Spilly why he had a truncheon in his shorts which like a pendulum swung from left to right at each step he took, like a metronome during piano lessons!

The Vrijdagmarkt was also a popular short cut from one shopping centre to another and with a multitude of passers-by provided a colourful convolution of regulars. One couple particularly added to this palette. They ran a long established family firm and shop of white linen garments for industry and schools in one of the adjacent shopping streets. The husband was a slightly built and short chap. His spouse was Amazonian with a voice like a foghorn and sweeping theatrical hand movements during speech. They would cross the square to visit 'their local' and meet friends in an adjoining road. She took exceptionally long strides, in accordance with her size shoes, but he almost tripped like a ballerina and virtually hung on her arm, his head bent towards her opulent form, his little hands clasped almost as in prayer over her forceful arm. Spilly would comment, in her Antwerpian wit, 'She sucks him in, then spits him out' . . . The Amazone would nod at all passers-by, whether recognised customers or total strangers, within the perimeter of her hawks' eyes, like a queen to her people. The routine of their local never varied. The waiter would approach their table. The little man would ask his wife 'Mama, what would you like?' 'A Trappist, Papa' (this being a Belgian beer brewed by the Trappist Monks). 'Waiter, two Trappists'. After a while - 'Mama, what would you like now?' 'I fancy a coffee, Papa'. 'Waiter, two coffees'. This went on and on with the two always ordering identical beverages and/or snacks. Spilly swore that, if Mama had asked for a bucket of horse-pee, the order would have been 'Waiter, two buckets of horse-pee'.

Shortly after moving in at Vrijdagmarkt my grandfather, who had lived with us ever since Spilly's mother died, also passed away. Spilly had promised her mother she would look after him although he was her stepfather. If ever one needed an example of someone dying of a broken heart, he was the personification thereof. I was very fond of him, partly because of his kind nature, but perhaps too because of his harsh life. Prior to his retirement, he had been a 'barrel roller' at the Port for a well known firm of petrol dealers and the harsh work through all sorts of weather had left him with a lung complaint. He was forever helping himself to 'tar-sweet's which he sucked all day swearing they helped him to breathe. I, too, loved the tarry taste and he regularly shared them with me. To my horror I heard afterwards that tar-products can contain a cancer forming ingredient . . . He was what is generally known as a 'healthy eater' and I once witnessed him devouring 7 small plaice for his supper accompanied by a small loaf!

Apart from his daily beer intake, he would periodically visit a strange winery, no longer in existence, situated in a cellar under a shop. The wine served in this establishment was mainly of a cheap red variety which the populace had baptised 'pinar' and after a session in that Bacchanalian sphere, Grandpa would return home zig-zagging along the pavements, crossing roads where heavy traffic abounded. It strengthened my belief in a special Guardian Angel for drunks!

During the summer after my fourteenth birthday, I and my school pals completed our studies at the Girls' School for Official Education. Prior to leaving, I sat a voluntary exam both for City and State which I passed with 'great distinction' as the diploma proclaimed. Spilly had urged me to take part as it was an essential element in successfully soliciting in the future for a career with either the City Authorities or Government. Fate decreed otherwise, and both diplomas remained rolled up with their ribbons with never a need for their use!

I had always yearned to become a doctor. I was soon to be made painfully aware that, not only were my parents lacking in financial means, my mentality and character were not conducive to this profession. No sooner would I detect someone in pain, then I would cry in sympathy and it did not look as though this compassionate trend would harden.

Next, as far as teaching was concerned, I showed little of the patience that is a prerequisite for this calling. Languages and the mystery of shorthand did attract me and so I landed at the High School for Commerce, a department of the University. In order to assist my perfecting the French language, Spilly had recruited a young teacher who had not yet obtained a permanent position. She called twice weekly and I made great strides, important enough in a bi-lingual country especially if one's background was Flemish. If Gainsborough had known her, he would have put her on canvas. She was elegance personified in her dark velvet dress, fitted to a perfect figure, its only adornment, a long, golden chain with hanger, her golden hair beautifully brushed back, culminating in a heavy knot resting on a slender neck and with a smile like an angel's and the patience paired to it. Strange how we remember certain people and completely forget others.

After school hours our square proved to be a safe playing ground for the kids from the neighbourhood. We would stand in groups and chat and start to flirt with the boys and although some of them sometimes dared to tell us a risqué joke, we were nevertheless rather naive. Although by then getting on for sixteen, my parents were very strict with me and it was quite a feat when Spilly allowed me and my girlfriend to walk out on Sundays to Antwerp's shopping avenue, the De Keyserlei, where in summer, the pubs and restaurants arranged terraces on the pavement in front with tables and chairs cushioned in gay colours; one could order anything from a refreshing drink and cold salad snack to a hot meal with wine or a galaxy of ice-cream dishes at all hours of the day and these establishments are now more splendid than ever. Adjoining the Century Hotel, we discovered the first 'Automatic Bar' with shelves containing a variety of sandwiches and snacks behind glass. After inserting coins, the attractively presented dish would automatically descend in a kind of miniature lift. Most of our pocket money would be spent on the mouth-watering concoctions, or on the maple-syrup wafers we obtained from a 'Crémerie' which, incidentally, was also famous for its Italian style ice-cream displayed in various colourful containers, and which was full of pieces of real fruit or nuts.

Yvonne, my early school friend decided not to continue studying and had become friends with another ex-pupil, Tilly, whose parents owned a garage in the south sector of Antwerp. Her father, in addition, acted as chauffeur and was a good-looking, neatly dressed man. One day his wife discovered he had an intimate relationship with one of the barmaids in a pub called La Cigale adjoining the garage. In fury, she grabbed hold of the revolver he had purchased as a safety measure during night duty, opened the door to the café and shot him. Considering she had never before fired a gun, he died instantly, a chance in a million, and later on the jury acquitted her, one of the first 'crimes de passion' in the annals of Antwerp legal history. Afterwards, the boys of our group would often taunt Tilly if she happened to pass by, except for one, who later became my first boyfriend.

His mother happened to be the best saleswoman I have ever met. She ran a furniture shop for her brother and worked on lucrative commission which doubtless inspired her seemingly inexhaustible patience. The expression 'Able to sell a fridge to an Eskimo' was coined for her! A potential customer would have to possess the hide of a rhino to withstand her sales talk and most of them would leave having purchased something. Her merchandise was manufactured from solid oak which appealed to a certain strata of the market, mostly bargees as their craft regularly docked at Antwerp. During the ensuing war years, she mainly sold to black-marketeers who made their way to the city from their farms in the country, loaded with produce or the profits thereof. As a matter of interest, it was widely known that small farmers would purchase expensive walnut or rosewood dining room suites from the more exclusive furniture shops and deposit these in their barns for lack of space in their hitherto primitive living quarters . . . Exchange barter was also rife and 'sober Mieke', as she was called, was thus in a position of bringing delicacies to her table which few people could then afford! I can still see her bottling a variety of foodstuffs such as roasts, chickens, wildfowl, expensive fruits and rare vegetables. There always seemed to be white bread, real butter and cooking fats in abundance in her larder. Come Christmas or the New Year during those war years, I was lucky enough to be invited to partake in the odd meal.

In later years, British friends denigrated the existence of the black market on the Continent. Controversial as it might seem, it was the only thing that kept the underprivileged classes alive as it was through their efforts that foodstuffs were regularly smuggled past German guards and the profits they made on the resale in turn sustained them.

Rick, the boy to whom I was attracted from the start, was a member of the Royal Sea Scouts, and so too was one of my cousins Anthony. The latter was a few years older and as I became more aware of my obligations and responsibility towards myself in these developing years, Spilly gave her permission for my attending the occasional Scouts Ball or 'Thé Dansant', chaperoned by Tony if my girlfriend's mother was unable to comply. He faithfully took and safely returned me after each event accompanied by his love of the moment. At the appropriate age he joined the Merchant Navy, happened to be aboard his ship berthed at New York during the outbreak of war in Europe, and took up residence in the USA. After his marriage to an American subject, he took American nationality. He returned to Belgium, however, in the late 1980's and died in the country of his birth . . .

One could say it was 'calves love' at first sight between Rick and myself and if much later at a more mature age I had not encountered my beloved Englishman, who knows, - this my first love, certainly not less intense in its innocence, could have led to marriage. I particularly liked him because of his decency for, during those early, formative teens, everything seemed to be wrapped in a romantic cloud as far as I was concerned. That our relationship remained platonic for ten years, and we even became officially engaged, vouches for this innocence. Perhaps it stemmed from his inexperience and my reticence in experimenting. After all, I was for the greater part aware of Spilly's warning: 'You can lose your virginity but once and, in order to avoid any reproaches with the man who will ultimately marry you, you had better lose it to him!' That was the pre-war philosophy upheld by a vast strata of society. I ruefully smile now in these modern, promiscuous times . . . Be that as it may, I knew most answers theoretically and even consulted my favourite married cousin who taught me a multitude of various ways in which to sexually please a man as those were things I was just too embarrassed to ask Spilly, broadminded as she was, and which I was told were of paramount importance in marriage.

Spilly, in the meantime, realised that she hated each moment spent at the Vrijdagmarkt pub. The difference from her beloved The Scheldt was too much, in spite of the occasional visits from some of her old British customers who, after enquiring about our new abode, found their way there during the rare calls of their ship at Antwerp. However, no light appeared at the end of the economical crisis tunnel. Trade exacerbated at Beliard & Creighton too. In addition, Spil had an argument with his immediate superior, a Scottish gentleman, peeved because Spil had pointed out a fault in his engineering plan which could have let to a calamity. When this Chief was requested to complete a list of 'superfluous personnel' Spil's name was on it.

He was desperate and replied to an advert from a British shipping company in need of volunteer seamen for sailings between London and Spanish ports where, in the meantime, war had broken out. Provisions and a variety of goods were to be shipped for the Spanish Government troops. He was accepted on the basis of his diplomas and previous experience. While his ship was berthed in the port of Bilbao, German Stukas, on the side of Franco, flew over and bombarded the town and port. Spil, busy looking after the machinery in the engine room became suddenly aware of heavy, thudding reverberations. Having climbed on deck he immediately grasped what was happening, fled like a hare from the gangway and was just in time to observe from a farther and safer distance, his ship being hit and sinking on the spot! After his return, he was mustered on another British ship with its next destination a Russian port.

As I stated before, Spil was what we called a fiery 'blue one', meaning a real Liberal. During his youthful years, prior to an election, he would go poster sticking, armed with a bucket of paste and a long handled brush. Once he even returned home from one such outing after he had had a strong argument with a member of the Socialist party, likewise inspired and equipped with his propaganda material. Spilly opened the door to her husband's ring and beheld a perplexed looking appearance, covered from head to toe in paste which dribbled in thick rivulets from his hair into his collar, minus his paste bucket (which by then was draped over the head of his competitor) and with the majority of his posters still intact!

Having been made redundant more than once, not by his own default, there nevertheless crept into Spil's political debating from time to time a pinch of rebellious resentment. His arguments would contain a tint that bordered on the Red, which in itself was quite a paradox in view of his in-born Liberalism. It needed but one single voyage to that Russian port to cure him from any of the leftist leanings - however incubating - he might have had. Indeed, during discharge of the cargo, he witnessed something which in its full incredulity

64

epitomised the inhumanity of the Stalin regime. A Russian dock worker secretly hid in his clothes a packet of cigarillos handed to him by a member of the crew in pure friendship and which happened to be similar to the cargo discharged. One of the uniformed guards had noticed this, brutally searched the unfortunate man on leaving the ship, not only confiscating the cigarillos but shooting the man in cold blood on the spot . . .

When Spil, in the meantime, offered some oranges to another docker, the man virtually crammed the segments in his mouth in Spil's cabin, his eyes rolling in furtive fear, then washed his hands and mouth several times with ship's carbolic soap to eliminate all traces of the strongly flavoured fruit with its treacherous give-away smell. To eat an imported orange meant . . . stealing from the community.

When Spain's Government ceded to the overwhelming Fascist odds and fighting ceased, Spil left the British shipping company and was able to muster with a minor Belgian one. Their ships, however, were small and very old. In fact, the Antwerpian seamen baptised them 'the floating coffins', but Spil had no choice; the dole, for as much as it existed, was distasteful to him. As there was a noted absence of any form of lifesaving equipment, least of all a lifeboat, as a precaution Spil had purchased an old car tyre, keeping this in his cabin. During a heavy storm in the North Sea, the inevitable happened, the ship went down. Only two out of the five crew were saved by a fishing boat. Spil could not swim - something always beyond my understanding - but he kept afloat in his car tyre. The ship's cook, a native of Ostend, jumped into the rough sea, could not swim either, and kept shouting 'Spil, help me, I'm, drowning!' With the tyre around his waist, Spil tried to reach the cook using his arms as oars. The whipped up waves thrashed him back time and again and with indescribable horror, he witnessed his shipmate drown. He suffered nightmares for months on end and would awake sobbing. After his return, he never sobered up for a full week. Among my souvenirs, I still have the original telegram received after the shipwreck which reads 'Ship lost, Papa saved'.

∗

By the end of my second year at the Commercial College, our financial position had gradually worsened. The curriculum at the college covered a multitude of subjects which had little in common with the commercial office routine per se, in my opinion at least. A certain private commercial Institute specialised more intensely in those subjects of manifest importance those days to office personnel, such as shorthand, typing, correspondence and bookkeeping. The first three subjects were taught in up to four languages. Provided one studied seriously and passed the intermediate mini-tests prior to the final exams, a diploma per subject was guaranteed after three months. In fact, lazy or disinterested pupils were simply expelled, not just to save the parents from unnecessary expense but foremost to uphold the Institute's reputation vis-à-vis their promise of a 'diploma in three months'.

I was able to persuade Spilly of the fact that, whilst the initial outlay of fees, etc would be enormous, within the next three to six months this could be recuperated quite early in the event of my finding employment. One minor drawback I luckily soon overcame. It was the variant of shorthand method taught at the Institute as against the Commercial College and I had to start from scratch, forgetting all I had learned before. However, shorthand had a fascination for me and, faithful to my promise to Spilly, I graduated with diplomas in Netherlands, French, English and German (the latter I had been studying at the College) for shorthand, typing and correspondence. In order to attain the prescribed typewriting speed, my father had come to an agreement with one of his acquaintances, a member of the same Liberal Association he belonged to and who sold typewriters in his well established shop near the centre of Antwerp. I was allowed to exercise on one of his personal machines after school hours.

Although employment during the immediate pre-war period was not easy to find as the recession was still rife, I was lucky and, after but a few soliciting letters, was engaged by a firm of Laboratory Equipment Manufacturers, at the 'encouraging' salary of B.Fr.250 a month (at present day values about £5 per month) for a 9-hour day . . . Saturdays till 12.30. Shylock reigned supreme those days insisting on his half pound of flesh! My workload consisted of taking shorthand, and typing letters in Netherlands, French and German and making tea for the other office staff. Once every fortnight, the huge display window at the front of the premises would be emptied, all items dusted and replaced and that, too, became part of my duties.

Rick, in the meantime, had been called up for his National Service and his regiment happened to be situated not far from my employers. On their return from manoeuvres, the regiment would often pass the firm and if I happened to be in the display window at the time the din of the wolf-whistles was quite embarrassing until a harsh command from the accompanying officer strangled the noise.

As luck would have it (precious little seemed to come our way at that time!) my parents were able to sell the pub and we duly moved to a small self-contained flat in a private house practically under the spire of St Aldegondis Church, in a select little street known by its flowery name of Geraniumstreet. My entire 'enormous' salary went to the rental and every Saturday afternoon I would visit my aunts and uncles who invariably gave me pocket money which my parents simply could not afford. My Uncle Jeff, married to

Spil's sister and a member of the Board of Directors of Mercantile Marine and Graving Docks Co, which was one of Antwerp's leading ship repairing firms, advised me shortly afterwards of a secretarial vacancy at the British American Tobacco Co at Merksem, a suburb of the city.

Upon receipt of my application and as a good knowledge of English was necessary, after conversation and ensuing written proof, I was accepted at the princely salary of B.Frs500 per month. Not only did this represent an entire month's rent, but it meant shorter working days. Incorporated in the factory was a printing department where all the packaging for the BATCO's cigarettes and tobacco was being manufactured, called Les Grandes Imperimeries Belges. It only took me 20 minutes walking to reach the office, via back streets, and I soon felt entirely at home, growing accustomed to the monotonous beat of the off-set printing machines.

My immediate superior, Mr Nietvelt and his colleague were constantly vying with one another and as the former had taken me under his wing from the start, I learned my first lesson in diplomacy and followed his instructions, sweetly talking his competitor out of the counter-orders with blissful innocence and a dose of guile. The latter also wished to be known as Mr Kemmelle but his name was spelt Kemel (which in Flemish means camel!) The remarkable thing was that both managers had a gammy leg, the one his left, the other the right one. When walking side by side through the gangways between the machinery, they invariably leant rhythmically towards each other at each step and, being somewhat on the heavy side, it looked like the clash of the Titans especially when involved in one of their numerous disputes when eyes would bulge, faces beetroot red in anger, arms gesticulating, and the machinists would hum the little ditty 'Sunday, Monday, drunk but never had a drop day' ...

On the 3rd September 1939 war was declared between Great Britain and Germany and Belgium called its General Mobilisation.

The London branch of our firm had sent two Britons, sons of Directors, to train in every aspect of the industry. I soon befriended them as I was getting quite fluent in English by then. In addition, under the leadership of a musical director-cum-technician of the works, a small orchestra had been assembled and as I loved singing - undoubtedly inherited from Spilly - I soon became an active member. We were often invited at week-ends to perform for our troops 'somewhere in the field' and also held musical evenings at the factory itself. Occasionally, out of politeness but for the better part to rescue them from boredom after their office hours as they lived in digs, I accompanied the Britons, one at a time, to a cinema in the town centre, followed by a coffee for me and a beer for them, at one of the frequented and luxuriously furnished drinking establishments of Antwerp's main thoroughfare, the De Keyserlei. They dutifully took me home and politely left me at the entrance to our flat. Initially I received beautiful bouquets delivered at home to thank me for a pleasant evening. These, however, were soon accompanied by flowery love letters from one of them so that I felt obliged to put an end to our little jaunts. Very much amused, in a melancholy way though, I sometimes still recall the highly romantic style of his notes with expressions such as 'I worship the ground you walk on' . . . and 'At night I fall asleep crying out your name in hopeful prayer' . . . Spilly commented: 'That one swallowed the Blarney stone, for sure! This was by no means my first experience of the English romantic. I always suspected that a raging fire burns under the so-called cold reserve of which he is all too often accused, outside his island. An opinion formed, no doubt, by those who meet him superficially or once travelled through his country at the speed of Epsom salts . . .

I inherited my love of opera and operetta from Spilly and preferred singing these. Italian operas and German and Austrian operettas featured daily on our radio programmes and through the BBC output I became familiar with the unforgettable, though lighter genre composers of this century; Gershwin, Cole Porter, Hoagy Carmichael, Irving Berlin, Jerome Kern, etc. 'If music be the food of love, play on' manifested itself where I was concerned! Indeed, good music can soothe disturbed hearts; it brings hope for those standing at the abyss of depression; can sustain love in its intimate intensity or fill one with love for his fellow man. It calls forth the sun over darkening clouds. And if one could perambulate the diversity of that which is old and that which is new, without taking too much into account the cultural caucus of what is nowadays called 'creative youth' and could imprint this from the early years in one's offspring, who knows it might possibly help create a less aggressive society. Free from destructiveness, from the instinct to hurt or even kill, free from the misdirected, blown-up *ego* . . . It is said that preaching outside the church is useless, becomes a voice in the wilderness. Shouldn't those leading our society ask themselves whether the caprices of the modern pop bands, inclusive of the wanton destruction of expensive musical instruments on the platform, the aggressive beat which fills air and ears monotonously hour after hour, the madly sinister words of certain modern songs (if one can understand them in that cauldron of cacophony), the drugs in all their varied forms, haven't finally come to their conclusion. Or has it all gone too far? Two generations never knew anything but this inciting beat. No wonder that the romantic musicals of the present British composers and lyricists enjoy such enormous success world-wide! Lloyd Webber's Evita, Cats, Phantom of

70

the Opera, Aspects of Love, Les Miserables and Lionel Bart's
Oliver, to name but a few.

Chapter Two

War!

Time never stands still . . . I awoke one beautiful clear 10th May morning 1940. The sun had fashioned my bedroom into a sphere of gold and I jumped out of bed crooning. We were never bad tempered in our little family first thing in the morning and I was, after all, a chip off the old block. Strange, although we had become accustomed to regularly hearing planes passing over our territory, the repetitious drone of a multitude of motors drove me to the window and I witnessed an air battle in progress. In the distance, like the dull thudding of faraway thunder, I heard the unmistakable sound of bombs dropping. During my hasty breakfast, the NIR, the Belgian equivalent of the BBC, announced the sad news that the Nazi hordes had violated our territory and so we, too, were at war!

After arriving at the British American Tobacco Co, I noticed that they had hastily lugged immense bales of paper and cardboard cuttings to the domed cellars to function as 'defensive fortification'. What irony, the whole place would have erupted in a veritable inferno in a vestige of time should a bomb have hit us! Virtually no work was produced that day on the factory floor nor in the offices. Sirens lowed in their high-pitched tone at regular intervals and we spent more time in the cellars than in the office. The two Britons virtually vied with one another in order to protect me from an invisible foe.

For seventeen long days, the Belgian Army fought a lost battle against an enemy equipped with the acme of modern weaponry; tanks, Stukas - the terror inducing planes of which few humans had any experience except Spil in Bilbao.

Night after night, after having been woken up by the screaming sirens, placed in and around Antwerp, and the incessant drone of countless planes, we fled from home to shelter in the heavily domed crypts of the St Aldegondis

Church nearby. The bombardment of London was in full swing.

Frightened witless, we listened to the thudding reverberations of falling bombs as one German bomber after another was forced to shed its load after having received a fatal hit by the fighting squadrons of the RAF. Enormous damage was caused on our territory on their way to the North Sea and beyond. Even after the bombardments over England had ceased we still had to shelter for the retaliating American bombers en route to German cities often jettisoned their deadly cargo on allied soil after they had been hit . . .

Until that too reached its conclusion.

I must mention that, before Belgium's capitulation, our soldiers remained fighting where they stood, more often than not until their bitter end.

Leading his army stood a King, beloved by his people who, like his father before him, remained with his soldiers until the ultimate humiliation - total capitulation. Whatever subsequent historians may write, the mothers whose sons fought in the Belgian Army could never forget that it was thanks to King Leopold III that the majority returned home safe and sound!

We were paid off at the firm prior to the closing down of the premises; the Britons were shipped out on the last boat to leave Antwerp bound for the UK. We never heard from them again. There were rumours that the ship, just outside the mouth of the River Scheldt, was bombed and sank with all hands . . .

*

On 28th May the inhabitants of Antwerp were ordered over the ether to remain indoors for at least three full days. Periodically looking out of the corner of our windows we only saw deserted streets, so alien to our lively Port. Early morning of the third day this order was rescinded after we had listened all night to the endless marching of heavy boots, in monotonous rhythm, spasmodically interrupted by harsh comments or distant rifle shots. Walking out after this imposed quarantine, we looked around with trepidation. The St Jansplein, a square normally noted for its bi-weekly open markets, was filled to more than capacity with armed panzers and tanks, as it swarmed with German soldiers clad entirely in black uniforms. It was unbelievable. We had not exactly expected Draculas with blood dripping jowls, though in our imagination was captured the image of an intimidating warrior, a triumphant conqueror with a most cruel expression, a hangover kept alive since the First World War. What we observed were tall, well-built Adonises, obviously dead tired, some were even draped physically over their motors, some leaning against their tanks, smoking, laughing in conversation with each other in normal speaking voices. If it had not been for the so hated sound of their mother tongue, we could have imagined them in khaki!

Later though, as time went by in a seemingly unending war, we realised only too clearly that these initial elite troops had formed part of the strategy of German Fighter Command and were not only chosen for their crack achievements in their tanks but to instil admiration in the defeated. Indeed, the ensuing infantry troops, clad in their dull grey/green with their ever present disinfectant smell, spoke volumes about the 'Herrenvolk'. Not to mention the hordes of SS troops amongst whom the number of psychopaths was legion!

Soon, however, daily routine took over. We were immediately strictly rationed and the population instantly underwent a Dr Jekyll and Mr Hyde metamorphosis so that a furtive food hoarding madness took hold of them; in later years whipped up by the financially better off for whom the

and witnessed my bare knee protruding from my new silk stockings . . Spilly's comment upon my tearful return 'It's still better than breaking a leg, child'!

As soon as the Belgian Army had capitulated and some Allied soldiers taken prisoner by the Germans, the local authorities looked for shelter for the many wounded amongst them. The hospitals in Antwerp were all soon fully occupied. One day I was told that an Auxiliary Hospital had been established in a convent forming part of the grounds of the St Carolus Boromeus Church, and that amongst the wounded were British prisoners of war, I hastened off to offer my services as interpreter and was recruited, in addition, as volunteer assistant nurse. All at once and for the first time in my life I stood face to face with terrible flesh wounds caused by bullets and shrapnel.

Apart from the very strict matron, there were a further six nurses and a few assistant nurses on duty. We wore white frock-coats and I was given a large square serviette to wear over my hair on which I had hastily embroidered a red cross. Each morning we disinfected the wounds and renewed bandages. Limbs with deep gashes (the bone was visible on some of the forearms I treated) were plunged into ether baths. Some bullet wounds seemed of a less serious nature being on arms, legs or shoulders and healed fairly swiftly. Most were Regular Army officers and soldiers from all over Britain; some from the Ardennes in Belgium. On recovering, some of them became my personal charges and I assisted with their physiotherapy exercises which were not too difficult for an inexperienced person as myself after I had been given a thorough demonstration by a qualified nurse.

It soon became apparent that we were getting short of food and so, after my daily shifts, from the early hours and on my way home, I would call on every baker, grocer and greengrocer begging free food for the wounded. On mentioning they were British prisoners, I was pleasantly surprised by the generosity of the Antwerpian traders.

British prisoners of war in hospital with their nurses including myself (an auxiliary) in the front. Spilly is on the left, having visited them with provisions.

With my special charges.

The soldiers anxiously awaited my return each morning and were more than grateful for the extras. One day, when it became obvious that the majority of them were well on the way to recovery, an order was issued from the German authorities to assemble a convoy for further imprisonment in Germany. It all happened so suddenly! We presented ourselves as usual in the early morning hours for our shift only to be told to our consternation that our patients were to leave practically immediately. After having ascertained that they would remain a few days in a barracks in Malines, which in addition was an assembly place for groups from hospitals in other Flemish towns, we hastily took leave of our patients. We then decided to cycle to the barracks the following day and loaded as much food and warm clothing as we could, borrowed from male family members or friends, onto bicycles, stuffing as much as possible in rucksacks. I hired a cycle from a rental garage and, loaded as a mule, arrived in Malines accompanied by my colleagues, sporting the most painful buttocks ever experienced and I could hardly move on alighting. The return voyage was sheer agony! Our patients were thrilled with our gifts and more so because of our presence. In the meantime, some romances flourished. One of my Scots friends handed me a parcel in gratitude for my care. On opening it I found a golden bracelet, ditto pendant and a small brooch in hand painted enamel set in a narrow golden frame. He sensed my suspicion but assured me had had found these trinkets after a bombing raid on the road they were taking, possibly lost by refugees. I wore them for years.

Later from their prisoner of war camp somewhere in Bavaria he regularly sent me short letters on specially provided forms informing me he was working on a farm. After repatriation he continued writing for a while but refused the return of the jewellery and after a year or so we stopped corresponding, the reason why was never very clear.

Whether some of the romances between the nurses and their wounded came to fruition was never confirmed as I lost touch with the other nurses. The move of our patients brought to an end my brief spell in the nursing field.

Chapter Three

The Resistance

I never knew how or where, but Spil became an active member of the Resistance Movement known as 'The White Brigade' Fidelio, under the command of Colonel Marcel Louette (then Lieutenant) when the group formed immediately after the capitulation of Belgium. Fidelio was Louette's code name, a name which would be chiselled forever and with pride in the annals of the history of Belgium. It seemed fitting that, as a ship's engineer, Spil was best suited for acts of sabotage at the shipyard. As already mentioned his brother-in-law, Joseph (our Uncle Jeff and husband of Aunt Stans, Dad's sister), was a director of the previously mentioned Mercantile Marine Engineering and Graving Docks Co, the leading maritime yard in Antwerp. As such he was able to set in motion the employment of my father. However, understandably, in view of his age and long service with the company, Uncle Jeff did not wish to know anything about Spil's activities in the Resistance.

Amongst my souvenirs I keep a certificate, written in English by Mr Callens, Social Secretary of the Resistance group, mentioning Spil's activities during the ensuing war years. Later on I showed it, unashamedly proud, to my British friends to prove that, in spite of being vanquished, our fight continued . . .

The majority of ships confiscated by the enemy were to be transformed at the shipswharf into veritable arsenals. Spil's resistance register reads:

'To sabotage ships' pumps so that they would cease to function after a short while;
passing on their departure date and nature of cargo;

also information about armed structures and weapons aboard;

adding sand to vital parts of the machinery of the mv Zinnia, (a ship that had cost the Germans millions of francs in repair and restructuring);

passed information about departures to a fellow member with secret radio. (It was later confirmed that from London, having been contacted, bombers were dispatched which sank the Zinnia just outside the mouth of the Scheldt on her first run from the repair yard!)'

distributed secret documents to other Resistance contacts, members of his cell, and passed on secret press communications;

supplied carborundum for use by the sabotage groups active in the field.'

As far as I am concerned, apart from the occasional delivery of secret press bulletins, hidden in my old school satchel, Spil strictly kept both myself and Spilly out of the underground activities as we soon learned of the indescribable tortures to which the SS subjected all captive resistance members.

Belgian personnel and workforce were either directly or indirectly employed by the enemy; one had to live. I joined another firm, Electrical Ship Repairers, situated only ten minutes' walk from our new abode, a much larger flat in a select street near the Atheneum College in the heart of Antwerp. Apart from shorthand and typing, my duties also comprised working out the wages of the electricians on a repaired, second-hand Burroughs machine which became the nightmare of my life because of its continuous breakdown. Mr Thys, the owner of the firm simultaneously acted as its Managing Director and, in order to justify his profits accrued by working for the occupying Forces, had his personnel regularly examined by a doctor to determine our state of health under the harsh rationing. Hot soup was delivered by an industrial purveyor of soup kitchens on a daily basis and when it became evident in late 1942 that I had become undernourished with far too low a blood pressure, bordering on anaemia, which more or less alarmed the doctor, he prescribed a daily diet consisting of soup, a large slice of bread thickly covered with raw, minced beef. Properly prepared it is one of Belgium's culinary delicacies especially when mixed with extremely finely chopped shallot, pepper and salt, and bound into a paste with either the yolk of an egg or mayonnaise, then finished with some added capers. This dish is called 'fillet Americain'. However, my allocation consisted simply of the plain minced beef. I would have voraciously eaten it if it had not been over salted by the janitor in charge of the soup distribution, etc. No matter how I protested, he kept liberally adding salt which made me puke. His motivation was never clear, perhaps plain unadulterated jealousy because he himself did not come into consideration in spite of his advanced age.

After the Liberation, I heard that Mr Thys had been arrested as a 'war-criminal-collaborator' which I found inane. Those days, though, in the minds of many people there only existed White and Black and the grey shades of life's gamma were lost in the often unjustified fury of the surviving Resistance members, many of whom had only joined up at the time when the Germans were already on the run . . .

My parents' honesty sometimes bordered on the ridiculous, and I have known my Pa to steal only once in his lifetime! At the Shipswharf much copper was in evidence for the repair of the confiscated ships. It had become most expensive and rare, very much sought after by the dealers of second-hand metals. Every evening he was able to pinch some piece of copper until he had quite a large quantity. The dealers paid a very good price. Mòst profits, however, he handed over for the Resistance in the Ardennes to where most of the saboteurs had fled.

It was by then Winter 1943 and Spil's footwear and clothes left a lot to be desired. He had been able to repair his workshoes with soles and heels cut out of old tyres. From his 'copper profits' he was able to buy a pair of shoes on the black market, an overcoat and an 'Eden' hat. This style was named after Sir Anthony Eden, one of the best dressed and most debonair Ministers of the British pre-war Government, and was very fashionable at the time. The first Sunday, going for a walk in the main shopping centre of Antwerp. Spil, proud as a peacock, stepped into dog dirt. 'Pa, that's money' Spilly laughed. 'No, blast it, it's shit' Spil retorted. Remarkably, a week afterwards Spilly was summoned to the office of a Solicitor to receive B.Frs.15,000 (then about £100) as part of an inheritance of an uncle on her mother's side of the family. The ensuing week we gorged ourselves on a small black market bacon roast, eggs at B.Frs.10 each (these days the equivalent of £1 each) and white bread, each bite of which I practically sucked!

Prior to all this, though, in 1940 to be precise and from mid-September, Hitler seemed ready to invade England with his hordes. We daily witnessed the many German bombers darkening the skies on their way to the British Isles in the first instance to bomb London. He was firmly convinced that, once the capital was completely devastated, it would crush the morale of the population, thus facilitating the invasion plans of the Wehrmacht. The only thing that marred his plan was a small group of pilots with their ever decreasing number of

Spitfires and Hurricanes. We often saw air battles above our fields for the gallant and outnumbered pilots flew towards the aces of a far superior Luftwaffe before these could succeed in their plan. The whole world now knows about 'The Battle of Britain' and its young heroes, sometimes saved within an inch of their lives from a burning plane by their parachutes and who, once returned to base, went up again the same day. The 'Few' are remembered in Great Britain with respect and Prime Minster Churchill could not have put it better than when he declared:

'Never in the history of human conflict have so many owed so much to so few.'

And then, when towards the end of September it was obvious that the British were more determined than ever to defend their island and measures were taken to create a 'fire-line' in front of their coastline in case of necessity, Hitler and his military advisers gave up. He turned his attention instead to the invasion of Russia, which ultimately added to his defeat. Every 15th September Great Britain commemorates Battle of Britain Day.

In the hope that Rick and I would one day get married, his father suggested that he should learn the art of the barber, being employed by himself, and that I should follow evening classes for hairdressing. I did not have much choice, so in addition to working that old Burroughs machine at my employers, hairdressing was my next bane. Ladies hairdressers did not then bear the 'elite' stamp of the crimpers of today. However, in accordance with my character (one huge paradox from the moment of my birth as my Zodiac sign is Fishes or personality traits of two opposites) and in spite of all this, I seemed to pass my exams with flying colours. I was able to create a distinctive style for each set exam as I was lucky enough to prevail myself of my cousin Mary as a model. She, as luck would have it, contentedly suffered the pink water rinses I applied to her bleached hair to add colour to each style. My manicures were always concluded with a gentle finger massage and the examiners allowed extra points for this. Rick's parents were proud . . . I was grateful not to have let anybody down.

When I received my (reluctant) diploma at the Hairdressers' College.

The work at the electrical firm, coupled with our monotonous food intake and my low blood pressure, brought me to the edge of neurasthenia. I went to work with leaden feet and hated the dreaded Friday wage calculating especially as the Burroughs would, regularly as clockwork, fail before many wage slips had been dealt with so that we were forced to send the men home without their pay packets. I knew how eagerly this was expected in their households as we all lived from hand to mouth, and I invariably returned home sobbing my heart out. Like thousands of housewives Spilly sometimes stood for hours in the queue, in all weathers and wind, for our miserable ration of butter, sometimes an egg or even herrings at the fishmongers which were coupon free but with limited supplies. More than once stock had run out before it was her turn. Frozen to the marrow, she would return home empty handed.

Spil's character, irascible at times, continuously under pressure by virtue of his sabotage activities, did not improve. The three of us were undernourished and the war news, where the allies were concerned, seemed daily to exacerbate. We lived on our nerves.

Spilly was still employed by Aunt Stans and the small quantities of extra nourishment which this kind lady gave along with her wage were the only intake to relieve the monotony of our daily diet. We started snarling at one another at the least provocation. Coming home from work one day when we realised Spilly had once again returned from a queuing session without the hoped for variety and we were faced with the same old dish of potatoes with boiled onions, we shouted our frustration at her. Spilly burst out sobbing, 'I wish I was dead,' she cried. Spil and I looked at one another in horror and so ashamed. We never moaned at table again . . . but the scene was imprinted on my memory for the rest of my life and I still can't forgive myself for having needlessly caused her such pain.

In our little dining room, the nucleus of our family life, Spil had nailed a large map of Europe on one of the walls on which he painstakingly ticked off the course of the war with pins carrying either a British flag or the swastika. We were not allowed to listen to the BBC although we daily heard people whistling the most popular and newest British or American tunes and our youth, except the pro-German ones naturally, sometimes even sang these in public. Every evening, before retiring, Spil would change the wavelength on our radio from BBC to the German sender 'Germany Calling' in English with the hated voice of the infamous Lord Haw-Haw, the British traitor in the service of the Reich's propaganda broadcasting.

The Nazi hordes relentlessly pushed their way through Europe: Russia did not escape unscathed. Great was our excitement when we heard Hitler had to forfeit his invasion plans of Great Britain after the victory of the Battle of Britain. John Bull made a plucky stand!

One evening Spil came home in a most agitated state. At Mercantile German soldiers, as well as 'black-shirts', the Belgian traitors in the service of the SS, were regularly acting as sentries. One of these was exceptionally brutal and hated by the entire workforce. He had more than once caught Belgian personnel stealing the odd item and denounced them to the SS officer in charge. 'Stealing from the Fatherland' was heavily punished, for German army personnel with the death penalty, for Belgians banishment to concentration camps, the existence of which we then not even suspected.

I was never able to discover detailed facts as Spil never talked about his activities, with a view to involving us as little as possible should the worst occur. However, it appears that on that particular day this Belgian SS-man was on duty at one of the connecting bridges between two dry-docks when Spil, at dusk, was forced to pass him. There had been a heavy frost on partly melted snow. The German sentries on duty stayed indoors, but a few Belgian workers were active in the open air. Spil, loaded up with discriminating material for the sabotage group, had to pass the SS-man and would undoubtedly have been frisked. He spontaneously reacted, feigned to slip on the ice and pushed the SS-man over the balustrade. When, alerted by his cry they eventually got him out of the hold, he was dead with a broken neck. The German authorities believed it to be an accident. The Belgians professed not to have seen a thing . . . Spil remained visibly upset and very quiet and seemed in deep thought for weeks on end; we hardly dared to talk to him.

What sublime excitement at the news of the Allied victory in Africa and the consequent defeat of the German General Rommel, whom the British had baptised 'The Desert Fox'! Spil simply pulled all his little flags from the map of Africa and nearly blew his front teeth out whistling 'Britannia rules the waves'.

Rommel's demise, during a so-called automobile accident in 1944, was preceded by the retreat from Russia of the German army, whose elite had long since perished or was crippled and hospitalised. Those still trying to hold out in the raw Russian winter consisted of the hard-core of SS-men, or soldiers nearer the retirement age as well as youths not long out of their short trousers, all of them forced to continue lost battles with the Mausers of their officers pointed at their backs.

Spil at 'Mercantile Marine Engineering' where he sabotaged repaired ships confiscated by the Germans. Just one of his 'activities'.

Spilly, myself and 'infamous' cousin Netta.

1943 hallmarked two happenings in my life.

For the first one I have to refer to our pre-war Vrijdagmarkt pub so reluctantly managed by Spilly. One day a modern open sports car arrived at our front door. Out stepped a smart well-dressed woman. Spilly couldn't believe her eyes; it was a cousin she had not seen for years. 'Cousin Netta' as she later on was called by us all, had gained a certain notoriety in a Bohemian circle of the 'quartier Latin', a district surrounding the French Opera at the Leopoldbrug in Antwerp, (now the Bourla Theatre) and frequented by all types of artisans, ladies and gentlemen of doubtful nature and mien, etc. At the time of her appearance she was 'enjoying the protection' of a well-known Industrial Ironmonger who had installed her in a delightful bungalow in Schoten near Antwerp. She was charm personified and obviously very pleased at finding us again after many years. She became a most regular visitor and I liked her very much, admiring her sophistication and open emancipation.

One night, though, returning unexpectedly from a reception, her much older lover caught her in bed with a young rival. He did not hesitate in throwing her out and she was forced to flee with a few hastily gathered items of clothing and some cash.

She was obliged to rent a small room somewhere in town, made the acquaintance of a cheese merchant and soon went to live in his flat at the back of his small shop. Joe, her new lover, was a broadminded, hardworking man-of-the-street, full of nervous energy. At the onset of war, with the strict cheese rationing and confiscating of stocks by the Germans he sold his business and joined the staff of the Erla Works (a branch of the Mercedes chain of Germany and run by the equivalent of the REME of the German Army) as a warehouse clerk. Blessed with the gift of the gab, he soon instigated friendly relations with a German Major in charge of buying tools and metals. Shortly afterwards, Joe could be seen accompanying the Major on his regular trips throughout the Province of Antwerp, later in Flanders and the Campines, purchasing metals and tools from the wholesalers and manufacturers. Soon their trips extended to Namur and Liege, the industrial parts of Belgium, and the Major began to depend more and more on Joe's enterprising nature.

By chance they also came across a small workshop near the Royer Sluice, north of Antwerp, where many small industries were established and huge wood storage hangars were erected. Pre-war the place was owned by a Briton and after he had fled to Great Britain, the Germans had confiscated it although it now stood empty. With the permission of the army hierarchy, the two decided to re-open the place and to install it as a Workshop with a view to turning out steel braces, matrixes, accessories and precision tools. The necessary machinery was purchased by the two, by then partners, with German capital from the Erla Works. Strange enough they kept its name intact: Workshops Ronny. A workforce was recruited and all correspondence and general office chores were taken care of by Cousin Netta.

Orders not only emanated from the Erla Works but from the Ford factories at Austruweel, likewise confiscated by the German occupying Forces. In addition, the Kriegsmarine whose headquarters were situated in the Antwerp Navigation College practically next door to the Workshop, also commissioned small repairs, etc.

Cousin Netta's education sadly left a lot to be desired and her knowledge of French was picked up in the twilight zone which she frequented for many years. She didn't have a clue about office work, the correspondence in both languages was full of grammatical mistakes and filing was a haphazard jumble of documents.

Joe who, in the meantime, had asked me to call him 'Uncle Joe' moaned in frustration as it took ages before he could make sense out of the hotchpotch of documents and invoices in the chaos of her filing. During one of their visits to our home, Uncle Joe heard how extremely unhappy I was at the Electro Navale firm and took advantage of the situation by offering me the position of his secretary at a salary of B.Frs.650 a month, the highest amount I had earned to date!

It took me two full days before all papers appertaining to the business were properly filed, after I had nearly burst a blood vessel laughing at the atrocious grammar and composition of Cousin Netta's French correspondence!

Joe was on cloud nine. Whatever information he requested, the reply was at my fingertips and I soon found myself thoroughly at home in that little office. 'Workshop' actually defied description. The building had been manufactured from corrugated iron and wood. The work area was situated in a square area. An old staircase led to a smaller space for the storage of tools and accessories, stocked by a storekeeper and next to a tiny office containing a huge square desk occupying the whole of the centre floor space, a cupboard to house the files and office requisites and two office chairs. It looked ridiculously small and primitive but offered a challenge to me and was, after all, a financial improvement. Unfortunately as the loo was communal and, furthermore, downstairs - in the open - Cousin Netta suggested that, as we were the only ones in the office and nobody would ever enter without knocking and our consent, we would place a small bucket between the desk and the outside wall so that we could respond to the lighter calls of nature. I was speechless, had never experienced anything like it before, but had to concur under the circumstances - she was in command after all! An odd job man, well advanced in years, was lumbered with the task of emptying and disinfecting the receptacle twice daily. This, in spite of my protest, as I thought it most humiliating but as far as he was concerned he took it all in his stride.

When it became obvious I could 'hold the fort' on my own, Cousin Netta appeared for only a few hours daily. Even so, during the hot summer, the little bucket soon became full as she was of fairly large build with, I suppose, a comparative bladder capacity and the old boy was not always available to see to it. An unpleasant smell of urine would regularly invade my senses, sharp at anytime. The only window in the office looked out onto the workshop downstairs, the choice being between the heavy oil machine smells or the occasional bucket smell as the combination of the two was pestiferous.

At that time we were regularly visited by a buyer from the Ford Motor Co, a most handsome man in his late thirties and Cousin Netta flirted outrageously with him which he completely ignored. He conducted himself most businesslike, though friendly and polite. One unbearably hot summer's day, I was just about to secretly empty the smelly receptacle, behind Netta's back, when to my horror in walked the Ford rep. I suggested she served ice-cold beer from the cellar as refreshment, but mainly with the hope that the hops smell would pervade. In the middle of discussions, before we could say 'cheers', 'Mr Ford Rep' suddenly stepped past my chair to telephone his office . . . with permission. The telephone had been installed at the left side of my desk allocation near the outside wall against which the infamous bucket had been placed. The man naturally had not got an inkling of the existence of this repulsive presence, kicked it over in his efficient haste, filling the hot atmosphere with a cloud of obnoxious urine fumes one could have cut with a knife. Gentleman as he indubitably was, he did not pay attention nor show disgust. However, I never dared to look him in the eye again during his subsequent visits and sidled out of the office like a thief until he left . . .

In the attic above our office, they had hoarded a stock of Dutch cheeses and German salamis which the old boy daily inspected and turned for safe preservation. My own daily lunch consisted of the invariable monotony of two slices of ration bread and a thermos of 'ersatz' coffee, called 'knijp' in the vernacular as it was brewed from roasted barley, real coffee beans, not yet transported for the German home front, fetching a fortune on the black market. Sometimes the thermos contained 'whistle milk', milk with all the nutritious content extracted; or 'porridge' made with oats and light table beer just so that I would put on a little weight although the bitter taste made me heave.

As I sat chewing my sandwiches with a filling of artificial apple preserve (this seemed to be the mainstay of all our daily lunches) Cousin Netta would daintily nibble hers filled with cheese and salami. She often left part of it and threw this in the wastepaper basket. As it was wrapped up, I fished it out after she had left, practically sucking each bite before swallowing. I seemed to be continuously hungry but dared not tell my parents for fear they would have shared their meagre ration even more than they already did.

The workforce finished at 5pm daily and as the storekeeper had the key, I too was allowed to leave the office. A special short train daily transported personnel from the Mercantile Marine Engineering Co, situated about five minutes drive to the north of our office, from and to the Orteliuskaai almost opposite to where I was born. When it reached the Royer Sluice just past the Workshops Ronny, it slowed down to go over a bridge. Spil would stand by a window, I waited by the bridge and, as soon as he spotted me, he would open the compartment door and, assisted by my Pa's strong arms, I would jump in accompanying him to the terminal. Together we would march home, arm in arm. We used to laugh with the jokes he had heard at Mercantile that same day. It always amazed me how plentiful these kept coming in spite of the overall war misery. Sometimes, we would even kiss one another on sheer impulse . . . how I loved that man!

Spilly was one day accosted in the street by a well meaning new neighbour; 'did she know her husband had a young mistress with whom he walked about unashamedly and on a regular basis?'

In the meantime, as Uncle Joe and Cousin Netta's financial situation had visibly improved, they moved to a most luxurious apartment at Isabellalei, an exclusive neighbourhood. The interior decorating was tastefully executed and fine furniture bought - on the black market naturally. Netta's wardrobe became extensive and expensive. Once she even turned up at the office dressed as a rider complete with whip . . . the horse we never discovered though!

Joe came visiting one Sunday and asked me if I would be prepared to compile and type some invoices at their private address during the ensuing Sundays for which he was prepared to pay me B.Frs.200 per session. This again would ensure a roast purchased on the black market. No real need to state, I snapped at it like a shark at bait.

I would generally start at 11am and finish by 4pm after which Rick would fetch me so that we could spend the rest of the Sunday together.

The bona-fide invoices were completed but not stamped as they were exempt from tax in dealing with merchandise destined for the Erla Works, ie German Army Services. I was handed blank invoices with letterheadings from the same firms. The prices on the original invoices were then to be increased by either 25%, 15% or 10% and the new prices typed on the blank ones next to the description of the original goods supplied. Somebody would then put a pseudo signature at the bottom under a 'paid in full' stamp. It was obvious there was a fraud going on. Uncle Joe and the German Major paid cash to the firms in question, at the prices quoted on the original invoices. The falsified ones where then sent to the Erla Works who promptly paid. This went on for several months until I resigned pretending that I needed my Sunday rests but in reality because the dishonest transactions of which I had by then become all too fully aware became repulsive, extra meat or not . . .

Then came the second happening in 1943 which hallmarked an extension to our family. Here I must recall Spilly's youth. When she was about eleven years old her mother found herself in the unfortunate position of having to leave her husband, Spilly's father. His drinking, womanising and regular physical abuse became too much. Spilly chose to remain with her mother in spite of the temptation of living with a financially well endowed father. Plunged into poverty as they suddenly were, she presented herself at a well known poulterers situated in an exclusive shopping centre of Antwerp for employment. Although he at first hesitated to taking on a mere child for lugging about the heavy baskets with poultry and game for delivery to various customers, the owner was soon overwhelmed by her cheerful handling, unbounded energy and reliable deliveries. Sometimes clients would pay cash and on returning to the shop not a centime would be missing. Her wage was 50 centimes (half a franc) per week plus tips. Her employers would occasionally give her left over pieces of chicken, game or rabbit, etc or invite her to partake of their midday meal. The couple were childless and very caring and Spilly was treated most generously by both of them. As life and subsequent events changed, she nevertheless kept in touch with them over the years.

Many years later, during the war period, my parents would sometimes spend their Sundays roving the countryside in order to buy from one farmer or another some black market food. Having heard some years prior to the war that the couple had sold their poultry business and retired to their property in Hove near Antwerp. Spilly had visited them from time to time. In due course the wife passed away and one day on their way back from visiting some farms, my parents called on the husband. To Spilly's consternation she found him almost unrecognisably aged. The little house was filthy and cold. It was clear that the man was ailing and had neglected himself. It appeared that he had worn the same underwear since the death of his wife more than a year before, hardly washed and only shaved periodically. Spilly rolled her sleeves up, helped the man to undress, placed him in a zinc bath which Spil had filled in the meantime with hot water and literally scrubbed him clean. Spil had brewed some coffee, cut some bread that had known fresher days, fried him two of their own black market eggs and were relieved to see the colour return to the man's cheeks. Wrapped in clean underwear, warm food inside, he duly fell asleep. Spilly wrote him a note promising to return shortly, wrapped his dirty underwear in newspaper and went home in deep thought. It took her three full hours to scrape off the thick scaly substances before boiling the lot, for he did not seem to possess sufficient coupons for new underwear!

She afterwards visited him on a regular basis, kept his house clean, bathed him frequently and prepared and fetched as much food as his coupons would allow and from whatever else she found in his cupboards. After a few months, however, it became apparent that his health had deteriorated. He caught a chest infection and the doctor, summoned to his bedside, advised Spilly to place him in an old people's home. This went against Spilly's nature especially as the old man started to sob pitifully. The end of the story: Joseph, the old man, came to live with us. Spilly vacated their own bedroom for him and moved the parental bed to mine. It proved afterwards that she had her hands more than full with the upkeep of her own home and that of Aunt Stans, looking after the old boy, cooking whatever food she could obtain and queuing up regularly for rations etc. There seemed no end to the carousel of routine. Although his health improved slightly, our guest hardly ever left his armchair except to go to bed.

One day he asked Spilly to summon his solicitor. Apparently he had a sister still alive somewhere although she never visited him. Just once did she appear on our own doorstep after having found out he no longer resided at his old address. His first visit concluded, the solicitor returned shortly afterwards accompanied by two witnesses and Spilly surmised that Old Joseph was having a Will drawn up. Shortly afterwards his mental condition deteriorated and for Spilly it seemed akin to looking after a mentally deficient child. Each evening found her exhausted. The old chap continuously tried to get out of his armchair with her aid: he was no lightweight. Then, once up he would drop heavily back into the chair, not knowing what exactly he wanted, unceasingly up and down like a yo-yo, for as long as Spilly was available

In the meantime, all seemed well at the Workshops Ronny except that Cousin Netta was getting more than fed up with Uncle Joe's constant praising of my services. When exactly the little green eye of jealousy finally spouted like a festering wound is irrelevant. The fact is she began to search for a reason to discredit me. When the telephone rang one day, a voice like a virago accused me in shrieking staccato that Rick had gossiped about their clandestine invoice activities with some of the customers in his father's barber shop. I knew this to be a brazen lie as I had never dared even to tell him that I had, albeit temporarily, assisted in this fraud. She started being very abusive and I thought I was going to burst with fury when she threatened to have Rick deported to Germany for compulsory employment. I had no choice but to resign after first having shouted a counter threat that if she were to propagate such perfidious outrage, I would personally denounce their falsifying to the German Kommandantur, after which I literally threw the receiver down.

A very flabbergasted Uncle Joe rang me shortly afterwards. I assured him that I could never perpetuate any such betrayal and that I had only grabbed the first available option in defence to save Rick. He fully accepted my version but failed to persuade me to remain in his employ. Back home, when I tearfully told Spil my story, he grabbed his coat and rushed to the home of the couple. Cousin Netta, in satin relaxing housecoat, opened the door, saw the fury on Spil's face and ran like a hare upstairs to their living room, hastily bolting the door. If it hadn't been for Uncle Joe's arrival, Pa would have kicked the door in and I fear he would have momentarily forgotten that Cousin Netta belonged to the female species . . .

*

As time passed more and more of the Belgian workforce, irrespective of age, received their orders for compulsory employment in Germany. Females, still studying, or already employed, were exempt. This lead to a further development in my life. Afraid that I too would be sent to Germany now that I found myself unemployed, I contacted one of the teachers at the hairdressing school who was able to recommend me for a job as a manicurist at the barber shop of the Hotel Century which was occupied by the German High Command. My lessons at the evening classes for hairdressing had not been in vain and, although I preferred office work, I was grateful.

Much to my disgust though, our clientele consisted exclusively of German officers using the hotel as a stop-gap. After my manipulations, many left the salon with one or more nicked cuticles . . .

My weekly wage did not exactly give rise to jubilation but tips plus 10% on all sales of perfume or toiletries, doubled the weekly sum that I took home so, in fact, I earned even more than at the office. Most officers on leave and en route to their fatherland were eager to purchase French perfumes which they bought in abundance.

My colleague, a barber called Omer, enjoyed a lucrative income from his percentage on 'frictions', the perfume rub after a shave or haircut. He was an unforgettable clown speaking atrocious German speckled with Flemish which made me howl with laughter. In addition, he all too often ran a dangerous risk with his ribaldry directed at the Hun. He would call 'Fraulein, a manicure please for Herr Major' and then, half turning himself at sotto voce, 'Shrivelcock' which not only shocked the breath out of me but filled me with dread in case it had been overheard. Worse was to follow. The barberchair would be moved down and backwards and the face of the client covered with shaving soap. Whilst soaping he would ask, overpolitely, if the gentleman required a 'friction' but, as he posed the question, he would simultaneously bring up his left leg and motion as if he was taking a certain part of his anatomy in hand in order to respond to the call of nature. I'd sit there, with my fist in my mouth so as not to explode with laughter in spite of my fear of his being caught out in the act.

One quiet afternoon, I sat reading a book. Spil and I would hire these from a small shop in our neighbourhood owned by an old lady with a hate for all that was German, unbelievable in its ferocity. My books came from 'under the counter' as they were written in English by British, American or Canadian authors, for I was determined to keep improving my knowledge of this language. All of a sudden a shadow fell on my book and a voice said " 'A Farewell to Arms' by Hemingway? and in English, why don't you read German books?" Instinctively, without thinking clearly, and in genuine innocence, I replied 'It's not worth it, you only come every 20 years!' The German Major, by then a fairly regular customer, accepted this as a joke but nevertheless laughed from the side of his face. That day, dare I say, no nicking of skin!

Not long after the German occupation, our Jewish population were ordered to sew a yellow Star of David on their clothing which initially somewhat surprised the Antwerpians. A fairly large contingent of Jews lived in Antwerp and although the majority were occupying an area around Kievitstraat in the immediate vicinity of the Jewellery Quarter, a ghetto as such did not exist. Most of them were either employed in the diamond industry or owned successful businesses such as furriers, tailors, jewellers, bakers, Kosher butchers etc and were very well integrated and many lived in residential areas. The riddle was soon solved when we heard that their civil rights had been taken from them and we were beginning to feel uncomfortable. To be quite honest, apart from a certain preoccupation with our own worries vis-à-vis the then disheartening news from the front, a low percentage of the population was anti-Semitic and impassive to the situation. The arrow found its mark though on the day that we heard that Jewish families and individuals had been rounded up from their homes or in the streets, loaded onto lorries or rail wagons and forcibly taken away. It happened in the usual 'blitz' style of the enemy, declaring that they were being taken to selected locations to be employed in special work camps. Initially we swallowed this tale. (After all some British subjects, still in Belgium after the capitulation, had indeed been accommodated at appointed receiving centres, ie in a mansion just outside Antwerp known as the 'Little Castle'. One of Spilly's friends, a British subject by marriage, wrote to us regularly from this place, even advising us of receipt of parcels from England through the Red Cross).

Until, via the White Brigade Resistance movement, near the end of 1943, we learned that these selected sites were, in fact, concentration camps deep in the heart of Germany or Austria. Although the inhuman conditions in those camps and the massacre of the Jewish race was still an unimaginable horror, arrangements were made either by individuals or Resistance Groups to take escapees to safety.

Today the whole world is conversant with the unforgivable inhumanity of the Holocaust and of the bestial way man dared to treat his fellow man. As far as I am concerned, the heartrending grief I experienced after witnessing the filming of the liberation of these camps, and the sorrow that we just could not offer more efficient help much earlier, left a burning mark on my conscience, a feeling of guilt that will remain in my soul until the day I exhale my last breath. I can still see clearly before me those large, bewildered and begging eyes of one of the Jewish children, so 'enthusiastically' filmed by the German SS camera gang, prior to him being marched off to the gas chamber. Each time this documentary is repeated on TV, even after all these years, an overwhelming sorrow fills every fibre of my body and mind, its intensity somewhat reduced by the marvel of the creation of the State of Israel. My greatest consolation and salving of my conscience exists in the knowledge that never again will Jew or Israelite meekly walk the path to a gas chamber nor dig his own grave, but will fight to the bitter end; honouring his fallen brothers of the Warsaw ghetto and elsewhere in Europe during those dark and beastly years, and with the same passion, I sincerely hope a peaceful solution will be found to assist the Palestine refugees, existing in their inhuman camps.

∗

The hunt for the members of the Resistance intensified towards the end of 1943. The Germans knew of the leader of the White Brigade, Marcel Louette, code name 'Fidelio', but initially he was far too clever, often creeping through the proverbial eye of the needle.

My memory of the war years is irrevocably bound to that gentle hero and writing without honouring him with a chapter would, where I am concerned, run parallel with ingratitude.

Prior to the events leading to the Second World War he was active as a teacher, in the densely populated area of the Schipperskwartier in the Boys School of the Keistraat to be precise. At the outbreak of war he was called up as a reserve Officer. After Belgium's capitulation on the 28th May 1940, he was demobilised but remained determined to serve his country. He was president of a sports club and its members met in one of the conference rooms above a pub in the heart of Antwerp. It was there, on the 23rd June, that he told them of his intention to form a network of volunteers offering fierce resistance to the occupying forces and assist the Allies in every possible way.

Although one of the first German proclamations covered the prohibition of meetings of groups of more than three people, the members of the club met regularly in that pub. It was not complicated. One entered, ordered a drink and disappeared through a door marked 'WC'. A staircase off led to the meeting room and it was there that Louette recruited the first members of his Group, later known as 'The White Brigade'. As a result, the activities of this group spread throughout the entire North of Belgium and France, with part of Limburg, over Brussels to the Ardennes. Each sector had a responsible leader. The leading committee was formed by experienced combatants, the members chosen in accordance

103

with their special skills; administration, medical services, sabotage, espionage, radio transmitting, etc. Each member was known by a number and liaised with others through a cell system. Louette had read about and studied this from a book regarding the secret activities of dissidents during the Tsarist regime in Russia and this cell idea impressed him. He reviewed the original, however, and replaced it with a chain system whereby each member was conversant with the number, not the name, of the one with whom they had contact, either in receiving or passing on messages, etc.

Meanwhile, he had already formed a committee of leaders from the first six applicants who, in their turn, recruited suitable newcomers, and the membership steadily mushroomed.

Later still, blacklists had been compiled of traitors and Gestapo torturers and if, after having been found guilty of the charges by the leading committee, they were condemned to death; they did not escape justice. Executions took place resembling 'accidents' in order to avoid reprisal measures against the population.

London was regularly advised of movements of military trains. Traffic on the waterways, ditto, to the extent that anything on the move in the Port of Antwerp. or whatever took place, was radio signalled. The vehement bombing by the RAF towards the end of 1943 and the beginning of 1944 of certain crucial junctions of the Belgian railway net prior to the invasion, were undoubtedly designed by and facilitated through information received from The White Brigade. This was by no means a solo performance.

London received plans and information about troop movements, installations and methods of anti-aircraft sites, factories and defensive works, targets for bombing in Germany, etc.

Our saboteurs ran a dangerous gauntlet; nevertheless bridges were blown up, trains derailed, motors of cars and trucks belonging to the German army damaged; sharp nails were strewn on roads when German convoys of lorries were signalled, central electricity networks dismantled. No holds were barred.

In spite of Fidelio's exemplary organising and his careful course of actions, a few members were arrested by the Gestapo. Some had been betrayed by the occasional infiltrator, although the majority of these never succeeded in their hateful intentions due to the continuous vigilance which Louette had literally drummed into everybody, but mainly because of the shrewd interrogation methods of the members of the council. Others, as human nature will prevail, in alter ego or bravado, boasted about their activities and . . . walls will have ears! We now know that these wretches were cruelly beaten and mercilessly tortured in order to extract information. Their suffering put paid to their folly.

When at last the identity of Louette, alias Fidelio, was known after long and inhuman torture of two of his captured agents, his wife and parents were taken into custody. He was subsequently forced into hiding but remained unwavering at his command post. He directed all his operations from an attic in the house of one of his most faithful followers, a lady whose family living in the same abode did not even suspect his presence. When visiting his sectors by nightfall he did so mainly when it rained as it reduced the risk of running into a German patrol and he was always accompanied by a volunteer, armed bodyguard. He organised aid for the families of the arrested members as well as for those who had gone 'underground'. Pilots of allied planes and escaped Russian or Polish prisoners of war, were housed by members of The White Brigade, fed and clothed.

Contact was made with the group responsible for assisting in the escape of British pilots shot down over the northern territory of Belgium and, via a special Brussels headquarters established specially to that end, they were given full assistance for their return to England. Some members of the Jewish fraternity who escaped from the mass abduction were equipped with false papers, and 'exemption forms' for forced labour in Germany were printed as well as false ration coupons and even money. These were all issued through a printing plant confiscated by the Germans, where certain members of The White Brigade were employed. 'La Libre Belgique' and its clandestine sister paper of The White Brigade 'Unis Toujours' (Ever United) were also printed at those premises and distributed by the members and activists. The population found renewed hope from their editorials.

One day Fidelio went to a pub situated at the Grote Steenweg near Schoonselhof, Antwerp's largest and most magnificent cemetery. He was supposed to hand a sheaf of falsified food coupons and money to a contact man for the members gone into hiding in the Flemish Kempen and Walloon country, as well as instructions for one of the active saboteurs groups. His contact did not show up at the arranged time.

In the meantime the pub was filling up with German soldiers who had already had a skin-full and heartily threw themselves into songs of the fatherland. Fidelio had just decided to leave when the door was forcibly thrown open and two SS men fell in pulling along the almost lifeless form of his contact. He had already been beaten black and blue. 'Now point out your contact man!' shouted the officer in charge following the apathetic group. Fidelio ducked behind the enormous back of one of the drunken soldiers, jumped to the back door and escaped over the railroad into the Schoonselhof, pursued by the SS men. He was able to evade them and spent the night in a family vault which had been used for some time as an arsenal for the group.

In spite of the intense vigil, many White Brigade members soon languished in the torture cellars of the Gestapo and, although the group was shortwinged as a result, Fidelio was able to complete, in all its intricacies, his plan of action geared as it was to the allied invasion schedule. To this effect, on D-Day, and at that time bereft of their leader, The White Brigade was able to fully execute their duties and, although the Antwerp section was somewhat crippled during the first hour or so, its members reformed and found each other swiftly, while the other sections in the north of Belgium fulfilled their tasks assigned by Fidelio without further delay. The White Brigade was by no means the sole resistance movement in Belgium but the population at large called all the resistance groups by that name, which was indeed the highest tribute they could pay them.

Our most bitter pill to swallow came in the form of certain Belgians - our own fellow men - donning the black of the SS uniform who executed their duties with a zest far exceeding that of the SS itself!

On the 5th December 1942 a fairly large group, commissioned to sabotage the Antwerp-Essen railway line, was arrested, informed upon by a Belgian Gestapo agent, code name Alex, after he had infiltrated the group. He was present during all the terrible interrogations. He finally discovered Fidelio's nightly accommodation presumably by secretly following him. This, however, he only succeeded in on the 9th May 1944 when at 5.20am Fidelio was finally arrested. The house was completely surrounded and the whole area staked out including the roofs. He was beaten and kicked mercilessly until he was hardly recognisable and brought to the infamous Gestapo building at the Koningin Elizabethlei. He was again subjected to interrogation by a further 'élite team'. The beatings continued, pitilessly, with everything that would hurt and they kicked where they could reach. The 'gentlemen'; had previously and triumphantly presented him to all their personnel. Fidelio refused to speak. More beating, this time by means of a bamboo covered iron bar. After half an hour his body lost control of all its functions. He could hardly move, yet they forced him, still with his hands bound, to clean up his faeces. They tried to make him talk by working on the tenderest parts of his body with the use of electricity, causing heavy shocks, excruciating pain and ugly burns. That same evening, bruised and injured over the whole of his body, they covered his wounds with iodine. Half naked, he was pushed into a car and brought to a supposed Resistance rendezvous near the St Michael's church in Antwerp. The so-called contact luckily had smelled a rat and never turned up. By that time, suffering also from a heavy cold, Louette was taken back to his cell at the Koningin Elizabethlei where he was again subjected during the entire night to 'interrogation' . . .

With the emphatic promise that 'he had not yet experienced anything untoward' and that the following day he would be tortured 'in earnest', they left him lying on the floor. The consulted German doctor professionally declared that Fidelio still had feeling left and that the gentlemen could continue with a good chance of success . . . which indeed they did only without result! In desperation they drove him to Breendonck, another Gestapo prison for the 'tough ones'. Again he was beaten and then left for the duration of the night hanging from a hook by his handcuffs. When let down they plunged him with his head under water until he almost drowned. His mouth, nose and throat were then burned with a spoonful of ammonia they forced him to take, only to spoon feed him immediately afterwards with almost boiling soup. His fingers were broken, nails torn out and then both legs broken as well. On the 10th July 1944, a full month after the

Allied landings, he was taken to the St Gillis jail in Brussels where members of the Wehrmacht, normally more humane in their approach, had received formal orders not to nurse 'the men from Breendonck'. Two doctors - also political prisoners - were nevertheless able to attend to Fidelio and, due to a trick had him taken into the infirmary on the 17th July. By then his condition was serious and he weighed only 37Kg. On the 20th July, the Antwerp Gestapo arrived and literally dragged him away over the ground. He was by then quite lame. He was taken back to Breendonck where, this time, he was not only interrogated by members of the Gestapo but in addition by the Feldgendarmerie (their Military Police). The reason for this latest outrage - apparently certain messages, sent to London by the as yet undetected White Brigade members had been intercepted. On the 29th August, he was again subjected to a colossal interrogation, this time by the *whole* Antwerpian department of the Gestapo; some of them had travelled especially to the city for this event.

Even then, he did not talk in spite of a certain Lieutenant Crauls, one of the most feared guards of the camp (the prisoners called him Mathurin) boasting that during the three preceding days he had personally kicked to death three Fidelio members. 'Today I will administer your last sacrament' this self-appointed executioner told him 'but before that you fill a few pages with your statement'. As luck would have it, at 7am the following morning the camp had to be evacuated due to the advance of the Allies. Two buses transported 130 men. They were pushed under and between the seats so that passers-by would think these empty. During the entire journey the prisoners were being kicked, pushed by the heavy boots of the guards on all parts of their bodies. On arrival at Vught, Fidelio had to be placed on the floor, he just could not stand. A German SS man kicked him viciously in the head and seemed surprised that he had not kicked through it! Fidelio was loaded onto a wheelbarrow on which the torturers had painted the letters 'WB' (White Brigade) and wheeled him triumphantly throughout the camp. The political prisoners of Vught afterwards put all their efforts into easing the situation of the new arrivals and carried Fidelio on their back in turn.

Incessantly during the nights of 3rd and 4th September, friends were shot. News spread to the effect that Fidelio would be shot on the 4th September. It did not happen as the camp was surrounded by a group of Americans. They thought they were free at last but something went wrong. The Yanks marched on and shortly afterwards the prisoners were again surrounded and 80 of them pushed into a cattle wagon. Each man was issued with one third of a loaf of bread, each wagon with one bucket of water. It was a horrendous journey. Some drank their own urine.

On the 8th September they arrived at Oranienburg. Fidelio was saved by some White Brigade members already imprisoned and the only ones able to reunite in the camp. They succeeded in constantly hiding him from the SS guards and got him to the hospital where he was splendidly nursed by doctors, political prisoners too, who were able to treat him with electro-massage and inject him with vitamin solutions, bartered from the German guards or stolen from their private ward.

On 15th January, over four months later, he was able, for the first time, to take some steps again with the aid of sticks. The spirit of The White Brigade lived on even in that camp. In the hospital, where in the meantime he was able to assist, they managed to construct the basics of a wireless after having obtained the parts from one of the guards on duty, again through the bartering method. Fidelio listened carefully to the news items regularly and drew maps easily showing the advance of the Allies which renewed for many the hope and determination to stand fast to the bitter end.

At the end of January 1945 the Russians had advanced to such an extent that it was decided to vacate the camp. Those men who, according to the SS could still walk 30km, were forced to march to the camp of Bergen-Belsen near Hannover. Fidelio, whose name featured on the list of incurables, and thus doomed to the crematorium, was rescued by a fellow countryman. His identity was exchanged for that of a corpse and they were finally rescued by the Russians. He immediately offered his services as a male nurse.

Dutch prisoners were able to confiscate a boat in order to repatriate their co-prisoners, followed by the French evacuated at the end of June. The Belgians left Sachsenburg-Oranienburg where they had met with others on the 11th July. Only then did Fidelio decide to leave as well. The sick were transported to Berlin (or what was left of it) where he remained to nurse for a little while longer, at the Weisengrund camp. On the 20th July 1945 he finally arrived by ambulance at Antwerp and was taken to the Stuyvenberg Hospital.

Irony over irony . . . his own house had in the meantime been totally devastated after a V-bomb hit. After his complete recovery, Marcel Louette, alias Fidelio, unceasingly strove for full assistance to the invalids, sick, widows and orphans of The White Brigade. His regular visits to Belgian post-war Ministers bore fruit. It was due to his continuous efforts, often akin to a bulldog-like insistence at the right sources, that the immediate families of those White Brigade fighters, never to return from the hell camps of the Hitler regime, received an adequate pension as indeed did the survivors. Shortly after his return he was promoted to the rank of Colonel. The Belgian King and Queen held him in very high esteem which is obvious from the numerous photos taken of the trio during ceremonial occasions. He kept The White Brigade together as a staunch brotherhood, until his untimely (for us at least) demise in 1978.

Colonel Louette, the efficient and heroic leader of The White
Brigade Resistance during a ceremony. He held the respect of
many, especially King Baudoin and Queen Fabiola, who made a
point of singling him out wherever they went.

*

Spil also fell foul of the Gestapo. During the night of 14th/15th January 1944, we were woken by loud ringing of the doorbell. The milliner trading from her ground floor flat fearfully opened the heavy wrought iron front door. Two *Belgian SS* men roughly pushed her aside, followed by a short, shy German solider of uncertain age, his rifle over his shoulder. They ran upstairs two steps at a time.

Although immediately awake and alert, I could hardly wake my father and by the time he was aware of the situation, the SS were already in the open door. Escape was impossible. When we stepped onto the landing we noticed the silhouette of the German soldier. Spilly got such a shock that she instinctively pushed her fist into his stomach. There was, however, no more gas in that little man, the tears were about to burst forth. It must have been his umpteenth experience that night and, as an obvious family man himself, he could not swallow the sorrow and suffering of the families of the prisoners to be taken, his little war seemingly having been a short one. Indeed, by that time Hitler's élite troops were either prisoners of war themselves in Africa, rotting corpses in the steppes of Russia or were hobbling on a miserable retreat.

One of the SS switched on our radio in the living room. 'This is the BBC' he said, a rather largely built man sporting carrot red hair just visible under his kepi. 'No', barked Spil, 'It is the German station 'Germany calling'.' The renegade Briton baptised Lord Haw-Haw sent his German propaganda and vituperous anti-British remarks through the ether, addressed to the fighting Allied troops always encouraging them to capitulate. He was subsequently hanged after the war.

The two SS-men could hardly comment on Spil's map on the wall as he had simply left the German flag pins with their advancing route into Russia, where they had been prior to having heard the good news of the German defeat in that country via the BBC!

After Spilly was allowed to cut a few sandwiches and parcel these with a packet of tobacco and some change of underwear, and we were told 'It would only be for a few days', Spil's remark 'Yes, we've heard that before' preceded our adieus. Spil's glasses steamed up; I heard a dry sob; was it his instinct telling him this was the last time? We clung to him for a moment. I could not speak. So often I had told him I loved him . . . this time the words would not come, but he knew . . . With others in the Black Maria he was taken to the Antwerp jail in the Begijnenstreet, which so often previously and in the vernacular of the Antwerpians, he had called 'Hotel the Wooden Spoon' and where he was reunited with his chain contact.

As we were told, long afterwards, they were subjected to regular interrogations until the 6th June 1944, the day of the Allied invasion, so longed for by the peoples under the German boot. Every time they called him from the cell for interrogation he used to remove his glasses, handing them over to a fellow prisoner for safe keeping, knowing full well he too would be beaten. He played even then the role of a stupid innocent and betrayed nobody.

After the Normandy landing all prisoners were transported in buses via Brussels to Buchenwald. Every morning, shortly after 7am, Spilly would be positioned at the entrance to the jail with a parcel of food, tobacco, clean underwear and a few sweets. We had heard that sometimes a group of prisoners were transferred at that time of the morning and that there was a chance of handing over a parcel to a loved one. On the morning of the 6th June all roads were blocked by endless rows of army vehicles and troops, en route to the French coast as reinforcements. By the time Spilly got through and arrived at the heavily guarded jail, the contingent of The White

Brigade prisoners, including Spil, had already been bundled into buses and were on the way to Germany. They too were having to stay hidden under the seats and at the least movement to ease themselves from their cramp-inducing positions, were cruelly stamped on. Whilst in custody at the Begijnenstraat jail, Spil kept high the morale of the others. Afterwards we heard from the lucky few returned from Buchenwald concentration camp that he continued there in the same vein.

Bill, Ma Jacob's youngest son, recruited to The White Brigade by my Dad and also arrested the same night, died in the camp of malnutrition and deprivation.

Once the Allies succeeded in breaking through in Normandy, their advance moved fairly swiftly with the exception of the initial battle for Caen, shelled during a day and half by the retreating Germans, and bombed by the Allies in order to annihilate the remaining Nazi resistance nests. Ironically this also caused a great number of casualties amongst their own troops. When finally the Liberating Forces swept across the German borders, all Buchenwald prisoners one morning were called to assemble on the plain within the barracks. They had often stood there for hours on end in the most atrocious weather conditions before the 'Herrenvolk' dismissed them. This time, however, they were ordered to leave the camp. Jan Zom, one of Spil's friends and a contact in The White Brigade, found himself ensconced in the camp infirmary and tried to dissuade Spil from joining the marching queue, feigning illness. Spil refused as he was of the opinion that the camp could well become a target for Allied bombing in their mistaken belief it was a German barracks. Furthermore, he was hoping to escape on the way. With those prisoners still able to walk, their guards marched towards the Czechoslovakian border. They were unbelievably cruel, continuously beating them with the butt of their rifles and shooting in the head everyone falling in utter exhaustion by the wayside. The prisoners were poorly dressed in a thin white and grey striped, cotton 'uniform' over what was left of their underwear, inadequate as protection against the bitter night frosts. Their only food consisted of a handful of corn a day. At night they were forced to lie down at the roadside often in grassy meadows covered each dawn in thick frozen dewdrops as it was still April 1945. Spil continued to encourage his friends and supported with almost inhuman determination those nearing exhaustion. 'Don't let the bastards win, now that the end is near, boys, keep going in God's name', one of the survivors told us was Spil's constant goading, and these would appear to be the last words he spoke.

One morning they realised that the guards had fled. When the morning mist cleared the prisoners saw a farm nearby. All of a sudden Spil collapsed, at the end of his tether and with a high temperature, presumably pneumonia. His friends stumbled towards the barn of the farm and found a wheelbarrow on which they heaved Spil's by then shivering form. It took four men, for in spite of the fact that he was but skin and bone, they themselves had little strength left. The noise of the artillery fire and shooting came nearer. Spil, by then, was in a semi-coma. All at once the prisoners spotted khaki-clad figures in the distance sporting helmets like round overturned cooking pots. 'Spil, look!' they cried, 'Americans, we're free!' Spil opened his eyes, feebly waved in greeting like he saw his friends do . . . and died. My everlasting and all prevailing consolation - he died a *free man and knew it!*

I never saw my dear Daddy again - the memories of his love and the humour he personified, warts and all, lives in me stronger than ever. I can recall his face as clearly as then, often relive experiences shared with him and above all, his sense of humour. The way he would beg for a kiss after he had first surreptitiously smeared his lips with a strong smelling

Brussels cheese (akin to Gorgonzola - only stronger) - this to my acclaimed disgust. The day he had promised to get me a bicycle during a very cold winter, so that I would not have to wait for ages in the Siberian like snow for a regularly late bus to the office. Full of expectation I had run upstairs, fleetingly thinking it funny that he should keep the bike up there, only to be met by Spil with a large piece of paper in his hand on which he had drawn . . . a bike! The way he anxiously waited at the carriage door of the Mercantile Works train in order to heave me aboard when it slowed down at the Royer Sluice and a few months later when, at last, I had been enriched by a second-hand bike and I rode alongside the track, he would not move from the window until the train stopped. We would walk home, he pushing my bike along and chattering non-stop. Then there was the evening he returned home after his Bilbao experience, drunk as a newt and Spilly afterwards opened the bedroom door for me 'So that you can admire your Dad!' she laughed. Pater was lying on top of the bed, naked as the day he was born except for his bowler which perched half on his forehead, half on his pillow, his tie as a lonely piece of string, loose but still tied in its knot around his neck, hands folded over his manly part . . . pity I did not possess a camera then!

Sometimes I look with pride at his medals, posthumously accorded by the Belgian Government. These were the Military Cross Political Prisoner 1940-45 with Palm; War Remembrance Medal 1940-45 with two crossed sabres; Medal of the Resistance; Knight's Cross Order of Leopold II with Palm; Volunteer's Medal. In the grounds of the Mercantile Marine Engineering Works, where he was employed during the war years and was able to conduct his sabotage duties, a monument has been erected to the Resistance members, shot by the Gestapo, as well as those who never returned from the concentration camps. His name is carved in large bronze letters for the next generations to read. To the remark of a sarcastic and ignorant acquaintance, 'Fat lot of good it did him', I had but one reply, 'Yes, perhaps, but I can look anyone proudly in the eye . . . where were you when it mattered?'

Life is indeed stranger than fiction. A few months before Spil's arrest, 'Uncle' Joe one day warned me over the phone that his colleague at the Erla Works, the German Major Wilhelm, had been arrested and Joe would have to be present at a tribunal, presumably as an accessory. He had never dreamed that a Court Martial would one day be on the calendar! He begged me to bear witness in his favour. I had little choice - between Joe and the German, the latter was 'an also ran'. After spying, stealing from the German Army was the ultimate crime. It was obvious that the Major was already condemned to death in theory and slightly manoeuvring the impetus towards him could conceivably help the Belgian.

The memorial to the fallen soldiers and Resistance members, in the grounds of the Mercantile Marine Engineering works near Antwerp.

As expected I duly received a summons from the German High Command to appear at the Palace Hotel in Brussels, and it was with profound trepidation that I practically tiptoed into the foyer of the Palace Hotel. The year 1943 was gradually coming to its end. The German sentry carefully perused my letter of introduction, more of a summons really, and told me to accompany him to the handsomely appointed room where the Court Martial was to be held and which, in normal times, would have served as the restaurant.

My heart was beating like a steam hammer and I was scarcely aware of the repetitious clank of the soldier's boots on the floor, spasmodically interrupted by the odd stretch of carpeting which, by virtue of its wear and tear, had escaped from the 'art-collecting' zeal of the occupying enemy. We climbed the wide stairs to the first floor. (Long afterwards I could neither recall the decor in the form of wall coverings, panelling, chandeliers, nor the multitude of prints, all of which under normal circumstances I would have been able to vividly describe). I felt like a zombie and must have acted as one as the sentry kept looking back at me.

All of a sudden we came to an abrupt halt in front of an ornately carved front door flanked by two armed soldiers who scarcely gave us a look. After a sharp rap, the door was flung wide open and I entered somewhat hesitatingly. My mouth became cork-dry, I could hardly control my shivering and my skin was suddenly covered in goose pimples. I was, however, politely led to the 'witness box'. The members of the Tribunal were seated behind a long table and were obviously older officers of very high rank; their uniformed breasts richly adorned with multi-coloured medal ribbons; the lapels of their jackets embroidered with silver or gold filigree. This was indeed the panoply of military power!

Two SS Officers, clad entirely in black, were the only interruption amongst the general 'feldgrau'. Their Iron

Crosses dangled from red-white-black silk ribbon around their necks. They looked formidable. I became faintly aware of a hubbub of voices, the rustling of papers and my thoughts, already caught in a maelstrom of horror visions, furtively recalled the immediate past. Would this be the end of my relative freedom? Would I be able to save the life of a Belgian, a fellow-man, and because of my testimony tip the balance to the inexorable demise of another, albeit an enemy? Although by then the latter was already a foregone conclusion in this, even in accordance with military procedures so impressive a trial, I would afterwards not exactly keep thumping my breast in mea-culpa. In my conscience, however, I have remained ill at ease throughout the ensuing years of my life and wish I could have avoided this irreversible deed; this slur on my Christian inspired and, otherwise, unimpaired existence!

A book was pushed under my hand (I wondered if it had been a German bible?) 'Do you speak German or do you need an interpreter?' To my affirmative reply to the first question, an officer proceeded to read the oath for my repetition. When I came to the part 'So helfe mir Gott' (so help me God) my voice broke and I had difficulty fighting back my tears. I had no intention of committing perjury in the actual meaning of the word. Bending the truth a little, yes, after all I found myself in the proverbial lions' den and refused to acknowledge the jurisdiction of the Occupying Forces. Unobtrusively I kept my fingers crossed against my thighs.

Suddenly a door was flung open wide and Major Wilhelm was brought in. I hardly recognised him, battered as he looked, very thin, his hands manacled, ankles in chains. His attendant, an ordinary soldier who, months before, would have kneeled in the mud at the command of his present prisoner, pulled him viciously and kicked him to the witness box opposite, like a dog on a chain. They asked me if I recognised the prisoner as the officer present during my Sunday work. Also what exactly the task covered and I told them as near to the truth as possible. 'Did I not realise that I had assisted in a fraud?' 'No, buying and selling for profit was bona fide trading in my vocabulary'. In addition, I declared to have been under the impression that the management of the Erla Works were in agreement, in view of the presence of their own Major.

'Who assigned the work to you?' I crossed the fingers of my other hand. 'The Major' I replied without hesitation. 'Not Jacobs?' 'No, he was present but did not give me any instructions'. 'How much were you paid?' 'Two hundred francs per Sunday'. The eyebrows of some of the Council members rose an inch or so. 'Is that all?' 'Yes, sufficient to buy a piece of bacon on the black market, for that was the only thing my parents and I longed for'.

An hour afterwards I found myself outside in the fresh air, taking deep breaths to tame the tumultuous tempest in my breast. I thought my heart would burst and, in spite of my deep hatred for the German Occupiers, I cried tears of compassion for the manacled man whose destiny had so irrevocably been sealed. Uncle Joe went free. Major Wilhelm was duly executed a few days later in Germany. Sometimes my conscience still pricks me and I even ask myself if fate had a hand in the fact that my Dad never returned from his imprisonment. As the saying goes: 'Man proposes, God disposes'.

*

One of the Master Hairdressers, a teacher at evening classes, and owner of one of Antwerp's leading hairdressing salons, offered me a position as First Worker in his salon as he seemed to think my practical demonstrations satisfactory and promising, in spite of my hidden dislike for this profession at the time. I accepted as, in the meantime, I had come to loathe the personal contact with the fingers of the German officers at the Century Hotel.

The increase in my salary, added to the generous tips, was well worth my while. Every evening I would empty the pockets of my white overall onto Spilly's kitchen table and on Saturday evenings, exhausted from standing up all day (those days clients were still accepted at 7pm) I would return home shining with pride as I deposited a full salary was well. Such are the complexities of life: since Spil's arrest that fateful night, Spilly never knew the hardship of financial worries, as though fate wanted to compensate for the loss of our provider.

Chapter Four

Liberation

The phenomenal advance of the Allied Forces was being followed with impatience. The BBC continued to be the source of dependable information. On the 3rd September we heard Brussels was liberated and on the 4th the noise of artillery sounded nearer and nearer. After a lull, I ran outside as though persecuted by demons, straight to the Frankrijklei, a direct route from Brussels, as some neighbours had signalled the British were on the way. My heart was beating at full throttle; my excitement so intense that I could hardly breathe. At the Teniersplaats I saw the first British tanks, the laughing faces of the crew, the first khaki uniforms since 1940 and I feared my heart would burst! I could not speak and just managed to squeak 'At last, at last'. The crew consisted of Belgians, however, from the Piron Brigade, part of the Free Belgian Forces who fled to England after the Belgian capitulation.

Running home to bring Spilly the wonderful news, I observed several Antwerpians pulling down the hated German notices and boards and after briefly having helped with the demolition of a 'Zum Luftschutzraum' board (To the shelter), I returned to the Royal Opera House where I witnessed a scene right out of 'Orpheus in the Underworld'. The hotel, next to the Opera, requisitioned in 1940 by the German military, was being systematically plundered of anything not nailed down. There was a hectic traffic of seemingly demented pedestrians. Windows were open on each floor. The entrance to the hotel literally spewed people out loaded with foodstuffs, drinks, household linen, chairs, small items of furniture, vases, lamps, you name it! A man threw a mattress down from the top floor at the same moment that another staggered outside, arms and pockets full of wine bottles. The mattress landed on the head of the wine enthusiast with such momentum that he sagged through his knees; the bottles broke in smithereens onto the pavement, the blood red contents spilling onto the street and there he sat, staring about like a blood wet sack. Only momentarily though as, before one could bat an eyelid, he had again disappeared through the entrance searching for more booty.

All of a sudden rifle shots sounded near, curing me immediately from all proclivity to the act of pilfering. An open armed truck, steered by a German officer, was being driven at top speed towards the plundering crowd. A few hotheads booed and shook fists and even made ready to run towards it. The officer, with wild eyes and fear written all over his face, fired in panic. Everyone down on the ground! And like an arrow out of a bow, the driver steered around the Benoit fountain back into Frankrijklei - presumably after the British tanks? The whole episode seemed more like a scene from a silent film.

The following morning, not long after the salon had opened, we heard loud cheering. Running outside we were faced with our actual liberators on their way to Merksem, a suburb of Antwerp. Their advance went very slowly as everybody wanted to shake hands with them and the ladies kiss them. Suddenly I stood before the first one in the line, a young soldier with cheeks like red apples, lips like ripe cherries and eyes shining with pleasure, his helmet jauntily placed on his head, not at all as the regulation had prescribed. Lucky for me, he too was of smallish build but even so, I stretched to my full height and planted a resounding kiss on his cheek, throwing my arms around him. 'Thank you, oh, thank you so very much' I sobbed, shaking hands only with those following him otherwise after having kissed the whole platoon, my mouth would have sported a continuous pout!

Sadly, though, it was in Merksem, near the canal, that they and some members of the Antwerpian Resistance met with a determined enemy fighters nest and many soldiers and White Brigade members were killed. My first contact with my liberator - that sunny, unforgettable English soldier, the epitome of my freedom - is chiselled in my brain for eternity; woulds't that he survived . . .

Not long after our liberation, walking in the vicinity of the Koningin Astridplein, a tremendous tumult assaulted the ears and walking towards the noise I discovered a mob in vociferous activity. Nosy as ever I edged my way to the front only to be confronted by two queues of people forming an arrow passage through which collaborators and enemy soldiers' sweethearts were being pushed, the latter crudely shaved bald as coots. They were jeered, beaten from both sides with umbrellas, walking sticks and bare fists. The mob howled and roared like lions and the prisoners were then pushed towards the Zoo where they were jailed in the lions' den and other wild animal enclosures, the animals having been disposed of at the outbreak of war.

I could not believe it; there we were acting in the same inhuman way as the Nazis! Again I fought my tears of sheer frustration and pity and shouted for them to stop, pleading that I had more reason to hate the collaborators than any of them as my father had not yet returned from the concentration camp; shouted in vain that we were now ourselves acting like the Nazi bullies. The mob turned on me and I had to flee or I too would have landed in the Zoo! I felt as though a knife had been twisted into the perpetual question mark; of what is *man* ultimately capable?

Spilly and I were temporarily embroiled in a pink haze of eager expectation as, day by day, we expected Spil's return. Unfortunately the elation brought about by the Liberation lasted but a short while for the Antwerpian population.

October started with the first V-bombs transforming areas famous for their architecture into heaps of rubble; whole residential areas disappeared from the map. Hitler wreaked his vengeance in the most devastating way as the bombs fell in unprecedented quick succession. The biggest horror was without doubt the V-2. Their predecessor the V-1 at least was audible as their motors droned like a plane. When this abruptly stopped one could assess approximately whether it would fall far or near, often allowing people to shelter before the tremendous explosion 'somewhere' would make the survivors heave a sigh of relief in spite of the devastation and death it had caused. The V-2, however, came like a thief in the night, silent as the pestilence, and its eerie silence coupled to its phenomenal explosive power caused a hitherto unknown panic among the population. Within a relatively short time, the once so beautiful city of Antwerp experienced an almost uncanny metamorphoses, its neat streets and avenues showing unsightly gaps, naked walls, still standing as lonely witness to man's madness. Tattered pieces of wallpaper blew listless over broken, marble hearths and wrecked bedsteads and other pieces of furniture dangled precariously in the breeze.

Understandably the vast majority of the population fled the city to seek refuge with relatives in less targeted areas of the country. We dared not move fearing that Spil would eventually return only to find a deserted abode or a heap of rubble and we wanted to save him this additional trauma. Whenever we heard the ominous sirens go during the day we fled to our cellar, I with Molly the cat of the milliner in my arms. The latter had in the meantime moved to relatives and left the animal in our care. Rick's parents too departed accompanied by their son, daughter and son-in-law to the country seat of the family. We were not asked if we would like to join them even though we would have refused. Only the 'Sauve qui peut' (save yourself first) seemed to motivate the family and presumably I no longer counted . . . Maybe I misinterpreted this. Fact is that it remained stuck in my gullet so to speak and might well have been the straw that broke the camel's back of a love affair already dying in the face of maturity. Indeed, my feelings towards Rick had slowly but inexorably cooled off. It was nobody's fault, simply a conjunction of circumstances based on life's experiences during the previous war years which had matured me beyond Rick's naiveté.

We were not spared. A V-1 landed on the houses between Van Maerlanstreet and our own in Van Stralenstreet. The percussion of the explosion not only shattered the glass panel behind the heavy wrought iron entrance door but somewhat distorted the hinges. At the moment of impact Spilly had been in our kitchen on the second floor. Our old guest, Joe Persoons, was still in bed. The windows smashed to smithereens, pieces of wooden window frame flew everywhere, walls cracked, some furniture simply disintegrated and the air filled with greyish dust. After assuring herself that the old boy was OK (he slept soundly through it all like a baby in his cot!) Spilly ran downstairs. The heavy door would not budge however hard she pulled. In the meantime, British soldiers billeted in the Antheneum College in our street, ran past to free victims from the rubble. When she called for help some returned at once and wrenched open the door. Afterwards they came back and salvaged household items still intact, brought woollen blankets which they secured to the white washed walls of our cellar. They drilled a hole in the ceiling, pushed through it the pipe of the anthracite stove which they had brought down in the meantime, coupled the gas cooker to the gas pipe, hammered the top of the broken kitchen table to the wall using sturdy hinges so that we could let it down after use, and brought our double bed down as well as some of the chairs still useable.

We lived there, rather snug and safe, until the end of the V-bombardments. The only sour note was the fact that we could not bring our old friend Joe down. He had been senile for some time and we had found that, during Spilly's absence for shopping, he had tried to warm some coffee, fiddling with the knobs on the gas cooker. Luckily Spilly had entered in time before he had gassed himself! The doctor advised us to leave him in bed especially as he obviously weakened. Two nuns from the nearby convent came every day to bathe him and put him in clean pyjamas and bed linen as Spilly possessed neither the nursing skill nor the strength. One morning, shortly after our installation into the cellar, as was my habit I ran upstairs with his breakfast. I found him dead, peacefully gone in his sleep but an emotional shock for me. The funeral concluded, the solicitor told Spilly that she was the sole beneficiary of Joe's will. One could have knocked her down with a feather as we expected it all to go to his sister in spite of the fact that she only once visited him.

In the meantime, Spilly had preserved the black market eggs so carefully purchased over the last months, in a substance called 'Waterglass', hoping Spil would benefit from this food upon his return. The British soldiers who so generously helped us had become friends and it was they who enjoyed them instead. She supplied them with 'ham and eggs' (with the ham supplied by them) as their army issue of eggs consisted of the powdered variety. They regularly brought us food, mostly in tins, and enjoyed their 'evenings at home' away from the barracks' militarism.

The regular passage of Jeeps past our house and the other open transport carrying the bloody remains of the victims of the V-bombs on their way to the Stuyvenberg Hospital, especially after the enormous catastrophe when a V-bomb landed in the centre of two adjoining cinemas, the Rex and Scala, in full performance, as well as those of the V-2 fallen on the Teniersplaats in the very centre of Antwerp, frightened me into a state of panic. I decided to offer my services to the British Employment Service for civilians at Pelikaanstreet as my employer had, in the meantime, fled the city. Philosophically, I hoped to gain some courage from the presence of my liberators . . .

I donned my new winter coat made from a once white, now beige dyed blanket, then borrowed Spilly's one and only hat, a black satin toque with short tulle veil and sparsely scattered small velvet balls, some red, some yellow (our tricolour). Women would wear a black skirt, yellow blouse, red scarf or any garment in the three Belgian colours . . . (Thus attired, and meeting friends in the street, we would give the Hitler salute and say 'This high lies the s..t in Germany!) The British officer who received me seemed a little taken aback when I addressed him in perfect English and, after having perused my typed letter following his dictation, he promptly telephoned the Port Superintendent whose suite of offices was situated in the Herbosch Building at the Van Meterenkaai. This building equally housed the offices of the Port Superintendent and other military authorities of the Royal Navy concerned with the re-opening and management of the Port of Antwerp as it had become an important liaison for supplies to the advancing Allied Forces.

Chapter Five

Lieutenant Evans

Due to the V-bombardments, more and more intensified on the Port, the entire area had been declared a military danger zone. As one needed a special pass to enter the place, somebody had to collect me. I sat down on one of the benches and waited . . . and waited . . . and waited . . .

About an hour afterwards the door was flung open with a loud clang. The tall, erect form of an officer filled the door opening. Let me deviate for a while -

Amongst the books written in English which I regularly and eagerly read during the years of occupation for the sole purpose of perfecting the language, I often chose those written by a Canadian author, Ridgwell Cullum (or McCullum?) His stories evolved around personae known as Fur Trappers in the Canadian wilds. His heroes were of a stereotype: tall, wide of shoulders, square chin. Had he worn the Trapper's uniform with fur lined and collared anorak instead of his khaki uniform, I would have thought that the officer I perceived was one of Cullum's heroes!

As he introduced himself he profusely apologised for the delay. He had apparently been on the phone for longer than anticipated with one of the Port services, after which he had completely forgotten there was a small bundle of humanity to be collected. He was extremely polite and charming with the friendliest blue eyes, in short a real English gentleman was my impression. The Port Superintendent duly employed me doubtless due to the Lieutenant's favourable report. Not only was my salary much higher than anticipated but as we were employed in the 'danger area' we received in addition an extra bonus, which the Antwerpians promptly baptised 'bibbergeld' (shiver-lolly). Canteen facilities, however, were the jewel in the crown for we were allowed to partake in a daily hot midday meal served in the pleasant canteen and with quantities of foodstuffs we had only dreamed of these last four years, even if some of them came out of the tasty M&V tins (meat and veg army issue). Furthermore, the afternoon tea was an added speciality with as many slices of fresh white bread and butter as we could eat with lashings of marmalade and other jams, cake and tea by the gallon! As far as I am concerned it seemed like a daily banquet . . . white bread, dear me, I could not get over it!

Although my duties kept me in a different place throughout the day, the work entailed regular calls on the Lieutenant in his office. Strange though, whenever a V-1 dangerously throbbed over the building and everybody, even the soldiers, outwardly indifferent but inwardly in fearful anticipation, stopped working for a while, my steps would lead me as swiftly as a swallow to his side. He always knew how to calm me as we waited with baited breath for the bomb to drop 'somewhere at the quay side or on the Left Bank'. As the days passed by we found ourselves more and more in animated conversation and I soon realised he was a man of the world, somewhat embittered by his battle experiences, but extremely kind of nature. He seemed most interested in The White Brigade activities mainly through my father's role as I related known facts to him, especially as we knew by then that Spil had been in Buchenwald. (His friend, Jan Zom, the same who had begged him to stay behind in the camp hospital had in the meantime returned, weighing just over five stone!) Furthermore, the Lieutenant had already experienced dealings with the French Maquis as, during the liberation of Caen, he had met members of the French Resistance. Amongst them he had encountered a young woman who, just before his arrival, had personally shot dead two SS men. It was remarkable how very little the average British soldier knew about the existence of Resistance groups in the occupied countries.

Ronny as he was when he stole my heart.

Ma and Pa Evans, Ronny's parents, with Bijou.

Sometimes the Lieutenant would bring me home after office hours in the spacious staff car or requested the driver so to do if he himself had to remain behind. Coded messages from other military bases were often sent over the phone quite late in the evening for him to decode. To thank him for his kindness to me Spilly invited him one evening to partake in one of her tasty fried plaice dishes, for, born in a seaport, he was probably reared on fresh fish. Such delicacies were not exactly served in the army and certainly not during active service at the front when the men were lucky if the supplies of tinned food, the 'K' rations came through. From what I gathered this was a complete meal in a receptacle cleverly designed by removing a small knob which would trigger off a heating device capable of warming the contents. If the fighting became unceasingly heavy so that the field kitchen personnel could not provide them at all they were grateful for the special dry biscuits they carried in their pack.

Ronny (after his visit the 'Lieutenant' was unceremoniously dropped except at the office) paid more than homage to Spilly's mouth-watering plaice fried in butter. From the first moment that I reported our meeting to Spilly and spontaneously compared him with the Cullum-model heroes, she had been dying to meet him and listening to my report she had already realised, deep inside, that 'her child was sold' which in the Antwerpian slang means 'in love'. Remarkable really as I could swear that, at the beginning, my feelings had not the slightest amorous connotation! Perhaps she knew me better.

Shortly afterwards he asked me to accompany him one evening to a well-known café at the De Keyserlei, Antwerp's main avenue and still functioning in spite of the bombs. Trouble free conversation in cosy surroundings, listening to music, acted like a sort of therapy for him away from the Mess which was always full of officers. (A 'military home' was normally situated in private houses or apartments, owned initially by Belgians or British nationals employed by branches of their firms in Antwerp prior to 1940 when the war broke out for us, and later confiscated by German officers and requisitioned by the British after liberation). The majority of these 'Mess Officers' were of the Rear HQ type, never actively engaged in warfare at the front. Ronny had essentially been a fighting soldier with landings behind him, at the decisive moment, for the invasion of North Africa (with the Desert Rats of General Alexander, later to be replaced by General Montgomery), then Sicily, Italy and finally Normandy. Most of his colleagues at the Mess, unfortunately, were blasé and unbelievable snobs. Their military experiences were incompatible with those of the front-line soldier, and Ronny felt ill at ease amongst them. He, in contrast, had been ordered from the fighting area at the request of the Port Superintendent (in pre-war days this gentleman was the son of the Managing Director of Ronny's shipping firm and was anxious to secure experienced shipping personnel for his team). This decision proved to be one of the most difficult and heartbreaking for Ronny. Indeed, ever since the first landing on North African soil he had the same group of men under his command, men who were similarly trained, underwent the same heavy terror-invoking shelling and battles, and some of whom, tired out and miserable, hungry and wet for days on end, had shared with him the same foxhole. They were as dear to him as his own blood brother and a love existed between all of them of such unselfish nature that each one would have given his life in order to save the other. Some of the heavy casualties had died in his arms, others he was forced to leave behind during the relentless advance. When a rest period would finally occur he had found himself with the unenviable task of writing letters of personal condolence and praise for the fallen to the next of kin to somewhat alleviate the pain caused by the impersonal official telegrams sent from the War Office. He had been wounded twice, in Africa and Italy, once by a bullet, the second time by shrapnel, by chance in the same leg. As soon as he had been able to leave the military hospital, he had rejoined his regiment to be with his men. Twice he refused promotion for that would have meant either an assignment at HQ or commanding a totally new group. Fate, however, unexpectedly decided a different immediate future.

One of his fellow combatants told me afterwards that when 'our Ronny' had first arrived at the Mess, the gong was just announcing dinner. He had been pulled out of the front line on Dutch territory, helter-skelter, with no chance of changing. His battledress no longer looked regulation smart. His dress uniform, hastily bundled in his kitbag, had not yet been pressed by his appointed batman. The Commanding Officer, after welcoming the new member, advised him to join the company at table as soon as possible. Ronny had just sufficient time for a swift freshening up. Before joining the diners at the table he was perfunctorily introduced. One of the Majors present could not refrain from sarcastically remarking, 'Looks like we're scraping the bottom of the barrel. They don't even know how to dress properly anymore!' Ronny got up, visibly seething and would have floored the man but for the intervention of the Commanding Officer. Not being able to contain his anger though he replied, 'Sir, I have removed the blood from my uniform, the blood of my men killed in action. Do you know what blood is? Not to be confused with the stuff that runs down your legs when you hear very distant artillery fire!' The officer in question was later reprimanded by the CO and ignored by those who, like Ronny, had known the baptism of fire.

It was obvious, therefore, that Ronny wanted to leave the Mess some evenings, the alternative being to drink himself into a stupor. The establishment we afterwards frequented was called Quèllin, a 'brasserie' popular with Antwerpian society in the same named street. All windows and the entrance, long since minus their glass, were covered by wooden panels, a necessity repeated in all cafés and clubs along the De Keyserlei. Deprived of its pre-war neon lighting, this avenue looked sad and forlorn, until one pushed the heavy curtaining aside behind the entrance of those places still open to the public. A sea of light would welcome the visitor to the tunes of familiar music scores. At the Quellin a small orchestra and the beautiful voice of an excellent soprano would deaden the noise of the sirens and my fear of the V-bombs seemed to miraculously melt away. It was as though I knew nothing could happen to me as long as I was protected by this man. Furthermore, we tapped unbelievable enjoyment from our conversations as we found that our expectations and appreciation of life ran parallel.

Being able to pour out his heart about his experiences to a sympathetic ear was sheer therapy although he spared me the more traumatic events of his war. These were too cruel for my delicate ears, as he told me later. Referring to his pre-war past, it was soon obvious that he had been a keen amateur sportsman. Cricket and rugby were his forte and I was astonished to find that the British, in spite of the hard substance of the ball in the former, only wore knee-pads, shin covers and 'boxes' and no protection whatsoever in the latter sport which is more brutal. This in direct opposite to their American counterparts, equipped as they are with protective fillings over their limbs and body and an additional metal frame over their face resembling some torture device.

Membership of the amateur clubs Ronny belonged to entailed a varied social life: Matches at home and other towns, dances and annual balls. Ardent amateur sportsman as he was, both cricket and rugby demanded all his spare time and although anything approaching a sexual urge was at once expunged through sport, for these social occasions each player had his female partner, mostly girls they had befriended since school days. As time went by though, one after the other of his friends married their partners until Ronny remained the only bachelor. His parents, especially his mother, were not at all keen on Ronny's partner though his friends teased him continuously asking when he was going to pop the question. One evening, after an argument with his mother who categorically forbade him to bring the girl home, and tired of his friends' teasing, Ronny named the date. Shortly after the marriage he realised he had made a grave mistake. Two months afterwards war was declared and he immediately enlisted.

After his first battle he wrote to his parents to say he would not return to his wife if he stayed alive but would make arrangements for her financial security. This was later confirmed to me by his father. Ronny told me all this without rancour, accusing no one but himself and totally without ulterior motives at the time.

Shortly before midnight we walked homewards. On leaving me, he planted a respectful kiss on my forehead, followed by the military salute and, gaily waving, went on his way. We repeated these evenings regularly, each one based on an identical pattern. I too laid my soul bare to him and told him about Rick and my mixed and mysterious feelings. His advice was to honestly and thoroughly discuss the situation with the young man. He wondered if the platonic nature of our long time association could be at the basis of my obvious dissatisfaction and anxiety regarding the controversial tumult raging inside of me.

Analysing the last two decennia with their promiscuous standards among the young, it seems almost incongruous that a platonic relationship could ever exist over a span of ten years, but we were after all practically brainwashed into controlling our sexual drive. Fear of pre-marital pregnancy most girls had sucked in with their mother's milk. The pill came on the scene but many years afterwards. Explicit books or films about sex and pregnancy prevention were absent from the school curriculum, indeed from our homes, unless hidden in locked drawers. Sexual awareness is evident in all generations from the earliest teens but many a young man found and still finds relief in wet dreams or, the more taboo subject, masturbation. Where the majority were concerned intimacy blossomed into sexual satisfaction either upon the day of the nuptials or on honeymoon, sometimes not even then. This naturally was not a general directive, certainly not a life doctrine for everybody. I still vividly remember with amusement a fiercely debated argument with one of my school friends who, pointing at a certain part of my anatomy asked, 'Do you think you only have it for peeing?'

As far as Rick and myself were concerned, we loved each other very much in an innocent sort of way and the possibility of ultimate intimacy simply did not arise. Truthfully, we did not search it out and the Continental 'chambres pour voyageurs' which in effect meant one could rent a room by the hour in specially appointed hotels for that purpose, and frequented by lovers (genuine or clandestine) were alien to our nature. To be honest there were flighty explorations of the female top and furtive ogling of the naked breasts on certain and rare occasions but that was all!

After having received news from Rick, I went to visit the family the following Sunday in their temporary country abode. Everything went wrong! My good intentions to discuss the situation in a mature way came to nothing. Suddenly, without foreplay, Rick just wanted to consummate our relationship there and then, during our country walk, in a field, which made me feel on a par with the grazing cows . . . No way was I going to succumb to that little adventure! On my return home, the penny dropped at last. I had learned to love the Englishman with an overwhelming emotion so profound that I could no longer control it. What I did not know was that in the meantime Ronny had equally been struggling with his own strong feelings for me. Quite by chance on my return I had heard from one of the soldiers in the office that it was to be Ronny's birthday the day after. In one of the tailor shops I bought a pair of leather cufflinks with his initials in gold leaf, fashionable at that time. In the morning I placed the parcel on his desk. He was visibly moved and later explained that he had never received a birthday present, indeed, demonstrations of affection were never forthcoming from his Victorian parents. To illustrate I feel justified in telling the following -

When he was 18 years old, during a rugby match, he was winded badly in the stomach by the ball. As he remained semi-conscious he was taken to a clinic where he was operated on for peritonitis and a scrofulous tumour. During hospitalisation he was to drink daily a bottle of Vichy water. When finally dismissed and arriving home, his father confronted him with a complete list of the cost of his operation, anaesthetist, medicines and . . . the daily bottle of Vichy. The total amount was divided into 12 and Ronny was to repay this at monthly instalments. When he told me the story, I cried. At that time his parents owned quite a number of houses, the rents of which afforded them more than a generous lifestyle . . . How different from my own parent's devotion which I had experienced on the occasion of my 18th birthday as related earlier.

On the evening of his birthday we again visited our by now regular haunt. As we afterwards approached the front door to my home the sirens went. Hastily he pulled me under a still existing lintel of a once heavy portal at one of the damaged houses further down the street and took me protectively in his arms while the V-1 flew over us. Being 6ft 2in he had to bend over me and I virtually disappeared in that safe lot of khaki. When the danger had passed he wanted to plant the habitual goodnight kiss on my forehead but this time our passion overwhelmed us. As far as I am concerned I felt as though I were afloat, my heart seemed to bounce up and down, my breath almost strangling me. And in that first, long kiss a fire exploded, burning us both up. His passionate kisses covered my face, my neck. I heard myself moan in ecstasy between his multiple 'I love you's', hungrily reciprocated by me, and those simple words became my span to the future. Borne on the rising flood of his passion I felt myself inexorably torn from the moorings of prudence, for so many years the mainspring of my life. When we finally calmed down and breathed normally, his sense of discipline prevailed and, although unwilling, we parted. Spilly had already gone to bed and was asleep, so no witness to my excitement. That night I did not sleep a wink!

A week later there was a party at the mess, then situated at No. 4 Jan Van Rijswijcklaan. Ronny was to work overtime but had given instructions for the driver of the staff car to fetch me from home. He would join us later. By chance that same day we had received news from one of the concentration camp inmates just returned, that Spil would more than probably soon be home as he was with one of the last groups to leave Buchenwald. He was almost certain that the Americans would have liberated him by now, not knowing Spil had been on one of the infamous death marches . . .

I was so excited that I told all and sundry at the Mess and one of Ronny's friends opened a bottle of champagne that had survived the German looting, and filled a beer glass for me to the brim. I drank it greedily, thirsty as I was. The party was in full swing. Champagne finished, I was handed a glass of gin and as it seemed that everybody present came over to congratulate me on Spil's supposedly imminent return, this brew followed the champagne. I spluttered somewhat, not much caring for its taste. By the time Ronny arrived, he located me in the loo . . . miserably spewing in an enamel bowl. I had never drunk any spirits, the taste of which I disliked, nor ever been drunk before, and had not the faintest idea of the acidity upheaval unleashed by this fatal mixture in an inexperienced stomach, not to mention my tortured liver! In less time than it takes to say 'Hello', he unceremoniously grabbed hold of me and marched me outside, homeward bound. Walking through the City Park, he decided to rest on one of the benches, hoping the fresh air would help me sleeping off my drunken state. Before he could reach his goal, my legs suddenly gave way. Looking up from my kneeling position, I pathetically said 'Oh, man, you're getting taller and taller!' About an hour afterwards, when I woke up, lovely and warm under Ronny's protective uniform coat, I became aware of a furiously smoking presence in shirt sleeves shaking like an aspen leaf. It was, after all, November.

During the whole of the walk home I had to listen to his sermon. Goaded by the knowledge that certain men find pleasure in getting a girl drunk in order to take sexual advantage of her, he was in effect more furious with himself for not having been present to protect me from the overindulgence of alcohol. It was not really necessary - his co-officers were just as correct as he was where I was concerned. When Spilly opened the door, Ronny's apologies and genuine concern, especially as by then I had sobered up slightly, seemed to amuse her. When she told him not to worry as she trusted him implicitly at all times, his tension eased and he never forgot this. From that moment on the bond between Spilly and Ronny was sealed.

Some days later the British and Belgian newspapers printed photos of the abominable sights of the liberated concentration camps with the heaped corpses and the disgusting gas ovens. For the first time during that war, the man in the street came face to face with the horrors of Nazism, and the enormity of the holocaust made its impact deep in the soul of even the hitherto most indifferent persons.

At the office everyone tried to give me courage - that famous British stiff upper lip disappeared in a sea of compassion. Many a soldier came to my desk for one excuse or another, pressing my hand in sympathy or bringing me innumerable cups of tea. Ronny took me to his office where he embraced me as though he would never again let me go. I howled like an animal not just for the Calvary Spil must have experienced, but for the, as we now know, six million Jews slaughtered like cattle. Did part of my love for my Dad transfer itself at that moment to this soft-hearted man, partially because he was so much older than I? Whatever the case may be I knew at that moment that I was irretrievably bound to him and no man would ever replace Ronny . . .

It followed suit that during Rick's unexpected visit, I had to tell him the sad news that our engagement had come to an end. There was no way by which I could assuage his pain and his grief cut me to the bone while remorse caused many a sleepless night. In life one can never embrace a finality without neurosis. As far as Rick was concerned, however, a good year afterwards he had married which was a great consolation especially when I later heard that he had become a father.

Our happy days in Antwerp soon came to an end for Ronny and myself. He was to be posted to the Military Port Authorities of Hamburg and received subsequent promotion to Captain. As the Allied advance by then was unstoppable that Port too was of great significance to the supply of provisions for the armies. It was a week before his departure for Hamburg that Ronny came to have a heart to heart talk with Spilly and told her, in honest detail, about his marriage. Via his father's intermediary, he had already filed for divorce and asked Spilly's consent for our wedding as soon as he was free. She was not even surprised and gave us her blessing, though with a heavy heart, and with the advice to me, 'Child, do you know what you are doing? If you burn your bottom *you* have to sit on the blisters! That evening we were to attend a military ball in, of all places, the Palace Hotel in Brussels. Spilly gave her permission for me to spend the night with some of the ATS girls I had befriended during my employ. For the first time in my life I betrayed her trust as the inevitable occurred. I spent the night at the hotel with Ronny. When we entered our room, all the colour seemed to shoot from my feet to my head. Gently and reassuringly he took me in his arms and covered my face with soft kisses. The whole of my nature responded to his and that night I experienced the satisfying culmination of my bodily needs, of which I had dreamed since heaven knows when, in an all-embracing mature love and passion totally strange to my hitherto hesitating nature. Later on in life, after each repeated occasion, I felt myself more and more obsessed by our love as though steered to as yet uncharted seas . . . Years afterwards, when I confessed my initial betrayal of her trust to Spilly, life's philosopher as she was, she replied, 'Well, it had to happen some time!'

One of Ronny's friends, Major Eric Allen and also posted to Hamburg, was engaged to be married to an Antwerpian girl, grandchild of the once famous British jockey, the late Fred

Archer, who had made his name at the start of the century. The couple decided to get married before the groom's demob. Ronny was asked as best man; I would accompany him. The winter of 1945/46 proved to be exceedingly harsh in all aspects and both men were supposed to arrive by plane. Freezing fog prevented the pilot from taking off and they were forced to drive in an open jeep to Antwerp. Jack Frost reigned supreme. When at one stage they descended in order to respond to the calls of nature, their frozen limbs literally gave way. The marriage was to take place the following day at the Antwerp Town Hall, one of the city's most beautifully preserved buildings full of artefacts dating from Antwerp's splendid and turbulent past.

On arrival we were ushered into a spacious and impressive hall but our eyes stood out like organ stops when we were given a card bearing the number 56. Fact is that during those post-liberation days so many soldiers of the various regiments stationed in Antwerp were getting married - there were British, Americans, Poles, Canadians, Australians, even from as far as New Caledonia - that the authorities had been obliged to marry them in groups. First group was called - 1 to 25 - and parents, uncles and aunties, sisters and brothers, all filed to the adjoining room where the ceremony was to take place; the service spoken in three languages; Flemish, French and English. It was hilarious. Such goings on the typically British groom had not foreseen! Never mind, the marriage was legal and that was of manifest importance. I swore, though, that we would eventually have a wedding ceremony which was more private and intimate.

*

At last the V-bombardments diminished in their intensity as their sources were relentlessly destroyed by the Allied bombers and the advancing speed of the Allied Forces on German soil. That Antwerp was battered but still not entirely destroyed was due to the efficiency of a black American ack-ack crew. At the height of the bombardments a V-1 or V-2 would fly over Belgian soil on course for Antwerp and the vital Port of London. The crew managed to shoot most of them down before the missiles reached their target, missing but a few V-2s with their incredible speed. Afterwards these boys received one of the highest honours the City and Belgian State could bestow on them.

Around Christmas 1944 though, panic ruled amongst the Belgian population, as the Nazis had forced an alarmingly successful counter offensive in the Ardennes. We held our proverbial breath and fear gripped us by the throat. An ingenious German military strategy had allowed for some of their English speaking military personnel to infiltrate the American held lines issuing fast orders of retreat causing utter chaos as they pushed their tanks through in an effort to surround the Yanks. They would have succeeded if it had not been for a most alert GI on sentry duty at a cross-roads. Immediate measures were taken to rectify the position; the infiltrators were doggedly pursued, killed or taken prisoner. The incident was later to become known as The Battle of the Bulge.

8th May 1945 and we could finally celebrate VE-Day. Germany had unconditionally capitulated. Europe was free from that most unspeakable psychopath whose name runs parallel for inhumanity with Caligula and Gengis Khan. No Hun since Attila has been so hated. We could breathe freely again and Spilly and I moved from our cellar to our flat upstairs. No news from Spil though and we were getting more and more worried. Then one day some of the prisoners, returned from the death march out of the camp, brought us the devastating news that Spil had died between Buchenwald and

Cham and had been buried, together with some of his friends, at Wetterfeld. Indeed, this was confirmed later on when we received the official document.

Chapter Six

Titch

Gradually the Antwerpian population returned to their city and homes and after the rubble was cleared, vigorous rebuilding started. Life was returned to almost normal. One sunny morning I decided to visit one of Antwerp's most picturesque Sunday markets, a colourful event existing to this day with fresh or cooked food displays, vegetables and flora and fauna, of such variety one could easily conjure up scenes out of a Breughel painting. There were stalls of clothing and leather ware as well and one section was devoted entirely to livestock and domestic animals. A certain moment found me in front of a stall with puppies on offer at bargain prices as it was near closing time. Suddenly the stall holder put a puppy in the palm of his hand and showed it around to the onlookers. The pup looked at me with the most appealing dark brown and startlingly human eyes imaginable and when the owner turned it with its back to me, doggie turned its head and fixed his eyes on me with such an imploring look that I felt my heart melt. 'How much?' I asked trying not to be too enthusiastic. 'Three hundred francs' was the reply. 'I only have 250 Frs left.' 'Well, if you want the dog, come and bring me the rest next week'. I could not grab hold of that little soft woollen bundle quickly enough. I soon realised it was a 'he' who immediately started to lick my hand, then my cheek, and that look in his eyes! Release? Gratitude? From that moment a never more to be denied devotion existed between us. He proved to be of such fabulous character that I simply have to devote part of this chapter to him.

I immediately baptised him Titch. On my way home, shortly after having carried him, I put him momentarily into the gutter and lo and behold he squatted for his first little puddle. Arriving home I made a triumphant entry holding

Titch high up towards the ceiling. Spilly curiously looked at him, then at me with a look of disbelief and barked 'Out with that dog!' She could not start this extra task of training him on top of her already many existing ones. I promised to take the dog the following day to the office and give it to a willing victim. In fact, to be honest, I had not the faintest intention to take leave of Titch and hoped to mollify Spilly's attitude.

During the first evening I continuously ran up and down the stairs with my doggie so as to teach him to use the street as his loo. Prior to going to bed, I covered the floor of our small ante-kitchen with newspaper. In the morning we found a little heap and a few puddles but everything neatly on the paper covering . . . On my arrival at the office I explained my vicissitude to the Colonel. No, he did not mind Titch remaining under his desk . . . where this ungrateful beastie promptly proceeded to leave a puddle on the cocomat . . . if only to keep the entente cordiale alive . . .

Spilly looked at me distrustfully upon my return home when I explained I had not yet been able to find a prospective owner for Titch. That same evening I again ran regularly down to the street with doggie in my arms. As soon as I saw him furtively sniffing around in our living room and trying to squat, I snapped him up like lightning and pinched his little willie with my two fingers. Outside I released it and Titch had learned his lesson at once as we never afterwards found any dirt from him which proves that little willies can be controlled . . . It was not long after that Titch sat on Spilly's lap and, actor that he undeniably was, used those alluring eyes on her as well! Three days after this identical routine - taking Titch to the office, returning him in the evening - Spilly was completely and hopelessly seduced by his charm. In the future wherever she went, he was, and vice-versa. New neighbours and people within the area not familiar with Spilly's surname called her Mrs Titch for everyone knew *his* name. He grew into a kind of English terrier but was obviously a mongrel of mixed parentage. (Ronny called him '57' after the Heinz varieties). Titch sported a short tail, somewhat square muzzle, undulating black pelt with milk chocolate coloured spots, fairly high legs and a white band round his neck. Spilly bathed him regularly and it was sufficient for her to fetch the special galvanised tub from under the sink for him to creep behind the armchair against the wall as a bath was the bane of his life! The remarkable fact is that, on taking the tub for any other purpose, Titch did not budge . . . where bath time was concerned, he possessed an instinct bordering on the supernatural. To keep his neck hair snowy white, Spilly rinsed it with Reckitts Blue!

This is me with Titch when he was a puppy.

Spilly, with Titch as a grown dog, together as they always were!

As he grew older Titch proved himself more than a Don Juan and as he often returned with his hindquarters soaking, I am convinced that he pleasured almost the entire she-dog population within a radius of at least one kilometre! Inexplicably though, we never encountered a pup or dog resembling his image. He was practically human in character. On shopping trips with Spilly, she sometimes lost him in one of the stores in the centre of Antwerp. When Titch failed to find her after having sniffed quite a number of ladies skirts, he simply returned home on his own, waited patiently at the traffic lights on the boulevards and roads leading to our abode, until the green appeared. He was the first to cross. Arriving at the Van Stralenstraat, he would rush to our front door and loudly bark. If nobody opened the door, he simply squatted on the threshold until he spotted her from afar, then came stomping and jumping, chatting to her in a plaintive bark whilst his little stump of a tail wagged like a dynamo. I too took him everywhere I went when not at work.

When Ronny arrived on leave from Hamburg and made Titch's acquaintance for the first time, he too was immediately captivated and again a deep devotion seemed to come to life. It almost could have had the opposite effect though. The dog had a habit of leaning against stretched out legs - his kind of comfort I presume - and to rest his hindleg on that of the 'beneficiary'. This happened regularly and we took little notice. Ronny installed himself in an armchair and stretched his long legs, Titch taking up his now customary position. Horror above horror! Was it excitement? Had we waited too long to let him outside? He promptly peed! Ronny jumped up, 'What . . . ?' he cried, 'No respect for the uniform of the King? You should be ashamed, dog!' and among peels of laughter and general jollity, the uniform was duly cleansed. Titch's sin was forgiven.

Every time Ronny came to stay with us after he was demobilised and prior to our wedding, he would regularly visit the Café Velodroom, the pub opposite, for his mid-morning pint. It was our local, a typical Antwerp 'Volkscafe' and, for as long as I can remember, owned by an old couple Fons and Leentje.

To momentarily deviate from Titch's story, a club of pigeon fanciers had established its seat there and once a year members would proudly exhibit their prize birds as much bartering and selling would take place. One can easily imagine Ronny's consternation, followed by amused surprise, when one morning he found himself surrounded in the pub by numerous pigeon cages stacked one on top of the other, covering all the tables. Small feathers floated about and one could hardly make oneself heard above the 'rookoo-de-koo' of the flying squad with their richly coloured plumage, proudly pointed out by their owners. Ronny could not get out fast enough . . . 'A speck of dust occasionally in my beer is acceptable, but feathers and pigeon droppings, no fear' was his comment.

A further idiosyncrasy of this pub life would take place during the summer months when members of the 'Vrije Antwerpenaren' (the Free Antwerpians), a long established brass band, would march through the streets of the city dressed in military uniform dating from the mid-19th century with helmets sporting magnificent white and red plumes; these colours representing the Antwerp flag. They would regularly stop at appointed pubs. After all, all that blowing dries one's spittle . . . Their last visit would generally be at De Velodroom, our said local, where they would arrive followed by the inevitable mixture of skipping children and enthusiastic thirsty followers. At the door they would play a tune of homage for the benefit of Fons and Leentje after which they trooped inside. A few glasses later they would leave and, as their ranks had long since ceased to proceed in an orderly fashion, the false notes triumphantly entered the ether, while the drummer would beat away in competition with the cymbalist irrespective of the written notes.

To illustrate the diversity of the clientele of the Velodroom, one evening Spilly and I were having a quiet drink with some friends. The place was packed. At the bar a very intoxicated stranger swung to and fro on his unsteady feet. Fons refused to serve him but the drunk remonstrated and refused to leave. Spilly, with her previous experience of running a pub, decided to assist. 'Come along, my good man, go to bed and sleep for an hour or so. When you wake up refreshed, do come back and I promise there will be one very big pint waiting for you.' The drunk squinted at her with bloodshot, drowsy eyes, looked her up and down as if she were something the cat had left behind and said, 'Little Madame, I wipe my b . . .s on you.' Spilly did not bat an eyelid, 'Big Sir, wipe them on a whetstone, I'll give a full turn of the handle!' she replied. I think the bottom part of my jaw then went on to say 'How do' to my navel as I almost cried, 'Maman, where the dickens did you get that from?' 'Child, we have a juicy language!'

Back to Titch. As soon as our midday meal was ready, Spilly would say to Titch, 'Go and fetch Ronny.' The dog would rush downstairs, bark at the door of the Milliner downstairs until she opened the front door for him, run across the road, bark at the door of the pub until someone opened it for him and rush in, straight to Ronny, at whom he would energetically wag his tail and proceed barking in a peculiar way, slowly traipsing backwards. Shortly afterwards, man and dog would leave. When Titch got separated he was then seen running from one of her regular shops to another, sniffing the air and leaving, until he found her. Many a female customer, either at an opulent Brasserie on the De Keyserlei or our humble local, whilst sitting comfortably, would look startled on suddenly feeling something moving under the table at the height of her knees. It would be Titch depositing his snout there and looking up beseechingly with those seducing brown eyes of his. He had carefully watched where coffee was being served as this was invariably accompanied by biscuits and sugar, normally forbidden by Spilly. His pièce de résistance, however, was his soprano reach. I had always loved to sing arias from my favourite Italian operas, and Mimi's from 'La Bohème', I could never resist. The higher the notes I sang, the higher he howled and our duet was concluded by Titch's dominant top note! Best of all was his dancing. At Spilly's request, he would roguishly bring his snout to his stump of a tail, bite it, then turn round and round as on an axle to the beat of any music we cared to play or croon. In the evenings he would stand near our apartment door, softly howling with pleasure even before I had inserted the front door key downstairs and his wagging tail welcome invariably ended in a kissing session as though it would be the last . . .

Years later, after my marriage and departure for England, when asked where I was, he would go to my portrait on the wall of our living room and mournfully howl in his dog conversational tone, as though he wanted to convey the time was nigh for my visit.

We lost him one day whilst visiting a park, the Rivierenhof, in a suburb of Antwerp. Crestfallen we finally boarded the tram and were disappointed on our return home not to see him there waiting. We need not have worried. All of a sudden a loud barking was heard; it was Titch. Eagerly I opened the door and was confronted by a man with an expression as though he had heard thunder in Cologne. 'Miss, is that your dog?' 'Yes, what the dickens has he done now?' 'Nothing, but what a clever one! He got onto tram 10 with me at the Riverenhof, did not want any fuss from anybody, but blooming well knew where to get off! I followed him as I simply could not believe such intelligence. He alighted at the Rooseveltplein and hurried here, unbelievable! In later years, when Spilly came to visit me in England, she used to take him to my Auntie Mits who had, in the meantime, moved to a countrified suburb. My Uncle took him for regular walks alongside a canal and decided one day to cure him of his water fear by throwing him in. Titch clambered out as fast as he could, rushed like the wind to . . . Van Stralenstraat where he barked for a long time and in vain at the front door. My poor Uncle arrived in the end, exhausted from his own run and decided to avoid the canal in future.

As he got older and our roads became pregnant with all kinds of transport, Titch developed a hatred for anything on wheels. Loudly barking he would chase them while we held our breath, afraid he might meet with an accident which luckily never transpired. He would also bark and chase running people, more out of playful inclination but this, nevertheless, panicked some of them. A heavily built man, running for the tram, was one day pursued by Titch, suddenly stopped in his tracks and kicked the dog's midriff with his heavy boot and with all his might. Titch howled 'pen and ink' and ran towards Spilly for sympathy. Ever since then he experienced periodical cramp attacks which made us suspect that something had either been kicked loose or badly hurt in his little tummy, although the vet could find nothing positive. I always seemed to be the first one to detect something amiss where my dog was concerned. For instance, after a more than energetic scratching performance lasting all day, I pointed out to the Spilly that he seemed to be plagued by fleas. The chemist recommended a powder to be added to the rinse after a wash. To make sure it would rid him entirely of this vermin, she decided to increase the dosage. While she was rinsing a by now more than miserable looking animal, the bell rang and she ordered Titch to stay in the bath tub and whatever she ordered him to do, he would obey - he was better disciplined than I. When she returned upstairs she carried on with the rinsing of a by then shivering being, thinking he was just feeling the cold. During the evening I remarked on the unusual quiet behaviour of Titch who was staying in his basket near the anthracite stove, ignoring our evening meal during which he normally begged for small morsels. We could not understand this, especially as all our loving words of encouragement only resulted in a weak tail wagging and his snout remained resting on his outstretched paws. Finally at the end of my tether I took him in my arms with his tummy uppermost. I burst into tears, 'You have burned by doggie's little testicles!' I cried. And indeed the skin was red raw and must have given him excruciating pain. The vet prescribed a powder to keep the wounds dry and Spilly was on duty all day to ensure Titch did not lick it off. The following day some scabs occurred and it all healed very quickly afterwards.

Another time, again after strange and unaccustomed behaviour of our four-footer, I detected a swelling under his jaw which seemed to steadily grow. The vet immediately diagnosed a painful abscess, presumably caused by a rat bite as Titch mercilessly hunted cats or rats in neighbours' gardens. We placed him on an old sheet on the kitchen table while Spilly explained to him that the vet was forced to cut him and would slightly hurt him in order to cure him . . . (I always said he was almost human!) Docilely he laid himself down, lamely wagged his tail, let out a soft noise when the scalpel cut through the pelt and skin but remained as still as death. After his wound was disinfected and bandaged and the vet softly spoke to him, he even licked his hand. 'That is the first time I have experienced such almost human reaction,' he said. A few antibiotic pills later, wrapped in his meat, and Titch was off again 'on safari', complete with bandage which, nearer recovery he unsuccessfully tried to bite off. A few days afterwards one of our neighbours came to tell Spilly, 'Don't search for your Titch, he'll be home soon being at present in the Dambruggestraat with a 'trailer' stuck to his rear'.

*

January 1946 and Ronny reported to Doornik (Tournai in French) to the Demobilisation Centre. In the meantime, full management of the Antwerp Port had been transferred to the private sector and Town Authorities and the British and American Army Depots and Headquarters were disbanded. Although the office of the Port Superintendent remained active for a short while longer, the Major then in charge advised me to apply for the position of private secretary to the European Manager of the British shipping firm, General Steam Navigation Co which, in the meantime, had re-opened its branch in Antwerp, at St Paulusstraat. The Manager was a Scot, incidentally a friend of the Major who had personally recommended me. After the customary interview, I was engaged at once. Not only was my experience of shipping to be enormously improved in that establishment, but later on it gave me a better insight into Ronny's efforts vis-à-vis his own shipping activities, and taught me what exactly was the definition in the then most chauvinistic world of business of a 'secretary'. Women were not half as emancipated as they are now, in spite of there still being room for improvement in the higher echelons.

As a 'humble secretary' (and I unashamedly borrow the following from one of the fact sheets doing the rounds in offices), I was supposed not to have the ability to do an executive job. I simply had to answer the telephone, take down letters in shorthand and type them out neatly for my boss. All - that is excepting - to know which personal letters were not at all personal, what was in them if they were and whether to remind him about an appointment I was not supposed to have seen. How to make someone whose appointment he had broken feel it was their fault, not his. And when he fixed an appointment a long time ahead, to remember to remind him that he did not want to keep it. To *look* nice enough, to be easy on the eye but not snazzy enough to disturb his wife; pleasant enough to be able to keep people away from his office, but not so pleasant that I brought them in. To realise - how often I could ask him to repeat a phrase I did not hear (as he was probably talking with a cigarette in his mouth) and whether, if I heard it right, I should alter it to good grammar. Or whether to cut out the ceremony altogether and write the letter myself. To manage to fill in the forms he could not understand, remember his wife's birthday, keep his Expenses Sheet, know in which pocket he had filed a vital letter, fix his travelling arrangements, check every figure and date in all his letters and . . . generally see that his genius was not stifled by any . . . executive work!

My dear chief, in addition, had an intake capacity for whisky that, even for a Scot, bordered on the phenomenal and his local was the 'Opti' in the same street as our office, but further down towards Van Meterekaai, and well known in shipping circles, alas no longer in existence. Many a time I would receive an urgent telephone call from one of the Moguls of the London Headquarters and, pretending our Scot was at that moment in the "little boy's room", I would run like mad to Café Opti, throw open the door shouting 'London'. The short legs of Dear Sir would soon run parallel with mine.

I remained with the firm until shortly before my wedding day, precisely for two years and nine months. Our team work ran smoothly. We had a slight tiff only once. During his regular diving expeditions into the whisky barrel, Sir's speech would sound not so much slurred as almost incoherent, as

157

though he had a fold in his tongue, accompanied as it was by the unavoidable, dangling fag end; he was a chain smoker. One day after he returned from a boozing session and after I had twice requested him to repeat a sentence, he shouted 'Whazza matter, are ye deaf, girlie?' 'No, but if you remove that dummy from your mush and breathe deeply, I may understand you!' I shouted back. Dear Sir jumped up to his enormous 5ft height and, leaning over the desk towards me shouted, 'You can't talk like that to me!' I too jumped up and we stood momentarily eye to eye. 'And who is going to stop me?' Surprised, we looked at one another and burst out laughing. Strangely, at the end of the month I received a substantial increase in my salary.

During my employ with the firm, I regularly met and received, during the absence of my chief, many of the regular ships' captains. One of them heard I had a fiancé in England with whom I could only communicate, albeit regularly, by telephone and letters. In 1946 a visa for entry into Britain, necessary at that time, was only obtainable by businessmen; tourism was still out of the question. The captain was a young man of 28. As so many seafaring personnel had perished with their ships during the war and a shortage existed of qualified commanders, the pre-war rule was waived whereby officers had to undergo lengthy training, first as 2nd, then 1st officer, and finally captain. Even then they had to wait a long time and step into 'dead men's shoes' so to speak. After the war younger men with captain's certificates were, therefore, able to secure such a position when a ship was available. One February morning, this particular captain, whom I had befriended in the meantime, told me his destination would be a port near Ronny's home town and said I could go with him. Initially I looked at him somewhat suspiciously but he suggested accompanying me home to ask for Spilly's consent and to reassure her of his honourable intentions. It was a fantastic suggestion and, as far as his career was concerned, extremely risky as it was obvious I would have to be smuggled into England. At first Spilly thought it rather dangerous but had practically no time to dither as the ship would sail that same evening. I should really call this a tub for she only had a 275-300 ton capacity, was as rusty as an old tin and drastically needed a coat of paint. My suitcase was swiftly packed and with a big hug and kiss and a 'be seeing you, Mummy', we ran out of the door; young, full of the fancy of adventure, not realising the tormenting fear taking possession of poor Spilly. If anything were to happen in a storm, would she lose her child as well?

I had sent a telegram to Ronny warning him to expect me on Thursday evening but under no circumstances to enquire anywhere regarding ships' movements. A taxi took us to the d'Herbouvillekaai where the tub was anchored. The first officer, beforehand advised, was waiting for us and took my suitcase aboard pretending it was his own. The captain told me to hang on to his arm as though I was his sweetheart. The policeman on duty let us pass unsuspecting and on board, I was duly introduced to the rest of the crew; the cook, the first and second engineer. I was allocated the captain's cabin and he duly installed himself into the chief officer's. Apart from these latter two, the other crew were of middle age. About an hour after supper, the boat shoved off and I felt warm and comfortable in the small cabin. Above the bunk hung a voice tube in direct contact with the bridge and so that I could communicate with the captain, was told to leave its lid off. Happy in the expectation of meeting my beloved again, I burst forth in song and went through my entire repertoire of opera, operetta and well known English ballads from before and during the war years, the lyrics of which I had learned from the BBC. I did not realise my voice could be heard all over the ship and was later told it had given a few happy hours to the crew until . . . we entered the North Sea. The barometer had turned to Gale 8 and I soon realised I was not fashioned from the same seaman's calibre as Spil! Lamentable as my condition became, I first got rid of my entire meal followed by ghastly gall until, like a wrung out dishcloth, I impotently sparred with the never ending movements, from left to right as well as up and down, of this cauldron of a tub. A few times the captain entered the cabin and in spite of my weak movements to keep him away, ashamed as I was of my continuous retching into a hastily picked up bowl, he placed himself behind me in the bunk and pushed both hands into my stomach to alleviate the pain. A brother could not have been more caring. His responsibilities soon called him back to the bridge, however, where he stayed for a full 12 hours without sleep, battling with the gigantic, grey fury of the North Sea, steering that bucking, metal seahorse as near as safety would allow within sight of the British coast, until we met calmer waters and took the pilot aboard. By that time the storm had abated and my poor, tortured stomach found some respite. Refreshed with a thorough wash and dressed, I settled on the bunk, upright with both legs outstretched. As per usual the pilot immediately proceeded to the captain's cabin for his regulation snifter, the latter by then being dead to the world in the chief officer's - and on opening the door realised things were different this time. The chief officer called him swiftly to his own quarters. When later on the ship berthed, and before leaving not having uttered a word regarding his discovery upon boarding, the pilot innocently remarked, 'I didn't know the captain had such shapely legs!' One has to go far to beat the subtle British wit!

When we left the ship at our port of destination, we followed the same method as before in Antwerp and I walked into the town with an uncanny feeling, an inexplicable 'déjà vu'. It was a cold evening and the habitual sea mist hung over the place, the street lamps shimmering on the damp pavements silhouetting a sparse number of passers-by. I could swear I had witnessed this view in one of my dreams. It was uncanny; had I been there in a previous life? Puzzled I remembered a similar experience when, as a child I had heard Tchaikovsky's 'Ballet of the Roses' for the first time in my dream and recognised it for what it was much later when an orchestra sent this lovely music through the ether.

We boarded the next train to Ronny's town after Mac had telephoned him requesting to meet us at the station buffet. He was accompanied by his father. The likeness was stupefying and the poor man perspired for fear that I would be found out as having been smuggled in like a bale of cotton! Ronny's mother, typically English I thought, looked me up and down when we arrived at home, opened her arms wide as she had decided there and then that I was a better catch for her son. I felt quite at ease with them and when later in the evening Ronny's brother arrived and welcomed me just as heartily, my bliss was complete.

All too soon we had to leave. Back on board for the return voyage, the crew had lined up with some presents. A book with extracts from Shakespeare's plays, another one depicting photographic views and descriptions of various provinces and picturesque villages of England, both individually signed by each member.

From the moment tourism was again set in motion between Belgium and Britain, Ronny and I regularly travelled to and fro. As far as I am concerned each time it proved to be a sickening ordeal for whenever I sailed, be it from Ostend to Dover or any other port on the East Coast, I invariably met with atrocious weather and I made the ships look like cattle transporters as I metaphorically hung over the side . . . and retched . . . Until I discovered pills to counteract it, normally prescribed for morning nausea for expectant mothers, in my case a great source of hilarity, but a splendid remedy.

*

When initially we were both fully convinced of our deep love for one another, Ronny filed for divorce but this had been categorically refused by his wife and for a while we were very unhappy. Again though fate intervened.

Ronny was still in the army in 1945 when he received a letter from his father enclosing an extract from Ronny's bank account. Apparently £200 was missing and unaccounted for. This amount was not a mere flea-bite at that time and from the records it seemed it had been paid out during Ronny's stay in the military hospital. At that time he had been listed as 'missing, presumed dead'. What happened was that during a counter offensive in North Africa, he had been hit by a heavy shrapnel burst and, heavily bleeding, had fallen down. Instinctively, and before losing conscience, he had crawled behind a rock. Immediately after the battle, the wounded had been taken by the medics and transported to a field hospital. The following day the special squads arrived to pick up the dead. One of them suddenly heard a moan and found Ronny hidden behind the rock. They hastily took him to the field hospital and he was operated on at once. In the meantime, the battle continued, enemy posts were taken, only to find the position reversed in retreat. By the time it was possible to warn Ronny's parents, as appointed next of kin, he was already placed on the aforesaid list. It was, therefore, impossible that during his sojourn in the hospital where all care was free and currency required for small extras shared amongst the wounded, Ronny would have found it necessary to draw £200 form his account. He had no need even for his regular army pay.

After careful investigation, conducted by his bank director, they came to the conclusion that a fraud had been committed. Confronted with the findings of the experts in the knowledge that she alone had access to Ronny's account, his wife could not deny the facts. His father threatened to sue her, which would have meant publication in the local press, unless she agreed to the divorce. The solicitor requested this on the basis of desertion and non-conjugal relations required at that time over a period of three years. The decree nisi was confirmed in October 1948 and the following 21st December, Ronny and I were joined in matrimony. Friends would afterwards tease me proclaiming I knew precisely what I wanted - the shortest day, the longest night! as they were wont to do. I had given my notice at General Steam at the end of October and although the manager was disappointed, he was pleasantly surprised when I introduced him to my successor - my very good friend Margie, part Danish, who had also worked for the British Army after the liberation. Her English was prima and she remained with them until she retired.

While awaiting Ronny's divorce, I never went out with my girlfriends. Every Friday evening though, Margie and her fiancé Charles would take me to the pictures and we had much fun. After they go married, I remained in touch especially during my subsequent holidays in Antwerp. There were times, especially during Sundays in the summertime, that I visited Yvonne, my erstwhile school friend at the Left Bank of the Scheldt where she and her husband had opened a Café-Restaurant. I often helped them when they were busy.

Also my cousins Irene and Arthur had a habit of visiting the horse races near Brussels and I regularly accompanied them. I loved them dearly for when they were courting I was a 2-year-old and Arthur used me as an excuse for baby-minding so that he and Irene could go out unaccompanied by cumbersome nosy parents, and they both spoilt me unashamedly. They could speak the real Antwerpian vernacular and we would howl with laughter. Arthur gambled modest sums on the horses; Irene and I just admired the outfits of the élite always draped in magnificent Paris fashions. As we used to return fairly late, I stayed the night in their home and we generally finished the day polishing off mouth-watering omelettes fried with onions and tomatoes.

Ronny, in the meantime, had been promoted to manager of the branch in Sheffield and at the beginning of November I travelled to the City of Steel. He had found lodgings with a spinster, a darling of a middle-aged lady who watched over her lodgers like a hen over her chicks. She arranged a neat room for me and I made daily excursions in search of a house. There was not much for sale as Sheffield had suffered heavy German bombing and all exertions had been directed to the priority of rebuilding their factories to the detriment of the private sector. As luck would have it I came across a neat semi-detached with through lounge which was just what we wanted. For days on end afterwards I scrubbed and polished until it shone. Ronny arranged for a magnificent open hearth to be installed fashioned out of beautiful mushroom/beige tiles. We had the lounge decorated and painted and five weeks later I returned home a few kilos lighter and with hands like sandpaper as rubber gloves had not yet been introduced on the post-war market.

I was somewhat taken aback when registering our wedding date with the Antwerp Town Authorities. I was told that the councillor conducting the ceremony was legally obliged to mention that Ronny was divorced. In spite of the fact that a more broadminded attitude was already prevailing with the younger generation, the older ones still attributed a stigma to the word 'divorce'. I was thrilled, therefore, when, during the actual ceremony, the councillor in question lowered the tone of his voice when he came to the crucial declaration and

164

nobody in the family nor my friends ever knew until much later when we told them. Nowadays I wouldn't have blinked an eye, we are after all of a more resilient understanding.

One more traumatic event took place in 1945 when our old friend Zucker returned from Buchenwald, lamentably alone without his loving family, his mind affected, never more to heal. The Jewish Community again looked after him. He found his brother-in-law and together they opened a small shop. Shortly afterwards Spilly and I visited him and our meeting was very emotional especially when he embraced me, his sons' playmate. He was to meet a Jewish woman in 1947, originally from Budapest, and in order to start up home with her he requested Spilly's assistance in finding a suitable apartment. It so happened one became free practically opposite us in Van Stralenstraat, and although initially the owner refused to let to a Jewish family (not because he was anti-Semitic but because for years rumours had abounded to the effect that some Jews always seemed to leave an alarming number of bed bugs behind!) Spilly was able to convert him assuring personal responsibility for the spotless cleanliness of the couple. Zucker was most grateful and insisted that we hold our wedding feast at his apartment which was much larger than ours.

My godfather, Uncle Frank, father's older brother, safely returned from his service in the Merchant Navy after twice being torpedoed, took Spil's place and 'gave me away to my bridegroom'.

A funny episode preceded this ceremony. Not long before our wedding Ronny went to officially visit my godfather requesting his permission, as is the custom, to marry me. As is also the custom amongst men, they shared a bottle of whisky. As the contents shrunk and the liquid oiled the tongues, it sounded as though they were suffering from verbal diarrhoea. The bottle empty, my uncle triumphantly retrieved from his stock a further receptacle containing Portuguese brandy. Before opening it, however, he threatened he would 'kill Ronny dead' if he should fail in his duty to me as a husband, or should cause me any sorrow. Ronny had only taken a frugal lunch that day and although his capacity for swallowing spirits was phenomenal (I always suspected he too had a sponge instead of a liver!) the Portuguese nectar did not seem to blend with the Scotch! Upon leaving, I noticed my fiancé stumbling and was surprised he could still stand as Uncle Frank was already blotto on the divan. Once outside, a short walking distance away, we boarded the tram but the fresh air must have affected the alcohol-filled stomach. All the seats having been taken, we stood at the rail that ran the length of the vehicle. To the amusement of the passengers, Ronny assured me in a loud voice of his eternal love for me - and this from my usually so reserved Englishman! No showing of emotion in public, please, we are British! In vain I tried to stop him but all at once he turned around, looked at the others, hiccuped more than coherently and said, 'But I don't give a damn that they can hear me, they should all know - I adore you!' When alighting at last, I stumbled home with Ronny half hanging onto my shoulders and that night I witnessed him being icky-poo in the loo for the first and last time in my life!

In the meantime all my friends and relatives had fully approved of my choice of husband. When Yvonne's father, the funeral director, met Ronny for the first time, he looked him up and down and declared laconically 'I'll not make much profit out of you!'

Walking in Antwerp during our 'waiting' period prior to marriage.

Chapter Seven

'War' Bride!

Our wedding ceremony was fairly short but most impressive mainly because of the unforgettable music of Mendelssohn's 'On Wings of Song' which was played quietly in the background. Once outside, posing for the photographer, Ronny smiled at me, 'It is too late now, my love, you cannot go back, you are mine at last!' to which I solemnly replied, 'Amen'.

Signing the register - happiness of a bride.

Our wedding breakfast, graciously offered by Aunt Stans and Uncle Jeff, was held at their house and was followed by the banquet at Zucker's apartment. The latter started at 3pm and ended at midnight. Ronny thought the successive gourmet dishes and marvellous wines were unbelievable as, at that time, rationing was still very strict in Great Britain.

We spent our wedding night in one of Antwerp's best known hotels, the Tourist, which was combined with the Century Hotel, in the opulent cellars of which I had at one time been employed. Although I had threatened Ronny with the refusal of all marital rights if he should get drunk that night, he remained reasonably sober but did stumble over the kerb when alighting from the taxi. My beautiful white satin nightie, finished by hand and edged with beige lace, was tossed into a miserable little heap at the foot of the bed . . . Our honeymoon, alas, was spent packing and filling tea chests with our household items, linen and clothing.

Our wedding group outside the Antwerp Town Hall with, left to right, Madge and Harry (Ron's best man) behind Spilly, the happy couple, Uncle Frank and Mr and Mrs Zucker.

Imported furniture and household effects were exempt from Purchase Tax, then levied in Britain, provided these had been in possession and used for at least 12 months. It was imperative, therefore, that we kept within this law. So just over one year earlier I had found myself in a position of acquiring both dining and bedroom suites, as well as a settee with matching armchairs and some kitchen furniture on my own, as Ronny's visits by virtue of his career were limited. With all due respect I lacked total proclivity towards the British equivalent, named the 'utility furniture', those days to be purchased with special coupons, when the alternative was such beautiful Belgian manufacture.

And so began my English adventure, my new life, which I would find was never to be switched to automatic pilot, although at the time I was blissfully unaware of this . . . I would learn that an evenly balanced life does not exist in this spectrum!

PART 2: ENGLAND

And there she lay, that miserable heap of scrap metal - in my opinion anyway - listed in the Lloyds Register as a Motor Vessel with a 750T capacity, owned by a leading shipping firm and as different from their generally luxurious cargo-cum-passenger fleet as chalk is from cheese! I had made her acquaintance many times before during sea-crossings, prior to my wedding, and our mutual dislike was obvious where I am concerned. I say 'mutual' as I swear she had a soul and made a pact with Neptune for blowing the worst storms over the North Sea waters the moment I boarded her.

My heart shrank to the size of a coffee bean as I was about to embark upon such an enormous step into the unknown. After all, I was leaving behind all that was dear and familiar to me: Spilly, friends, family, my beloved 'Gingerbread city', and all this for a kind of void yet to be explored.

Spilly had accompanied us to the ship and was valiantly fighting her tears; I dared not look at her.

We stepped aboard with our luggage; the container with our worldly possessions was already stored in the hold since the previous day. All too soon the signal was given to cast off and Spilly had to leave the deck. She remained on the quay side until the ship left her berth, courageously smiling at us.

A last 'write soon' addressed to me and a 'be good to her' to Ronny and her small figure became more and more diminutive as she kept on waving until she was but a dot, hardly visible in the falling dusk.

What a paradox love is!

On the one side it creates a total casting aside of self in free and complete sacrifice for the subject of this love. On the other side we metaphorically step on the feelings of those who, in reality and precisely, justify such unselfishness. Egotistical as youth can be I was utterly and completely submerged in my own immediate future.

And there she stood, the mother who, since my birth, nursed me in sickness, comforted me in all disappointments, reared and led me along the right paths to maturity. Her husband had only recently been taken from her, her only child left her to start a new life in a foreign country. She stayed behind, all alone, certainly bereft of everything that meant reason for existence. Nobody knows how raw she must have felt inside as she slowly left the quay to return to an empty home, welcomed only by a dumb animal, Titch, our little dog . . . We simply had not dared to bring him along prior to our departure; it would have been even more traumatic. No wonder that in years to come both of them, human and animal, became inseparable and he alone contributed to her keeping her sanity.

It is very easy to roll extolling superlatives over one's tongue, but with the emphasis on 'ups and downs' in life, I have met few women who have experienced so many 'downs' as Spilly. Full honours must be bestowed on her as, time and again, knocked over by fate, she would get up in renewed spirit, brushing herself off as the saying goes, and starting again after, it must be admitted, the customary female flood of tears, which in effect was her salvation.

Before the vessel left, I had taken pills against sea-sickness. However, in spite of having consumed a full meal as an added precaution (nothing is worse than being sea-sick on an empty stomach!) I found myself once again in my bunk battling with the elements responsible for the hellish movements of this tub. Ronny was in the bar with some of the other passengers, twelve in total. In any case, he was an ace at sea in all weathers. How else with, as I suspected, his inner organs presumably pickled by now! At times it seemed as though the whole structure would plunge to the bottom, rise up again from the water abyss, like a mad dog on a lead, to continue its rolling, this time from left to right. I held on like grim death to both sides of the bunk and could only think of the container in the hold with our precious furniture, meaningful aid to my new life.

At last, after a crossing of about 22 hours, the river pilot was picked up and we glided into the calm River Humber. A few hours later we were able to disembark after the Immigration Officer had stamped my Belgian passport under his written observation 'Landed as a British subject by reason of marriage to a British born subject'.

We spent the night at Ronny's lodgings in Sheffield and the following morning found us in our little property impatiently awaiting the arrival of the container with all our necessities. Shortly after midday a well known transport firm deposited it in front of our door. The Customs Officer did not turn up until we had finished an early evening meal, my first step into the culinary art: boiled mussels the Antwerp way, a dish adored by my man. I had purchased these crustaceans at the fishmongers a few streets away, and prepared them in a cooking pot borrowed from Ron's former landlady. The English Conway mussels, at that time, were enormous and very tasty, but were unfortunately supplied even now complete with barnacles and seaweed attached. Spoiled as I was with the excellent care the Belgian fishmongers lavished on this produce, I was naturally somewhat disappointed as it took so long to remove all these adherences in addition to the many rinsings in cold water prior to cooking. Luckily the result was most gratifying.

Already pleasantly attracted by the tantalising cooking smell, the Customs Officer became increasingly surprised when the container spilled its load of furniture, household goods, linen and especially the enormous case, filled to bursting by Spilly, with tins of salmon, crab and meats, sugar, soap, dairy produce (especially chip fat and butter), tinned vegetables and fruits, bars of chocolate and even some salamis. Strict rationing was still in existence in Great Britain and chip fat had all but disappeared from British larders.

After having partaken of a few whiskys with the head of the new household and but fleetingly glancing through our invoices for the furniture, the Customs Officer seemed satisfied and we sent him happily on his way with a pack of beef dripping, a tin of salmon and a bag of sugar. We remained friends with him and his family until we moved from Sheffield about two and half years later.

The ensuing days found me unpacking, storing or arranging nick-nacks for display and making the acquaintance of our local food purveyors. Luckily fish was not rationed, nor was rabbit 'during the hunting season'. The tame kind was a children's pet and not for eating. The fact that they were sometimes attacked and devoured by foxes during many a night after these cunning hunters had broken the chicken-wire around the hutches, was accepted by the rabbit owners with the customary British stoicism!

I had to succumb to the demand for a substantial sweet after a meal in the form of fruit pies, steamed puddings or cakes as the Brit is renowned for his sweet tooth and, in accordance with the custom, I learned to get to grips with flour . . . Fine confectioners, like we knew them in Belgium, were conspicuous by their absence. 'Coffee cakes', many years later obtainable in the form of Danish pastries, Belgian cakes and such, were still unknown. The only patisserie available at that time contained cakes baked by wholesale bakers and supplied to outlets such as grocers. One could get the occasional cream puff in tea-rooms of the larger stores but these were usually filled with an artificial cream. Jam or lemoncurd tarts were also on the tea-room menu or available at grocers but the cream slices made with puff pastry were of such tough consistency that one almost needed a chisel to tackle them. A Belgian 'Pattissier' would have made a fortune those days in a comparably short time. But then . . . would he have been able to get the ingredients? . . . The most mouthwatering pastries with melt-in-the-mouth crusts and the light-as-a-feather sponges and fruity cakes one found only at the table of the experienced British housewife.

And so you would have found me busy with the weekly Saturday chore - as indeed most housewives in our street and elsewhere - up to my elbows in flour or dough as I carefully followed the recipe book and wished I was in Timbuktu as my experience in that field was zilch. My first rhubarb tart was a proverbial disaster, dough and fruit inside still raw in spite of its gold-baked look! Marrying a foreigner nevertheless teaches one the art of compromise . . .

Chapter Eight

Adaptation - A New Life

The start of my life in England manifested itself predominantly in compromise. I found myself not only facing a different mentality but in addition a way of life dating back to at least half a century before.

In the suburbs of Sheffield for instance there still existed street lighting by gas lanterns and come dusk I witnessed the intriguing routine of the Corporation employee religiously lighting these. I found myself dreaming of horsedrawn carriages transporting ladies in crinolines . . .

Contrary to the legendary continental belief that the British are cold of nature, I found them extremely forthcoming in their hospitality, albeit sometimes steeped in old-fashioned ideas or even guilty of a suburban mentality. They accepted me in the friendliest way and provided neighbourly help without being intrusive. The housewives worked hard from early morning till late evening as cleaning ladies were virtually extinct. Few owned washing machines and, although in the majority of British homes there were more carpets in evidence than in Belgian ones, not many possessed a proper vacuum cleaner. While I found their cooking skills generally below zero, the pastries they ardently provided were manifold as this was the only way by which they could extend hospitality to their visitors: a lot of sweetness, little savoury.

Their open hearths, while creating a most convivial atmosphere required constant attention and involved a lot of work in the mornings when ashes had to be raked out and the fire remade, heavy coal buckets filled to the brim with large pieces of coal which one had to haul along. Then shopping for provisions, a time consuming task as the shops in the suburbs were few and far between. As far as the man of this island was concerned, being able to study them on a day to day basis, I very soon learned to confirm my previously established belief that he was more disciplined and, moreover, totally in command of his feelings. The basis thereto most probably lay in the fact that gentlemanly sport was taught in all schools of Albion. Cricket, tennis and rugby seemed to demand such strict rules of fairness that they unavoidably enriched the mind and, assimilated during the formative years, became part of the male mentality. When an Englishman is confronted by a provocative female, he is just as excited as a Belgian (I wrote later) and Mother Nature assuredly plays him the same tricks!

I also found the bond between man and wife much deeper in my adopted land and it was not just the 'bringing up' which was responsible for this. The keyword was hereditary. A Briton would help with the household chores; I even witnessed him washing his baby's nappies and pushing the pram during his free weekends in order to allow his wife some respite. A crying baby during the night was often soothed by daddy administering the milk bottle, walking up and down with it or helping it to get rid of the burps until dad would return to his disturbed sleep. And those days few women went out to work.

Each morning Ronny would light the open hearth fire until I knew the drill. After that it became his weekend chore. It was the only source of heating in that house (except for an electric plate built into the wall of the bedroom). Once lit and going full swing, the fire emitted a fierce and most pleasant heat and in addition an extraordinarily cosy atmosphere. It had, however, one significant drawback: when seated in front of it the flames would warm us from head to toe but . . . back and legs remained cold which explained why so many ladies here sported spotty shins like multiple reddish buds!

Tending of the hearth was not just confined to daily raking of the ashes. Coal was rationed, and, moreover, of the old-fashioned type. It was delivered in bags of a hundredweight.

As we only had one fire, our ration was adequate where the living room was concerned but upstairs it remained very cold. The walls of the bathroom had been treated with gloss paint and often enough during the first hard winter, icicles would form on them caused by dripping steam after our baths. We had a shed in the garden near the backdoor to the kitchen, partly for storing garden tools but mostly to house coal. Unfortunately, household coal came in the form of enormous blocks. Most people, as I learned much later, had taken the precautionary measure of providing heavy, iron hammers, except we innocents who were new to the game. It was Ronny's task each weekend to hammer the big blocks into sizeable smaller ones, in sufficient quantity for the rest of the week and suitable to start the fire. For breaking up those big blocks of 'black gold', we used a normal, though fairly heavy hammer, too inadequate for its task.

As the 'other half of my wedding certificate' became more and more aware of the fact that his bride was blessed with hands capable of tackling most obstacles that came her way - indeed he never exactly treated me as a delicate flower, more a question of 'throw her in the deep end and she will learn to swim' - it happened more than once that his task of coal breaking was forgotten!

That first winter - January 1949 onwards - was bitter in England and for days on end the snow remained thick on the streets and hills of Sheffield. The winter tableau, however, was breathtakingly beautiful as the morning sun created a golden halo over the snow covered boughs of trees and shrubs. The roofs of the houses lower down (we lived on a very hilly road) resembled shiny meringues and reflected a separate clarity in the air; snowy lace patterns formed on the windows and all transport sounded muffled as though everything was covered by a thick cloak.

One Monday morning found me standing in our coal shed, cold and miserable and crying in full Flemish fury whilst I tried in vain to break the heavy coal blocks into smaller ones with our unsuitable tool and which necessitated real men's strength. Some of my knuckles were already bruised to bleeding and to top it all, while boiling some of my washing, I had singed one of Ronny's detached shirt collars, to me a blemish on my efficiency as a housewife!

All of a sudden a voice, pregnant with compassion, sounded nearby: *'What's the matter, love?'* - in the North of England everybody is addressed by this pet-name which makes you instantly feel you are treated as 'one of us'. I started to sob even louder upon hearing this sympathetic voice and told my story of central heating, of anthracite-fed stoves that burned day and night in Belgium and where blocks of coal had disappeared with the crinolines, of a forgetful husband, etc, etc.

The Corporation employees, responsible for weekly emptying our dustbins, as indeed these two men were, came to an instant decision. While one of them kindly steered me to the kitchen door and politely requested the brewing of a pot of tea, the second one had already fetched a heavy hammer from the dustcart and they started banging away at the coal like souls obsessed. One broke the heavy blocks, the other formed an assorted heap. By the time tea was served with the appropriate slices of cake, my tears had long since dried. As veterans from the War, by chance having pleasant memories of Belgian hospitality after the Liberation, they promised to do their coal chopping act every week providing a pot of tea would be at their disposal.

About tea. I all too soon learned that, as far as the nationally tea-drinking Brit is concerned, this liquid represented the all-embracing nectar of their life, the truth-brew holding a solution in each cup . . . Have you got a pain anywhere? Have a cup of tea. Difficulty giving birth? Come in, have a drink of tea. Has your man absconded with your best friend? Drink a strong cup of tea. Tea, strong, sweet and with the exact quantity of milk, prescription from the Gods and . . . believe me or not, it does work! A cynic will declare that it is the symbol that cures . . . but tea and what it represents: friendship, consolation, the feeling that one is not alone in the world if brewed for you, the salve on a sometimes open wound. For all that, I remained a coffee drinker and Ronny too, although he was weaned on tea . . . and beer . . . and whisky . . . Our pals of the Corporation possessed the dry British wit so often devoid of atmosphere.

One day I was to collect the wife of Ronny's Managing Director from Sheffield Station as she was spending the day with me. We had met and become friends in Antwerp when she visited her husband, the Port Superintendent for whom I then acted as private secretary. We had got on extremely well from the start and hence her curiosity, natural in its form, regarding a typical Belgian home. I was dressed, according to Ronny, as a miniature fashion-plate and put my best foot forward, for I intended to make a good impression as the wife of a budding career-man with an eye on promotion. All of a sudden, upon leaving the station, I noticed a Corporation dustcart, rushing at great speed towards us. An earsplitting hooting filled the air and, half hanging out of the window, my 'coal-chopping benefactor' shouted merrily in loud baritone and unmistakable Sheffield accent *'Hello, love, you look smashing!'* For one moment I lost my marbles, admittedly ashamed for my embarrassment, but my guest found it fabulous that 'They were so gallant' in that sombre city of steel.

It seemed the norm in England that the husband kept his salary and handed the wife the agreed housekeeping amount, sufficient to his reckoning. (In Belgium it was the other way round.) As a rule many women would receive a monthly allowance for extras, clothing or shoes. It still exists at present but emancipation has allowed many women to decide and manage their own finances.

It was decided in our own household that I would receive a monthly salary to cover food, gas, coal and electricity and I divided this in four envelopes. We never received a demand from either of those instances during the time I was responsible for payments. Spilly had brought me up with a sense of reliability. Years later we changed tactics when Ronny would settle all bills and left me with adequate housekeeping cash when I too opened my first bank account.

I soon felt at home in Sheffield where we lived in one of the nicest suburbs, Ecclesall, with pleasant, caring neighbours and a beautiful panoramic view over the landscape. Sheffield was certainly no metropolis but the English had called her *'the ugly painting with the beautiful frame'*, for wherever you went, the view of the undulating hills and dales did full justice to Mother Nature. The county of Derbyshire is adjacent and has been called Little Switzerland by the endemic population.

However, no matter how happy in a foreign country, homesickness for one's place of birth and the pull of the blood cannot be denied. There were days at first - mainly just before menstruation when a woman is at her lowest ebb - when I would stand at the window, longingly looking down on the twisting road to the farthest corner. I would imagine my dad, Spil, to appear. His death had been a tremendous shock to me, feeling it far more acutely than I could ever imagine and time had not assuaged this loss. I would sometimes whisper 'My daddy is not really dead, any minute now he will step from around that corner' . . . Luckily, such moments of nostalgia only lasted from twelve till high noon and my fighting spirit, inherited from my Flemish forebears, asserted itself.

Once, loaded with shopping, I climbed the steep, hilly street to our house. The snow was lying knee-deep, the first Spring awakening already in the air though. Our neighbour's children raced downhill on hastily assembled wooden sledges. Ignoring the cramp in the back of my legs, I deposited my shopping bags on our threshold, and started throwing snowballs with them. After all I was but a 26-year-old ball of energy . . . The following noon, Ronny opened our front door to the constant ringing. One of the children with whom I had cavorted the day before eagerly asked: *'Can your little girl come out to play?'* *'No, darling, my little girl is cooking my dinner for she is my wife'*, Ronny laughingly replied. The obvious difference in our age was his continuous pride.

The politeness and nice manners of the British people reflected in their children. No child would remain seated on the tram or bus when a grown-up stood. When crossing the street, sometimes in a group-queue from school, the boys would remove their matching uniform cap to thank the driver of the car or lorry having come to a halt in front of the zebra crossing. Nobody would collide with you without an apology; if someone passed sharply in front of you, a polite 'excuse me' would be heard. Entering a shop, office or store, the person preceding you would hold the door open. There were slightly different rules regarding cutlery, etc during meal times to which I soon adapted. Biscuits were never loudly chewed but softened in the mouth. Sweets were to be sucked not crunched under the teeth. Once my mother-in-law looked at me disdainfully because I could not quite chew a piece of celery without sound, after which I told her I had, unfortunately, not yet mastered the art of sucking that particular vegetable!

Children had to ask permission to leave the table after a meal. Enquiries anywhere were always addressed with a *'Please'*; accepting or even handing anything always accompanied by a *'Thank you'*. A man always allowed a woman to board public transport vehicles, or enter and leave any premises, in front of him. On alighting he would go first and hold his hand to help her down. (Most amused, I remembered a scene I witnessed many a time in Antwerp: a man stepping from a tram behind his wife actually pushing her, being too slow for his liking. *'Go on, get a move on!'* was his friendly request . . .)

When walking in the street a man would take the side nearest to the kerb so that, in rain, the passing motors would not splash on her clothes, presumably dating back to the horse and carriage eras. If a lady got up from the table in a pub or restaurant, the gentleman too got up and repeated this when his lady returned. During a holiday in Juan-les-Pins, spent with some of my relatives, one of them scathingly remarked that Ronny looked like a yo-yo each time one of the ladies present got up. We all laughed but I knew in my heart whose good manners I preferred and was very proud of my 'yo-yo'.

As a driver John Bull could not be faulted! His Highway Code was strict and he adhered to it at all times. Upon waiting to turn into a main road from a side street, more often than not a driver, on the main road, would stop and signal for the waiting car to proceed in front of him. Then a wave of the hand in acknowledged greeting, a polite smile or a flash of lights from the beneficiary to show appreciation. No impatient hooting as I was used to on the Continent. Upon nearing zebra crossings, he would always stop when noticing a waiting pedestrian. Lorry drivers, seated much higher in their cabin than car drivers, would signal to following transport when it was safe for them to overtake.

The first year of my marriage distinguished itself in my memory mainly because of the regular malaria attacks Ronny suffered. He had caught this during his African war days, in spite of a regular intake of anti-malaria pills and quinine. To the uninitiated these attacks were frightening. Within a few minutes his night and bedclothes and pillow would be saturated with perspiration and he would shake uncontrollably. Suddenly I became Florence Nightingale and, for several nights, found myself washing pyjamas in the bath, hanging them on the line in the pitch dark garden, airing them in front of the open hearth in the morning, ready to wear. Due to the strict rationing of clothes, he only possessed three pairs!

I still wonder how on earth, during these attacks, I managed to dress and undress that big fellow on my own . . . On the floor, at the side of the bed, I hardly slept albeit on thickly folded blankets and under my eiderdown, as our guest room was not yet furnished. I sponged him regularly and poured liquid down him as fast as he was losing it. Finally, the microbes settled on his tonsils, causing the most painful quinsies which virtually prevented him swallowing. During the early Spring, our GP decided to have Ronny's tonsils removed. The operation, considering his age - 36 at the time - was a huge success and the few days of his hospitalisation were highlighted by the visit of a multitude of student doctors and consultants as such operations had hitherto only involved children. Since then he never suffered any malaria attacks nor throat infections.

The public house, decimated to 'pub' by the Britons, was a true revelation. Not always visited by all and sundry as, in the better circles, one got Brahms and Liszt at home! It was not just a small café pushed between other houses as I knew them abroad. No, they consisted of large mansion-like buildings with different rooms, one for Gentlemen only, one for Mixed Company and one for billiards or snooker. Children under 18 were not allowed but . . . dogs were!

The word 'café' above a shop-like window usually meant a not too hygienic looking place where weak tea and undrinkable coffee was served, the latter made from a teaspoon of a syrupy mixture out of a bottle and boiling water, the taste of which was pure chicory, the look of it weak gravy. Cold drinks were also available, together with sandwiches complete with curling edges, fillings of rubbery, tasteless ham and margarine. The later new trend of 'Espresso Bars' with their Italian coffee machines subsequently enjoyed a huge following, especially as the patisserie too improved, but they did not arrive on the scene until many years afterwards.

I thought pub names so poetical, sometimes related to historical events or personages. Opening times between 11.30am until 2.30pm and from 6pm to 10.30pm. If you were thirsty in between, tough luck. The atmosphere in the pubs, however, was extremely cosy providing your lungs could cope with the smog of nicotine, and in Winter, especially, when wood logs crackled in the open hearths in each room, and woe betide if you stood too near. Burning embers would fly around one's legs and respected neither men's trousers nor ladies' nylons. The style was predominantly old English, with centuries old, blackish-smoked beams, pewter beer cans sometimes hanging from rafters, and antique china plates exhibited alongside the walls high up on equally blackened, narrow shelves. Wrought iron chandeliers and olde worlde lamps, strategically placed, created an almost homely atmosphere together with inviting, deep armchairs and sofas which obviously had known better days. Hand pumps provided the two beers in evidence: Bitter and Mild and, apart from the cold drinks, a further dark and bitter beer, stout, could be obtained; also Spirits, Sherry or Port (no licence from Excises necessary!)

As the pub filled with thirsty Brits the buzz of voices grew to a staccato pitch and one had to shout in order to be heard. After a short while, the air could be cut due to the tobacco smoke as both sexes smoked like factory chimneys and pipe tobacco especially caused a heavy, albeit aromatic cloud at each puff. And it was there that for the first time, I found myself confronted with the intake capacity of the British female. I witnessed them drinking pint for pint or spirits with the men without any difference to their conduct and the only sign of their alcoholic consumption, at the end of the evening session, after the landlord had shouted *'Time, Gentlemen, please'* was when their one eye would say 'to hell with you' to the other . . . At the onset I often tried to emulate them with all the drinks and cocktails purported to be 'safe' but it simply ended with my head in the bowl of the little room, pulling the chain from time to time, with 'the mill' going around and around when I closed my eyes, my stomach two days afterwards still feeling as though the lining had been forcefully removed! I could not and will never be able to drink.

As a mere onlooker, and yet a very staunch royalist myself, I found the deep-rooted love of a Briton for his Royal Family almost incongruous. As the Scots, Welsh and English sometimes face one another like cat and dog, the love for the Royal House takes precedence. This fierce pro-royalism has existed for centuries. After perusing many historical books, I came to the conclusion that his adoration strangely enough seemed to stem primarily from the old wars. In effect, during the Crusades as well as the wars occurring around 1000AD and later, when the independent Scots warred on the English and Welsh in bitter conflicts, the Kings led their fighting men in the true sense of the word, during the heat of each battle. The King would fight side by side with a serf after his knights and nobles had succumbed. The Battle of Hastings in 1066 was a typical example when King Harold died after having been left with a soldier who had fought back to back with his Sovereign just before the arrow drilled Harold's eye. Henry V's example was typical, fighting the French, personally leading his men into battle and to date called 'The greatest soldier of them all' . . . (If I was wrong in my conclusion, perhaps I read the wrong books!)

Whenever George VI and his Queen, accompanied by the two Princesses, visited anywhere, the people would arrive in droves from far away to catch a glimpse of them or simply being able to applaud their presence. Many even spent the night, in sleeping bags, on the pavements *just to be* in front at the time of a visit. And, because everything was so very new to me, time just flew . . .

By the end of May 1949, Spilly honoured us with her first visit. Titch had been placed in the care of my auntie Mit, Spil's older sister and my uncle who looked after him very well. Spilly too had arrived via my pet-hate, that sea-bronco, but with one exception: during the extremely rough crossing, the entire crew and other passengers were deadly sick and Spilly, in the morning, sat calmly waiting for her breakfast, served by the only crew member still upright, a green-around-the-gills cook.

Ronny collected her in Hull and I waited with more impatience than I dared to admit for my mother's first visit. She seemed pleasantly surprised with our interior decor as she had never seen the furniture; it having been stored and wrapped since purchase. She fell instantly in love with the open hearth and its comfortable warmth and voted everything orderly and ship-shape. I went to the kitchen to make the coffee and returned, proud as a peacock, holding my home-baked cake. I burst out laughing when she congratulated me on the cleanliness of our abode (she had often berated me at home for my disorderliness), and confessed that just before her arrival I had once more dusted the skirting boards as I knew for a fact she would make a bee-line for them for testing!

England really is at her best during Spring, due mainly to the wealth of plants, bulbs and blossoms everywhere in evidence and Spilly's enthusiasm for the beautiful views and immaculately kept gardens, manifested itself in her many *'Oh, how beautiful'* exclamations, so that where Ronny was concerned the word 'schoon' (the Flemish for beautiful) for him too became a favoured word, only he pronounced it 'skoon'. A while back I had taught him to say in Flemish, *'I love you my little wife for ever'* and it sounded so quaint in his accent but when, after many trials, he could in addition recite a little rhyme and found to his consternation that it was not a polite introductory form of address but 'about the man in the moon wearing leather pants' his zeal towards learning my mother tongue categorically cooled!

The next Christmas and New Year we celebrated with Ronny's parents. They lived in a large, old-fashioned house outside Hull. Those days the Christmas holidays lasted but three days except when Christmas Day fell in the middle of the week, when 'the bridge' was made and the holiday extended to the following Monday. Some years later, the long holiday became a norm and often lasted a full week with shops and certain factories only opening the last few days before New Year's Eve. When, however, it fell on a Thursday, everything would close until the following Monday. (New Year's Day was mostly considered a full working day until many years later. In comparison with the Continent's two day Christmas holiday, I found it complex here.)

If, during those periods, anything went amiss with your electric appliances, you remained in the dark or without their use, by a mute radio (battery-operated were not yet designed) or, in later years, a blank television screen, while your fridge defrosted and the electric blanket failed to keep your bed warm . . .

Christmas Eve was not celebrated with a main Christmas dinner as is the fashion on the Continent. We did have small groups of children going from door to door and, having asked permission so to do, gave a rendering of the most popular Christmas carols, amongst which the international 'Holy Night' was one of the best known. It was extremely emotional to look upon those shiny little faces and hear their young voices, sometimes out of tune, and for days beforehand, Ronny would hold small change aside to fill their eager little hands while I would distribute bars of Belgian chocolate as this commodity was still rationed.

Pubs would be quite crowded and sometimes a half hour closing-time extension had been granted by the Local Authorities. In contrast to the Continent, St Nicolas was not celebrated but instead Father Christmas would call during the night of 24th to the 25th. Stockings would be dangling from each child's bed, filled with a variety of small goodies, an orange, nuts, a small doll for the girls, a few toys for the boys, etc. I had jokingly filled one of Ronny's socks too, but in view of his 'elegant size 13' decided it was too expensive a fad . . . The presents would be placed underneath the Tree, beautifully wrapped in colourful papers and these were opened prior to the main midday fare on Christmas Day.

Weeks beforehand plucked turkeys hung forlornly from the front of the Fishmonger's window, special poulterers' shops for poultry and game, as we knew them in Belgium, did not exist. Even grocers would sell chickens, some even fish as well. One would choose one's turkey, the shopkeeper would pluck it and keep it refrigerated until one collected it the day before Christmas, as few homes then boasted a fridge.

In preparation, geese or turkeys were usually stuffed with a mixture of breadcrumbs soaked in stock made from the stomach, liver, kidneys, throat and fore-legs of the poultry, squeezed dry and mixed with finely chopped onion, sage, pepper and salt. The roast turkey would be served on a huge platter, surrounded by chipolatas and small rounds of roast bacon, and accompanied by a bread sauce and red currant jelly. The former was a concoction of breadcrumbs to which the liquid had been added, obtained by boiling an onion stuffed with cloves until soft. Sometimes, the onion would be mashed and added to the bread sauce which by now resembled a smooth paste. Take it or leave it . . . I left it as a rule.

The pièce de résistance was undoubtedly the enormous Christmas pud triumphantly carried on a platter, flambéed at the moment of entry. It had habitually been steamed au bain Marie for hours on end as they were made with vast quantities of dried fruits, kidney fat, sugar and aromatised with brandy, sherry or rum and as black as a Negro's head. Each portion served with a brandy or rum butter sauce and, coming to rest on an already full stomach, would feel as heavy as a cannonball from the Battle of Waterloo! After eating it we felt we'd met this!

At the side of each plate, in all its gaudy splendour, rested a 'cracker', a tube-like parcel in multicoloured silver paper, closed at each end and filled with an innocent firecracker which would softly explode when opened. This would happen when two people grabbed hold of each end of the cracker and pulled. A paper hat, a lucky charm and a proverb or wise-crack written on a mini piece of paper would drop out.

In the evening, we were further served cold turkey and a variety of accompanying pickles and it seems as though the Brits held a monopoly on those as I had never seen such a variety! Even the common walnut was transformed into one of the nicest pickles I had ever tasted. (The ensuing days would test our patience for culinary imagination. Turkey was served in all possible ways, minced and fashioned into meatballs, covered with breadcrumbs and lightly fried, mixed with a thick milk sauce as stew, in soups . . . until it came out of our ears and nose!)

Then we had the traditional mince pies with which visitors were regaled innumerable days prior to and after Christmas. These sweet tartlets have nothing to do with meat in spite of the fact that the jars for their filling mentions 'Mincemeat', one of the idiosyncrasies of the English cuisine. Made with shortcrust pastry and served hot from the oven, they are distinct in taste and I soon learned to add a few drops of fresh lemon juice and a snuff of cinnamon to the mincemeat filling to enhance this even further.

New Year's Eve, as far as I was concerned, was like a sparkling drink without its fizz! We would visit the local for a few hours, were introduced to total strangers and listened to the much in evidence pub-syndrome: small talk from the ladies mostly of babies . . . Although the pubs were allowed an extension of opening hours, we were homeward bound long before midnight. At home, if we had invited friends to come along, at the stroke of twelve, we would stand in a circle, holding hands crossed in front of our body and sing the equally traditional Auld Lang Syne, while my little heart would be about to burst with longing for my parents, friends and my lively city and hot tears would run down my cheeks stemmed only when the two strong arms of my man folded lovingly around me and I silently and gratefully blessed Fate for that love.

As far as my in-laws were concerned, they had been travelling abroad since the year dot, right up to the start of World War II. If, as is proclaimed, one learns by travel and one's mind broadens, I fear they were not conversant with this tune! I do not think I ever met such a narrow-minded and prejudiced twosome and can only surmise they went through most Continental countries like a dose of Epsom salts. In fact, my dear mother-in-law was convinced my staple diet had been frogs' legs and snails. As snobbism goes, she was undoubtedly the top and a typical example of 'when nothing comes to something, something doesn't know itself!' This being a well known Flemish proverb, the equivalent of which I have not yet discovered.

But in spite of this, she was kind to me and we got on very well. After all she had given birth to a being that was more precious to me than life itself. Perhaps it was just as well that our meetings were but sporadic so that I was never put in the position of the proverbial 'bull in a china shop' as my candid nature might have directed. She had missed her calling though, for in everyday life she conducted herself as a star actress. Her alighting from the car was a revelation, elegant and majestic, with an almost royal forbearance. And I, as the young woman, stumbled out of it like an elephant forced through a keyhole! She always bleached her own hair and wore funny, beret-like hats out of which on her forehead peeked long, thin curls, set in iron curlers every night. Her face powder was white as the driven snow and it always seemed as though she had just blown into a sack of flour. Her large, beautiful, dark brown eyes would searchingly stare, as Ronny would say: 'Like two pee-holes in the snow' . . . Although elegant of stature, she dressed very conservatively in pastel shades. Black horrified her. Her culinary art was non-existent as in better, pre-war days, this was left to capable personnel who, as the war stretched into years, either joined the army or went for employment in war equipment manufacturing at higher wages.

At midday mealtime, every single day, potatoes would be steamed in a special steamer, as old as Methuselah, and dad's task was mashing them with a fork but without milk, butter, pepper or salt. Vegetables were boiled to a soggy mass. Meat, always accompanied by a large onion and crowned with a piece of hard fat, was unceremoniously pushed into the oven. The lovely juices were thrown away and the bottom of the roasting pan scratched, water added, usually the same liquid in which vegetables had been boiled, then thickened with a granulated substance tasting of stew and still on the market today. One day I witnessed mother-in-law placing a beautiful rump steak in a roasting tin in the oven. After about one hour's cooking, she prodded it with a fork, declared it was still tough and, to my horror, threw it in a pan filled with cold water, placed it on top of the gas hob, brought it to the boil and left it to simmer for another twenty minutes. A shoe-sole thus treated would have been just as tender and just as tasteless.

No doubt my parents-in-law were steeped in Victoriana. During the First World War, dad had been mustard-gassed, near Passchendaele. His lungs were in a pitiful state and his breathing suffered. It did not prevent him, however, from staying alive until his 78th year proving the well known proverb that 'creaking doors hang longest'. Ronny resembled him like the other pea in the pod and 30 years later, I would realise this even more: the same beautiful white wavy hair, the only difference that Ronny would always walk straight as only a healthy military man holds himself, while his father's shoulders were bent. This to the delight of their dog, a Pekinese, as while driving, dad would wear a veritable scarf of fur in his neck: the dog came along, resting partly on the top of the driving seat, partly in his master's neck. Indeed, I never did see a suit worn by dad bereft of dog hairs! The dog was already of advanced age and stank like the pest from both ends . . . He was baptised 'Bijou' and had a mania for passing ankles and legs at which he continuously snapped. Each outing in the car with that dog caused nausea and would leave me heaving.

After the Armistice in 1918, dad returned home and was re-engaged as an estate agent. It was in that capacity he was able to purchase a whole string of small houses at low mortgage-interest rates. After a certain number of years, these were paid off and became his property, the couple managing to live off the rents in a most comfortable manner. Years later he inherited even more property from his parents, resigned and retired. Unfortunately at the end of the 50s, Hull Council decided to modernise the town centre. Hundreds of houses were demolished to make way for dual carriageways, diversions and broadening of roads and entire streets simply vanished. Many of dad's properties (some already destroyed by bombs) disappeared and the socialist council, vigorously anti-landlord, compensated him for the value of the ground only; this calculated at pre-war land prices! Although not exactly ruined, the wings of their luxury life were considerably clipped.

I waited a year and a half before returning to my birthplace as I was determined to adapt myself to a changed way of life and to cultivate my marriage into a success.

My meeting with Titch, favourite family members and friends was bordering on hysterics and everybody thought I looked exceptionally healthy. Titch had been warned beforehand by Spilly that I was to arrive and, encouraged by her, stood for hours either babbling in his dog-language, at my photograph on the wall, or sat watching the door with endless patience. When at last, early evening, I rang the bell and at the same time opened the front door, he ran downstairs at the speed of lightning, howling like a banshee and alarming the entire neighbourhood. We met halfway and after my sobs accompanied Titch's howls, everyone in the building was in tears! He never left my side during the entire fortnight except at night as Spilly would never allow him in the bedroom.

Too soon my holiday came to an end and, although I yearned for my husband, it was exceptionally hard to leave Antwerp. I was hoarse with laughing and chatting. Antwerp, as a cosmopolitan and international Port, had enjoyed a veritable post-war boom. Neon advertising, especially in the city centre, glittered in a kaleidoscope of colours late into the night. The city swarmed with people and life until dawn, and the pubs stayed open just as long. Some of the larger 'brasseries' situated at the De Keyserlei, Antwerp's main avenue, and around the Central Station area nearby, had engaged small size orchestras or had juke boxes installed spewing out the latest melodies, non stop. Film enthusiasts would visit cinemas twice a day during the weekends and still walk into a café afterwards as drink and food were available day and night and many restaurants accepted customers even at 10pm for a complete meal, whilst others would close their doors but still serve drinks behind them . . .

Back in Sheffield, Ronny came to fetch me from the train. It was late and I was fighting back my tears when we drove through the sad and forlorn streets. In the very centre, we spotted a solitary flickering light at the façade of a store. *'You see, darling, we too have neon light here'*, Ronny joked. That did it! To Ronny's consternation I burst out sobbing. He quickly took me in his arms. *'What have I done to you, where did I bring you'* he whispered. *'Home*, I replied, *'and here too we will soon have a city full of neon lights and what's more we have each other'*. If possible at all, the bond between us became even stronger in that old taxi . . .

As a born city dweller, I had not the slightest clue about gardening, but, true to the norm, I started improving on the situation with gusto. With the first warmth of Spring, a small plant pushed its head above the soil in our front garden. I watered it daily and virtually willed it to grow. Even supported it with a stick and when it was about half a yard tall and it showed beautiful, mauve flowers later on, I called an elderly neighbour to admire it. His garden, by the way, was a picture of flowering shrubs and multicoloured flowers and bulbs throughout the year as I would later discover. *'Good girl'* he commented, *'There's just one thing - your beaut of a plant is . . . a weed!'*

I soon became convinced all Englishmen are born gardeners. While his Sunday routine generally speaking was repetitive - he cleaned his car each Sunday morning even in the coldest winter weather - he would spend most of his weekends in Spring until late Autumn, in the front and/or back garden and succumbed to an orgy of grass cutting, digging, planting, weeding, pruning, harvesting and, especially, creating. Perhaps the only arena where man and wife could work side by side in full co-operation without discord . . . even laying garden paths was a job he would tackle, on his own, as mixing cement is beyond most women's capacity. The results, more often than not, were really surprisingly pleasant. The colour palette of Spring with its undulating soft pastel hues would be followed by the warm, sunny Summer tints superseded in time by the rust coloured Autumn shades. It was not only the colour schemes but the ingenuity in planning the layout of the garden, with lawn for sunbathing for those not blessed with a special patio, or children at play, cosy corners in the shadow for those to whom the sun is more of a menace. Twisting paths would lead one past weed-free flower beds to the end of the garden where vegetables were grown. Some grew useful herbal beds near the kitchen door and the aromatic perfume would caress one's sense of smell at passing.

Just as I had dedicated my younger years to further education, evening classes and/or books, so I threw myself into the pursuit of British flora and, aided by friends and neighbours, learned to respect and know nature as never before.

My immediate neighbour had heard me singing, prior to my marriage, during a thorough cleaning of our newly acquired house. She encouraged me to join the local Operatic

Society and yet another neighbour with a piano allowed me to rehearse accompanied by her daughter. The Sheffield Amateur Operatic Society would perform annually either an American or British show operetta. Unfortunately, the Viennese or German ones with which I was familiar, were unknown. During the second year of my membership, as their regular leading lady had let them down, I was offered the lead, perhaps too because my voice had in the meantime been considerably improved by a well-known Sheffield baritone after private lessons. He had been performing for many years at the famous opera house of Milan, had reached pensionable age and retired to his native Sheffield where he proceeded to teach music and singing. After a while he advised me to study in Italy. However, I had not exactly got married to become a diva and was of the opinion that my little voice shrunk to nothing in comparison with my man's own career and comfort. Moreover, I had never really considered my voice as a prerogative, except to . . . chatter.

We had been most surprised to receive a cheque from my mother-in-law to cover these singing lessons. Musical evenings around the piano were still a regular pattern of English family life those days and she, herself, played the piano very well. We had spent many a convivial evening during our visits when she had heard me sing. Her financial contribution abruptly came to an end, though, when she realised my name would not be displayed above the entrance to Covent Garden, lit up as *the* star, and so I carried on 'amateuring' with much pleasure and glee in the chorus line until we left Sheffield. This generosity of mother-in-law had initially very much surprised us as Ronny's parents were not exactly famous for it! Apart from the case of Ronny's operation as the result of a heavy kick in his stomach during one of his sporting activities, of which I have already written in the first part of this book, and which he found himself repaying to his father, I must disclose the following. Before we took the matrimonial step, Ronny and I made a verbal agreement. By virtue of Spilly's generosity, I was able to purchase all our furniture from a well-known Belgian manufacturer. Furthermore, and for many months, she allowed me to keep the lion's share of my salary enabling me to acquire all linen, personal trousseau, nick-nacks and necessary housewares. Ronny, on the other hand, would pay for packing and dispatching of the container; shipping costs to be free, courtesy of his firm. The deposit on our house was also his responsibility. His parents presented us with a cheque for . . . £25 which just covered stair carpet and kitchen lino. The total amount for our complete Belgian household effects came to £1350, at the then rate of exchange of just over B.Frs.100 to the £. Prices of all commodities have risen considerably in some cases beyond reason, so work it out for yourself!

Chapter Nine

Journalism

It stands to reason that, when living in a foreign country, one tries to meet fellow countrymen. I soon met other Belgian brides and our group extended to five, three French speaking Belgians, a further Antwerpian and myself. We would regularly meet in each other's home. We sympathised with each other in our praise for England; sometimes we would criticise when comparison with Belgium warranted it. It was during one of these 'hen parties' that I came to a decision which would play a very important part in my future life and absorb a great deal of my leisure time. We were discussing the fact that, during our holidays in our native cities, we would often be unpleasantly surprised at the mocking attitude of some acquaintances on learning that we lived in England. In my own case, it was deemed unnatural that, after four years of strict rationing, and indeed hunger, I would still remain in a country where almost the same strict rationing applied, and leisure, in the form of 'going out', apart from London's West End, was virtually nil. Some of the first war-brides had already returned, disillusioned partly by their own insufficient stamina to face a new life in a foreign country. The difference in mentality for that matter also played an important part plus, in extremis, the living conditions of these girls when they were forced to live with in-laws, being alone with their husbands in private circumstances only late at night. Some people in Belgium simply did not realise that England, in that immediate post-war era, was virtually bankrupt and the financial depression of her economic policy would be slow to evolve towards improvement.

And so I decided, with the assistance of De Nieuwe Gazet, one of Antwerp's leading daily newspapers which had encouraged me from an early age to accept the familial and written example of liberalism, to enlighten the ignorant. To tell them about our life and how a child of the 'Sinjorenstad' (nickname for Antwerp) had got to know and love these so-called cold Brits. Spending and leisure after all were no sinecure for a happy life! Great was my pleasant surprise when the Editor accepted my contribution as the first of a series of three, with as title 'A 'Sinjorin' (female native of Antwerp) who became English, recounts . . .

Admittedly during my school days successive teachers would invite me to read my essays aloud in front of the class but to find my name under my article printed in a leading newspaper was 'another pair of sleeves' as translated from a Flemish proverb. When I was further requested to send regular articles (the Editor thought my 'natural enthusiasm most refreshing') - I found myself quite emotional. Newspaper readers were not as yet bombarded by the profusion of radio news bulletins regarding foreign countries, television had only just taken its hesitant steps, and any news items from Albion were eagerly perused. Fate played a hand in this shortly after, however, as Ronny was offered the management of the Birmingham branch, which was in dire need of modernising, and as our imminent move commanded most of my interest and time, further articles were sent but sporadically.

Just before our moving to Birmingham, my immediate neighbour passed away. During my younger years, true enough, I had fleetingly greeted the bodies of my dead grandparents prior to their coffin being nailed down but a quick look at their marble-like features left me with a peaceful memory. To my consternation, when handing our card of condolence to his wife, she invited me in to pay my last respects to her husband. In the open coffin my neighbour was serenely resting in his best suit, nicely made up, surrounded by a cloud of white satin, indifferent to the continuous caresses and kisses overwhelmingly bestowed upon him by his wife. She insisted that I too would caress his face . . . I had only met the man previously to exchange polite conversation and literally shivered in my shoes upon touching the ice-cold skin. When I regaled him with my story, Ronny was furious but humane enough to afterwards ignore the incident . . .

Photo which appeared above my articles written for 'De Dieuwe Gazet'. It was taken when I was 40. I sent one to Spilly - 'Your ugly duckling!'

In the meantime, the Belgian Authorities had commenced the repatriation of the remains of the 'political prisoners', either deceased in the concentration camps or during the martyrdom of their enforced 'death march'. In March 1951 Spilly was advised that Spil's remains equally would be returned. She was requested to come to an Assembly Centre at the Belgielei - ironically where the Nazis had their interrogation headquarters during the war - and where she was shown a piece of knitwear that she recognised at once as part of a pullover Spil had worn at the time of his capture. This, as a matter of fact, was the only warm clothing he had been left with to wear under the thin, grey and white striped cotton prisoners' rig-out.

Small crates containing the remains were placed side by side in a kind of ward. Spilly burst out crying and begged the nurse to allow her once more to look upon her husband. *'My dear lady, these people were not put in a coffin but buried in the soil. To be blunt only the skull and bones still exist'*. She replied, *'I'll know him, I swear'*. *'It is impossible, I can assure you it would not serve anything except cause you more distress'*. Spilly's heart was in an uproar. She could only recall her first and great love when married at the age of 17, living together through thick and thin for 33 years, and now not even able to pay her last respects.

She begged and so heartbreakingly insisted, refusing to quit, until the nurse gave in, herself shaking her head, full of pity and led her inside. Spilly went from crate to crate, hardly glancing at the pitiful remnants of what once had been much loved beings. Suddenly she stepped determinedly towards one. *'This is my husband'* she said. *'How is it possible?'* The nurse could hardly believe it. *'Look at that small, round skull and the broken front tooth, that's my man alright'* Spilly said. *'Please, please can I hold him for a moment?'* she sobbed. *'My dear, it is not permitted, come on, it isn't even hygienic!'* But Spilly pointed at some rubber gloves and apron on a table nearby and the nurse, by that time, also in tears, made her wear these. Lovingly the skull was removed from the crate and placed in Spilly's arms, like a first born. She pressed it full of love and sobbing deeply to her heart. An equally crying nurse then took it gently out of her arms and helped her outside . . .

That same evening I was advised by telephone that Spil's official funeral ceremony would shortly take place and I travelled to Antwerp the following day. On the day of the funeral, 31st March 1951, Spil's coffin stood resting on a dais in the Holy Heart Church. It was draped with the Belgian tricolour. The place was full of people, the service splendid and the priest transposed the long drawn catachismus litany into a moving synopsis with regard to the fight of the Resistance in general. When the Belgian National Anthem was softly played, 'En Sourdine' as it is called, while we walked serenely around the coffin, I thought I would drop with chagrin. Did I support Spilly's weight, or did she hold me upright? We held on to one another like grim death. The cruel truth was irrevocable, that small light of hope we kept alive in our subconscious had been extinguished for ever! We hardly slept nor ate for days and sobbed and sobbed.

*

Before leaving Sheffield for good, I visited Birmingham on several occasions to look for a house, accompanied by Ronny. Few were for sale. The building trade was in a pitiful state and building permissions allocated only by exception. Modernising of roads and laying of new ones, clearing up the rubble of bombed housing in many areas, took priority and house design was still an embryo in the pens of the architects. Add to this that many a builder, at the end of the war and where possible, had acquired areas or building plots at low, pre-war prices. For as long as possible they postponed applying for a licence to build, which was then the norm, speculating on enormous price increases in the private sector. I believe it is called 'feathering one's nest' . . . if you'll pardon the pun.

The majority of houses we visited did not appeal, either because of the style, the often sad condition or the unattractive area. One day we were told of a building project going up in Solihull, then a village situated between Birmingham and Stratford upon Avon, the Bard's birthplace.

Long before, I had succumbed to the inevitable stereotype of British house-styling. It was explained to me that this was precisely why the majority of Britons could afford to actually buy. Flats were, in essence, the exception to the rule although London boasted quite a number of apartment buildings. There were some near the centre of Birmingham and some owners of large, oldish houses had created a kind of self-contained flat in their abode, with availability of a communal kitchen and/or bathroom. As soon as the lodging couples had saved sufficient funds to put down as a deposit on a house of their own however, they moved . . . A Briton possesses an inborn mania for bricks and mortar as the ultimate investment for his future and the first ten years of repaying interest on mortgages could be financially crippling. Twenty years later they are laughing up their sleeve when the property has been completely paid off! Once a builder had acquired building land, either by permission of the Council or a sale by a farmer, architects would submit their plans and the winner would see the accumulation of his creation in the form of long streets and seemingly interminable areas of monotonous identically styled houses. That way building proved cheaper and, if all the houses looked like photocopies from the outside, at least the inside would bear witness to the individuality of its owner. To-date, with the influence of America and competition sharper than ever due to the availability of building land, albeit at phenomenal prices, this initiative made a complete U-turn and family houses are a revelation in their individual style, beautiful architecture and inner comfort.

Although we, too, decided on a newly built house, we were promptly put on a waiting list and, after having chosen our building plot from the plan, were told it would take 6 to 8 months to completion. Saying good-bye to our friends and neighbours in Sheffield was very painful . . . 'partir c'est mourir un peu' as the French say. One of our neighbours adopted our beautiful, ginger tomcat, of the snow-white neck hair and blue eyes. We had baptised him Ginny, short for Ginger, not gin . . . As a kitten he had been brought to us by a friend 'for us to look after for a few days until she could find him a home'. We had heard that one before! As the tinned cat and dog food industry had not yet reached its present boom and I did not like to see my cat suffering from beriberi, I fed him on thick neck cuts of haddock, wild rabbit or boiled lights, mixed with bread soaked in the stock, and added small pieces of green and the occasional vitamin biscuit. No wonder his pelt shone like a mirror.

That tomcat proved to be a character of his own. When Ronny climbed the steep, narrow lane at the side of our house as a short cut to his local, Ginny walked alongside, jumping like an experienced acrobat from low garden wall to wall. For as long as Ronny remained in the pub, Ginny stood guard and accompanied him homewards, frolicking from wall to pavement, around his legs, and back again. Come dinner time, I only had to stand at the back door, rattle the lid on the cooking pot and wherever Ginny was, sometimes streets away or even on neighbour's beds, he came running in, ass over elbow at the speed of a cannonball. He had learned his lesson at an early age, with a few sternly spoken words and the habitual light tick against his posteria and thus he shied away from either scratching furniture or sitting on settee or armchairs. His favourite spot at night would be on the rug in front of the hearth on his own towel. When we said good-bye,

I caressed him very tenderly but I swear I saw reproach in those lovely little blue eyes . . .

Awaiting the completion of our house, we were obliged to go into rented accommodation in one of the old houses in an adjacent suburb of Birmingham. Our precious furniture was placed in the depot of one of the only removal firms with centrally heated storage. Again I found myself cleaning furtively, this time somebody else's home for the previous lodgers had avoided this like the pest.

As the automobile and smaller industries for which Birmingham was known worldwide, had started production again at full speed a substantial number of women had found more lucrative employment and consequently cleaning ladies were as rare as pimples on fashion models. When all rooms were thoroughly cleaned, I closed them up with the exception of the bedroom, kitchen and bathroom. Fate, however, decreed we were to live there longer than we had foreseen. After a week or so it was evident that, without my habitual care for a proper house and garden, I was slowly dying of boredom in that old place. Perusing the advertisements in one of our local newspapers, the Birmingham Mail, I noticed a shorthand typist/statistician was required for a leading Chain Manufacturer with offices in the centre of Birmingham. Unhesitatingly, I solicited for the vacancy and in addition to my curriculum vitae enclosed a copy of a certificate handed to me in Antwerp by my erstwhile employer upon my leaving. I was summoned to an interview by the elderly Secretary of the Managing Director, shooting dozens of questions at me, almost discouraging, until I was casually asked when exactly I could start . . . this was on a Friday morning and the following Monday I joined them.

Back home I had to resort to all the diplomacy I could muster to reason with a man whose ideal in life was to solely provide for his wife and had always rejected the idea of my going out to work. I faced him with a fait accompli: I either started this job or would return to Antwerp until our house was completed as living in that uncomfortable flat without proper activities made me want to crawl up the wall, a candidate for neurosis . . it succeeded. I think he was secretly proud that I had been able to so swiftly snap up a position without anyone's assistance. He made me promise, however, that this was but a temporary measure and that my consequent earnings would be strictly personal. I had no intention of sharing these, I laughed, as I was determined to have fitted carpeting in the new house.

The technical reports I was dictated by the representatives were double Dutch at first but they soon lost their mystery as the recurring terminology became more familiar. Having keenly wallowed in English literature since my early teens and, after coming to England, I had further improved my spelling. The statistics were part of a new venture of the firm but as I had always liked figures (except in algebra!) I soon mastered them.

During lunch I was not only able to correspond with Spilly on a regular basis but in addition could type the occasional article for De Nieuwe Gazet, until I bought my own typewriter. For some considerable time, Saturdays had been non-working days in England long before this was introduced in Belgium and I would mostly visit one establishment or another for building requisites in order to choose specific items for the new house. This was sooner said than done. The manager of the building site wielded the sceptre and suffered from the then much in evidence 'English disease' which had found its origin during the war, namely: take what we offer or leave it, reminiscent of one typical Antwerpian command to babies: 'Pee or no pee, on the potty' . . . After all there was a surplus of keen buyers featuring on lists as long as your arm!

However much we insisted on purchasing better quality items or to deviate from the stereotyped, second-best hearth and bathroom structures, cash in hand, we encountered the blank wall of nefarious stoicism. The site manager was the Fuhrer . . . Nevertheless, one thing on which he had not counted was a stubborn Jampot (an endearing nick-name Spilly had chosen for the sweet-toothed Brits) and a tough little Sinjoor, whose aspirations could not be blunted! So the next Saturday morning, we stormed his office at the building firm's headquarters. Ronny demanded to see the owner or managing director saying 'he wanted to confront the organ grinder, not the monkey' . . . When he opened his mouth in Sgt Major's voice he sounded formidable. We returned home, triumphantly, with flying colours. I can still remember his tirade: *'Listen carefully, little man, a customer spending thousands of pounds is no small beer in spite of your long waiting list. That house means everything to us. I am not purchasing a rabbit hutch, and of more importance, if my wife wants to bathe in a pink bath instead of a white one, she blooming well will, whether it is written in your tripey rules or not!'* During this tirade, many heads appeared above the wooden office partition behind which the office staff were working in order to identify the bass voice which dared to stamp into the ground the strategy of the Great Mogul of the Building Section. As far as we were concerned, our requests were granted. When at last we breathed more easily, the heaviest blow fell out of the blue. Talk about the pericles of building perfidy! A few weeks previously we had been approached by the building firm asking our permission for them to take a long, narrowish piece of land, approximately 100m x 1.5m, from the side of what was to be our garden. As we had more than sufficient ground, we were most willing especially as it would mean an extra house could be built if every owner agreed to this proposition. If it meant a home for yet another desperate couple, why not, we reasoned.

One day our eventual next door neighbour rang Ronny's firm, urging him to inspect our site as soon as possible as a terrible mistake had been made. Indeed, not everybody had agreed to secede some of their land, in spite of which the builder had decided to still push an extra house into the original plans. This then stood diagonally next to ours. As a result our kitchen window, originally planned with a full view onto the garden, looked out instead onto the blind wall of our neighbour's garage. I dared not look at Ronny fearing the disillusion on my face would incite him to manslaughter. At that moment I hated England as never before nor since! This could only happen here. How we reached the firm's office I cannot recall but when the blood again coursed through my veins, I heard Ronny declare he definitely could not accept the present position of the house and, in fact, advised them 'to stick it where the monkey stuck his nuts' . . .

A few sleepless nights and miserable days later, we were offered a different plot in the next street to be built, with the result, however, that we did not take possession after 6 but after 12 long months!

＊

It was 1953 and a few weeks before the crowning of the young Queen Elizabeth II, whose father's funeral we had viewed for the first time on TV, to be followed some weeks afterwards by the imposing crowning ceremony.

As we had heard so much about the decorations in London, we visited the metropolis just a few days prior to the crowning. It was a unique experience as we had never before seen such luxurious and original adornments. We could have walked on the visitors' heads who seemed to have come in droves from all over the world. Flags hung everywhere in the cherry red, white and royal blue of the Union Jack and majestic mauve and purple which had been coupled for centuries with royal standards and flags. An excitingly happy atmosphere prevailed. There were floral decorations everywhere, draped silks hung from the façades of the largest hotels. The English Rose, the Scottish Thistle, the Leek of Wales and the Irish Shamrock were represented in gigantic, lit up decors and nailed to the lamp posts and illuminated columns. In the evening the entire scene miraculously transformed itself, creating a veritable fairy-tale world with all the colours resplendently accentuated by lamps fastened in the centre of the flower decorations.

Above the entrance to one of the larger stores in Regent Street, a replica in papiermaché had been erected depicting the Queen-to-be in uniform on horseback as though she were trooping the colours. The windows of another store had been draped like Arab tents in rich lavender and yellow silk; the luxurious Dorchester Hotel, where many famous people and film stars rubbed shoulders with Princes and other Royal personages, capped it all with its exceptionally rich decoration covering the entire eight storeys. Around all the windows shiny silks in rich mauve and gold were draped and in each window three gigantic candelabra had been placed which, together with a further twenty or so placed above the sumptuously adorned entrance, created a particularly golden glow caused by the oil wicks, recalling memories of a century gone by . . .

Bows in gilded wire and wrought iron, representing the Unicorn and Lion of the Royal Arms were placed over the wide avenues and lights curling around the lamp posts and draped like rose garlands added their bit, plunging everything in a cloud of mysterious warmth. It was just as though Anderson's fables had come to life.

If at all possible, London was even more cosmopolitan than ever! We heard Indian dialects, singing French, the deep, nose-twang of the Americans, flat English of Australians, the 'hing-hong-hang' language of the Chinese and Japanese and even . . . Antwerpian.

On approaching St James' Palace, I suddenly noticed a car on the opposite side of the street, a black Rolls Royce sporting a Belgian flag from its motor. I crossed with the speed of a hare and, after having made enquiries, the chauffeur told me he was waiting for Prince Albert of Liege, at that moment in audience with Mr Churchill after a visit at the British Admiralty. As he had just been promoted in the Navy, he was to join the British Navy as part of his training. When the Prince appeared at last, smartly dressed in a grey tweed suit of impeccable cut, I had the feeling of standing before a younger King Albert . . . It is difficult to describe what precisely went on inside of me at that moment. Here I was, far away from home (those days blood was still thicker than water) and yet so near that I could have touched Belgium by holding out my hand and touching the Prince. A few moments afterwards the car started up, the Prince already deeply in conversation with his companion and I stayed happy but somewhat nonplussed.

✳

In April 1954 we were at last able to walk over the threshold of our own home and remained there for 25 long years . . . When we took possession of our earthly goods from storage, it was as though we were greeting long lost children!

It took several weeks of scrubbing and scraping off paint spots and cement blobs before everything shone to our satisfaction. The plasterers and painters had not exactly been careful in their work and had used their tools and brushes to their heart's content. We were still lumbered with an open hearth, though again found one of a beautiful design, also lucky in being able to find a stockist of anthracite stoves of French manufacture which, once lit, burned day and night. We installed one in the hearth in the dining room. The fitted carpets to which I had looked forward to so much had been laid before we moved in with our fairly heavy furniture. The first evening I plunged into my . . . pink bath full of bliss . . . What has always pleased me about houses and modern apartments here is the fact that each bathroom has a window looking out onto the garden or the street. The wash basin is generally placed just below this and, most useful when applying make-up for the ladies and for shaving where the men are concerned; a magnifying mirror on the window sill or near the window being of paramount importance. Sadly enough in Belgium, in many houses as well as modern apartments one has to resort to electric lighting often in windowless bathrooms . . .

Chapter Ten

House Owners Again

Water heating systems by virtue of the open hearth installation or immersion heaters, I found to be very ingenious and effective. The entire neighbourhood had been built on the grounds of an old farmhouse, with acres of meadows. The bulldozers of the builders had passed, in gay abandon and all weathers, over the soil which was later to become our garden. In order to overcome the crater 'River Yser 1914-18' look of the area, they had phlegmatically thrown down what seemed like tonnes of bricks and planking forming a sort of hard path assembly and when extricated found to be sufficiently adequate to build dozens of Uncle Tom's Cabins . . .

As soon as we had moved in, though, the by then created 'exclusive neighbourhood' transformed itself into a wriggling ants' nest as we all furtively started to reclaim the soil for our garden layout. Again I was confronted with a new aspect of John Bull, cancelling the general opinion. Our neighbours were mostly of the 'professional class' or bureaucrats, for the majority 'pen-lickers' as the Belgians call office workers and the British 'pen-pushers'. My eyes left their sockets when I saw their soft fingers, normally so neatly kept, plunging into the freshly dug soil and saw those lily-white hands mixing cement, swinging the pick-axe like born navvies, saw them cart stones and bricks, heaving old rafters and carrying heavy stones for building the famous English rockeries, digging the soil and sifting it three or four times to get rid of small stones in readiness for laying the lawn. Those who could afford it had long strips of turf delivered and placed them neatly on the prepared soil. To flatten this they had hired heavy, metal rollers from specialised firms and could be seen pulling them over the earth in their enthusiasm, resembling slaves of old harnessed to wooden spokes.

We too were ready. During the first season we planted potatoes in both front and back gardens. We had two in the front because the house stood at a corner and the drive to the garage divided the ground into two. Growing potatoes cultivated the virgin soil prior to sowing the grass seed. After reaping what Ronny called 'zeppelins' in size, we dug all the earth over and the top quality English grass seed soon germinated in the rich soil when I would excitedly study the first green shoots peering above the earth each day in the warm spring weather. Our 'virginal soil' however soon returned to nature and in momentary depression I realised that the lovely green carpet contained more weeds than grass as the daisy seeds had awoken. A hastily summoned expert voted for one solution only: remove the weeds complete with root . . by hand. Two continuous days I sat on my knees from morning till just before six at night and plucked and pulled . . . until, on getting upright again, I must have looked like Charlie Chaplin in 'Modern Times', his famous film about automation, hardly able to stop my hands from carrying on plucking in the thin air . . . Ronny stayed out of my way for the sake of safety . . . Soon enough Mother Nature intervened and the ensuing months we were regaled with a marvellous carpet of healthy green, like a Chinese carpet to begin with.

We dug and weeded and fashioned flowerbeds, planted double flowering Japanese cherry trees, a laburnum (which a few years later fell victim to the widening of our drive when the garage was extended), a crab apple tree and a lilac in the rear garden where we also indulged in a small vegetable plot. We grew garden peas, runner beans, sprouts, a few cabbages and 'field lettuce', a winter variety the seeds of which I had acquired in Belgium and, best of all, a Morello cherry tree. The few strawberry plants we were given by a kind friend soon grew so prolific we had to eventually dig out and discard them.

Ronny, however, soon proved to be more of an armchair gardener and left it all to me except the grass cutting. As the rear of the house faced South, the sun seemed to shine that first beautiful Summer from early morning till dusk. I was able for the first time in my life to indulge in sunbathing on the patio which in later years we were to transform into a wider Italian inspired version to enhance the enjoyment of our Summer outdoor life. With the generous assistance of Ambre Solaire sunbathing oil (those days but available in France and bought for me by holidaying friends), I acquired the tan I had always admired on ardent and persistent sunbathers and by so doing unknowingly added to wrinkling of my face in later years! By all that I had not neglected the interior design and was able, through careful mixing of additives in emulsion paint, to create a flattering palette of colour combinations, restful and pleasing to the eye. The paint manufacturers had not yet overindulged the general public with the vast variety on offer at present, and my friends were more than amused to see me add Ricketts Blue to the water, added to a pinkish emulsion paint in order to obtain the lilac-rose colour I wanted, or to see me mix other pastel concoctions for the required result . . .

And what of the English Sunday? As different to the Belgian one as day to night. I just could not get used to it and as Spilly later proclaimed: if we had walked in the street poodle-naked, nobody would have been any the wiser except perhaps the Bobby on the beat who would soon have put paid to this. The Continental Sunday indubitably is *the* day, longed for during the whole previous week, a day of rest, leisure and completely different to the daily routine, so that afterwards the breadwinner would have absorbed sufficient strength and willpower to throw himself with renewed vigour into the following week. All this in theory of course.

Once in possession of our property, I no longer judged the sad British Sunday as a lost cause with deserted streets and seemingly sleepy houses. Indeed, with his heavy mortgaged heap of bricks around his neck, John Bull found himself in the unfortunate position of executing *all* the jobs in his house himself and I am convinced the DIY syndrome reached its swiftest growth to the present peak in Albion. And whilst, in our residential area, his Sunday tasks limited themselves to cleaning the car, gardening, painting or decorating, in the less élite districts - which I learned were called 'working class areas' (an expression that puzzled me somewhat as we were all working for our daily crust of bread!) it was a different sort of beehive.

In order to fully and humorously describe it, I am quoting from the book of my late friend, André Drucker. John Bull's Sunday - as enthusiastic house owner those days - was filled to the brim with exhausting duties, to such extent that, at the end of the day, there was no more energy left to indulge in that disapproving habit of his Continental counterpart: night-life. He would wake at the crack of dawn. Throughout the week he would have slept the peaceful sleep of the contented man, with few worries on his mind, with fewer thoughts on his work,. The alarm clock had to drum him out of bed. But on Sunday morning, the curtain of sleep went up early, rung up by a battalion of duties. Having dragged himself downstairs, yawning in the chilly morn, he would brew a cup of tea for the companion of his bed. This ritual performed, he would dress. He too had his Sunday suit which he considered befitting for the Day of the Lord. It was his oldest pair of flannels, thin over the knees, frayed at the turn-ups, patched in the seat, spattered and patterned with old paint, old cement, old oil, old soil. Sometimes it would be an old pair of corduroys, stiff and heavy with the ballast of years of usage. No shining shoes for him in this special day of the week. He would slip into old crusted boots or into flabby Wellingtons, ready for the toil of his leisure. Thus, fitted out in his bizarre Sunday armour, the Knight of the Household Regiment would launch his weekly, fierce attack upon the Holy Sabbath. The morning air would resound with the noise of his labours. There he would be, John Quixote, Esq splitting the air with his battle-axe (no, not his wife, my personal note!) chopping firewood, gathering splinters from his hands, raking the grate, sifting the cinders, disposing of the ashes, banging the lid upon the dustbin, smashing up coal, filling the bucket and making the fire.

It was on Sunday mornings, when the Men of England got their home fires burning, that the sky would be filled with charred newspapers, chimneys would erupt and the fire-brigades all over England stood posed at action stations. And John Quixote, Esq on the day when even the good Lord rested, would be throwing himself into the multitude of Herculean tasks which he had planned and designed during the lull of the weekdays. There he would be, while Continentals were still lazing in bed, already wheeling the loaded wheelbarrow, mixing the sand and cement with water and sweat, and making a concrete path and a crazy path and patching up holes and cementing the rotting gate post. There he would stand, in the neighbourhood of the clouds perched on a wobbly ladder, replacing that missing roof tile, scraping off paint and painting the woodwork, pointing the bricks, fortifying the self-made shed and strengthening the crumbling outhouse.

You would find him unstiffening the brushes and mixing the paints, emulsioning the ceiling and papering the walls, battling all by himself like Laocoon with the pythons, only encouraged by the wife's scathing aspersions upon his craftsmanship when he spatters paint on the sideboard and by his children entangled in the sticky mess of pasted papers, the

217

. . . baskets. You would have seen him mending the gutter, cleaning the drain, stopping up unstoppable draughts, putting down the lino, ripping up the lino, gashing his hand, swearing . . . This Knight in his Sunday suit would sharpen his tools and trim the hedge, cut the lawn and plant the flowers, weed out weeds, do skilful things to trees and spray and manure and prune and clip and water and turn and dig and rake and hack and double-up with pain and keep himself upright only by clinging desperately to his spade, a hero!

You might even have seen him dismantle his bicycle, his motor-cycle, polish and grease and weld and replace a part and make the part himself on his own workbench and shout for iodine and adhesive plaster . . . If he was the owner of a car - and who of the little men of England, even those early days, wasn't? - there he would be, under the car, over the bonnet, between bits of car, an integral part of it, oily, mud-caked. It is a glorious testimony to the robustness of English cars that they withstood this Sunday onslaught without disintegrating every Monday. The other little men, his neighbours, would stand around him, advise, exchange opinion on pinions and dive underneath the car and give him a hand and emerge oily, mud-caked and happy themselves. Don't think for a moment that his Sunday was then done! There was the shelf that his wife would want him to knock together, the door which wanted easing up. The boy's scooter needed attention, the girl's dolls house and pram, the swing in his stamp-sized garden. The dog would be ready for airing, the henhouse to be cleaned, the cat's meal to be cooked - oh the perfume of boiled fish heads! - the water in the goldfish bowl to be changed, the canary to be made comfortable, the rabbit or tortoise to be provisioned with dandelions.

There seemed no man on earth who succeeded so completely in surrounding himself voluntarily with animals that are the greatest nuisances to himself and everybody else within a radius of a bark or a cockcrow! When at last the sun was setting on his Sunday, John Quixote would still be at it. His mind blank by now, his palms blistered; he is sore and bruised and covered in a new layer of paint, cement, sawdust, oil, soil and sweat. In the fading light you would have observed him sweeping up the yard, knocking a nail in the fence, labelling a flower, collecting the rubbish and concluding with a bonfire which usually darkened the whole district, teaching a loitering foreigner in his Sunday suit, what a Sunday can smell like once the Englishman has finished with it and it with him.

Aching in every part of his body, you would have seen him stagger in complete exhaustion to his chair, turn on the radio and doze off at once over four to six Sunday papers of which he is a regular subscriber. Alas, soon though he would be shaken out of his slumber by the rasping call of his dear dynamic wife, who demands of him to get up and wipe the dishes, hang up the clothes line for Monday's washing, fetch more coal and make himself generally useful in the house as other husbands do . . .

And why was John Bull such a fervent DIY man, and still is? Because he is the helpless victim of two circumstances: the first is that he can put his hand to most jobs. He is a veritable Jack-of-all-trades and Master-of-most. He is a walking compendium of household craft and domestic engineering. He is the complete professional amateur when doing things for himself. No one else on earth can discuss, with the same balanced authority, matters ranging from Crownwheels and Pinions to French Beans and Onions. How he came to know in the first place is shrouded in mystery, but he knows it all. Which is beyond the grasp of most foreigners, who are already regarded as an authority if they can unscrew a burnt-out electric bulb without electrocuting themselves. The second reason is that John Quixote Esq was weighed down with a standard of living too great for the shoulders of one man. No little man outside England could boast the use of a house and garden, some even a car. The English Man owned too much and it made him a slave to his castle. Where our castle was concerned, I caught the exception to the rule and although Ronny had been laying our garden paths, mixing the cement himself, and, at their conclusion, looked like a skeleton (Spilly baptised him 'Pants, Bones, no Bottom') and dabbed a few coats of paint on some woodwork, gave the mower the occasional 'skip' over the grass, most of the jobs were allocated to proper professionals. As far as DIY was concerned, Ronny gave the impression of the proverbial 'fart in a colander' . . . the only man who looked at a hammer and . . . started bleeding. Indeed, when during the first Spring days he would start the motor mower in the garage, I was already at the back door with the elastoplast as my dear hubby would appear a few minutes afterwards with blood dripping from some wound on one finger or another.

*

A journalist on the Female Page of the Birmingham Mail and the local Solihull press, greedy for copy, had been told by friends about our Belgian interior and, after having visited us, wrote a substantial article, enthusiast as she was with our variance of the habitual stereotype. As often happens in life one thing led to another and it resulted in my writing a series of articles for this paper regarding life as it then was in Belgium with its different mentality compared to an England to which I had grown even more sympathetic. A cartoonist was responsible for some very funny drawings at the top of each article. The series was referred to as provocative . . .

In the meantime apart from my regular contributions to De Nieuwe Gazet, I had started with translations into or from the

Dutch for the Birmingham Chamber of Commerce, working from home. Although I was sent legal documents including contracts and judicial lawsuits only sporadically, they heavily brought to the test my grey material as no matter in which language, legal expressions are often Double-Dutch!

After a particularly difficult example, there came the day when I decided to find relaxation in putting my hands to use. As many of my friends and neighbours had started papering their own home, I too indulged in this pleasant task. A friend taught me how and, after having acquired a folding work-table and the necessary utensils, I commenced what became a hobby, providing me with many pleasant hours and a never ending pride after observing the created results. My first efforts in the art of paperhanging limited themselves to the guest room, followed, in my innocence, by the nightmare of the decorater, ie the loo. This generally smallest-room-in-the-house, with all its obstacles parried with the cistern's position, pipes, nooks and crannies, demanded contortions of a mamba.

My enthusiasm was boundless, however, and paperhanging became a sort of therapy, as gardening had proved to be. Luckily I never hung any paper upside down but I did fall off my step-ladder once during my first attempt at papering the ceiling. The first panel proved to be a veritable equilibrium exercise as I struggled to hold the pasted, folded strip with the left hand and, with the right one holding the dry brush, attempted to stick it to the ceiling in a straight line. As soon as I had succeeded, I had to step onto a stool strategically placed in order to continue. To my consternation, and halfway into this operation, the initially stuck part loosened and started to curl itself like a slow film, around my ears. Wrestling with paper, brush and balance, I finally ended up on the floor, hair and face covered in paste, convulsed with laughter . . . and started again, until I succeeded. During the ensuing years I happily indulged in emulsion paint ceilings and walls with the new plastic paints, so easily applicable with rollers, with paper hanging even in the hall where one strip involved a length of over 13 feet. I only asked Ronny's help for supporting this, pasted and folded, for fear its weight would tear the strip in the drop if I did it alone.

In November 1957, the management of De Nieuwe Gazet decided to amalgamate with Het Laatste Nieuws, another well-known Flemish newspaper and a Government Minister took over as Director-General. Shortly before this event I had been advised that my continued input would be appreciated and when, during my next stay in Antwerp, I visited the paper's Editorial office, realised, upon making his acquaintance, we had a lot in common, not least of all being born and bred in the heart of the Port on the Scheldt. Nevertheless, I was instructed, in future, to deviate from the personal and to resort to issues of a more political nature. When humbly confessing that I was groping in the dark where political matters were concerned, I was told: *'Learn, you've got a brain so use it!'*

In addition I was warned never to write a downright lie or that which could involve the paper in a libel case. This advice, issued to all journalists, was unnecessary in my case as I had instinctively followed these rules from the onset although, as a freelance journalist, I wore the stamp of my upbringing, education and personal convictions. (Sadly, nowadays, the truth is not always too near to the heart of the world press or audio and visual media and, with the exception of a few bona-fide newspapers in this country, becomes all too often flagrantly bent in the pursuit of phenomenal sensationalism in order to satisfy the inborn, human craving for another man's scandal, all for the sake of increased distribution and profit.) I was always under the impression that integrity and altruism go hand in hand!

During regular travels through the country for the necessary copy and interviewing of interesting personalities on the British scene, I was allowed to charge expenses.

The immediate future found me with my head buried into political newspaper reports, listening with monotonous regularity to the BBC's 'Today in Parliament', greedily viewing TV's political debates, visiting ditto meetings and debating for hours with friends until I no longer projected myself as the proverbial dunce on the political scene. Furthermore it was most amusing to follow the debates in Parliament as they not only showed to perfection the typical and subtle British sense of humour. While the discussions were absent of open defamation, their poisonous intonations and acidity of replies supplied the oxygen for the life-blood of democracy. Sharp-witted retorts such as 'Sit down, Honourable Member, you're a walking obituary for your Party!', or 'being supported by you runs parallel with being measured by a funeral director' were but a few examples.

The years 1958/9 were especially distinctive for my series of articles on the British Royal Family. I wrote successively about Queen Elizabeth II as 'Woman and Queen'; the role of Prince Philip as Royal Consort; the happy liaison between the Queen Mother and her reigning daughter, followed by the broken romance of Princess Margaret and Peter Townsend. I trust the respect I hold for all of them shone out of my work.

My honoraria were paid into a postal account which Spilly had opened for me and though these were not over-generous they paid for my expenses during my stays in Antwerp.

*

An annual event in the Midlands was the British Industrial Fair, usually at the end of April/beginning of May and the exhibition area was situated at Castle Bromwich. This Fair was visited by buyers from all over the world although initially confined to national exhibitors.

(In the 1970s this event was to be replaced by the National Exhibition Centre, near Solihull, now an internationally famous complex of over 20 halls, most of them intercommunicating and with facilities such as banking, shops, post office, public telephones, fax and telex access, restaurants, meeting places and convention rooms with film and TV screens, canteens, medical centre, etc. Firms of all nationalities come to exhibit their machinery, wares or technology. One of the halls, the Arena, has a 12,760 seating capacity and concerts regularly take place, often with pop groups or distinctive singers, famous throughout the world, not to mention the occasional transformation into a skating rink.)

One day in early 1957, over the customary 'bucket of beer' at the bar of The Midlands Hotel in Birmingham where all those involved in shipping, forwarding or travel industry, regularly conglomerated to 'keep the waterways of England open' (and their throats as a side line), Ronny was asked if I would assist during the BIF fortnight as an interpreter. And so the next BIF event found me at a kiosk at Snow Hill station. Looking more like a hastily hammered together stand, it bore a poster mentioning the four main languages I was then familiar with and under which one smart ass, much to my amusement, the same evening had written 'We speaka da lingo'. My other colleague was engaged at the Midland station and quite a character. She was 78, looking all but 55 years of age! To draw attention to her and her puny stand, she had dressed herself in a bizarre way for which, no doubt, her many years of residence in pre-war Berlin's bohemian quarter, supplied the inspiration. Her stage-like appearance, cyclamen coat bordered with two different kinds of fur, (boa and fox), gigantic hat covered in multicoloured flora perched on her white hair, dangling earrings and gold chains around her neck, made her stand out like a sore thumb. In addition, she carried a wide, satin ribbon over her shoulder with big lettering with 'BIF' all over it. She looked like a Christmas tree and created an unmistakable beacon not to be missed and most helpful to the foreign visitors.

There were hilarious little incidents those first days. The two Antwerpians coming to my stand and saying to one another in their unique vernacular. *'An Englishwoman with languages? That's a phenomenon! I'm sure ours is one language she doesn't speak!'* I straightened my hat, an obviously continental creation, and replied in the same vein; *'Wanna bet? I've forgotten more Antwerpian than you'll ever know!'* After which we exploded with laughter.

A group of gentlemen in meticulously clean raincoats looked forlorn until I accosted them offering assistance. They seemed surprised I had recognised them as foreigners and did not tell them that an Englishman only felt at home in a raincoat nearing antiquity status. A Dutchman had left his briefcase with all his papers in a taxi. After having reported it to the police, I found that the entire force, the office for lost property and half the station personnel had literally been mobilised as I could not rest before the proverbial honesty of John Bull had been proved. The briefcase was duly recovered, intact, and returned by a phlegmatic taxi driver who had decided a cup of tea was his prerequisite. Come rain, come shine, tea-time is religiously adhered to. Must add that the briefcase contained 10,000 guilders! I was unexpectedly rewarded with an enormous box of chocolates sent on from one of London's most exclusive stores. Ronny was the beneficiary as sour-sweet gherkins are my forte.

A few days afterwards a Spaniard needing accommodation was directed to one of my acquaintances with a fine Bed and Breakfast reputation. I had had difficulty explaining this, in view of the fact I had only just started to learn Spanish and was still very much in the dark with the language. He was so delighted that, upon entering the hastily called taxi, he invited me to stay with his family in . . . Barcelona . . . well, it's only around the corner . . .

The two Antwerpians returned just before closing and came home with me to partake in our evening meal, preceded by a stiff aperitif of Ronny's Scotch, adding to the bonhomie, and insisting they plant an aubrietia cutting each. One was planted in the middle of our celeriac bed, while the cat of our next door neighbour soon put paid to the other one . . . Well, such is life!

After a visit to a gynaecologist when we had been married ten years, I was told that, presumably due to my peritonitis operation as a child, I could not conceive and as medical science had not yet advanced to its present form we accepted the verdict especially as we were quite close and happy with one another. From time to time friends and family back in Antwerp would enquire about offspring but soon lost interest. Except for one little old lady, one of Spilly's neighbours. From the moment we had got married, she had accosted Spilly time and time again upon meeting, posing the same question: *'Well, no kiddies yet, and why?'* until Spilly got so fed up that she saw no way out of it but to answer, in her own dry humour; *'Well, you see, my dear, I'll spill the beans after all these years. My daughter is too deep and her husband too short!'* . . . Little dear never asked her again, indeed, when noticing Spilly approach, she would cross the road . . .

During the Winter months, in accordance with British business life, we found ourselves happily involved in official dinners, receptions, banquets, the former either taking place in our own home or elsewhere, having received invitations to dinner dances and balls given by business acquaintances or friends, members of Freemason Lodges.

Years later, after Ronny retired, he too became a Freemason with the Chevron Lodge, for veterans of the War. Although shrouded in mystery as they were, I was told membership was open to people of all religious denominations which is not the case in Belgium where a strict anti-religion rule applies. Prior to becoming an active member under the wing of his chosen Lodge, the potential applicant's background is investigated and he will be visited by a delegation to his home to satisfy that his wife is in accord. There are female Lodges as well. And so it happened that the Grand Master and some representatives came to visit us and consequently received him in their Lodge. I had, however, warned Ronny beforehand, strangely enough after having seen a programme on TV regarding this cult showing some of the so-called secret rites during 'indoctrination', telling him the only person he should kneel to should be his Queen . . . I am convinced, in retrospect, that Ronny joined half-heartedly, encouraged no doubt by the enthusiasm of one or two dear friends, themselves members of long standing or ex-Grand Masters. It took him two years to realise Freemasonry was not his scene and he resigned. However, never afterwards did he utter one word or show any sign about the teachings and rules and the little I learned about it in years to come I gained from various TV programmes on the subject.

As far as I am concerned, my memories of the Freemason balls are of pleasant dinners and dancing till midnight, healthy fun and the fact that, as a group, we considerably contributed to financing charities.

Chapter Eleven

Spilly's Happiness

Spilly's life too underwent an enormous change. While our house was being built and lodging facility was lacking in the flat we had temporarily rented, coupled with the fact that, having joined the Chain Manufacturers Firm in Birmingham so recently, I had no right to a holiday, we did not meet for over a year. She felt extremely lonely and in order to combat this would visit a friend of hers, the landlady of a pub not far from where she lived. We knew her very well and she was notorious, in an affable way, for her enormous chest. She had breasts like round farmhouse loaves although, strange enough, not as huge as those of another pub landlady in the same square, but sufficient to be in competition. The latter had been baptised by the Antwerpian populace 'Fanny Tit' whereas Ronny had called Spilly's friend 'Mrs Mosquito-bite', an anachronism that caused much laughter. The punters in Mrs Mosquito-bite's place were mostly neighbours and regulars on their way home from work and often visiting the pub in the evening with their wife and family. One of the regulars happened to be a widower, born in the Ardennes, the French speaking part of Belgium but since many years a resident of Antwerp. His wife had died before the war leaving him with two small girls he then brought up single handedly. The oldest, alas, was killed by a V-1 destroying her house. He was living with the other, married daughter, who with her husband and two children, lived in an apartment next door to Spilly. Within a comparatively short time of meeting her, Armand developed a soft spot for Spilly and pursued her relentlessly until, after a few years coinciding with her period of loneliness, she had got to know him better and to appreciate his kind nature and quiet demeanour. His grandchildren were growing up and as the necessity arose for them to have their own bedroom he felt he was in the way. We had a well-kept attic room and Spilly allowed him to arrange and furnish this as a bed-sitter. He was still active in his own painting business and her life once again had a purpose; cooking for two, another being to look after, going out together, once more a kind of family.

And I? Jeepers, I was green with envy!! How did that man dare to intrude there where my daddy should have been? In my possessive selfishness I forgot her loneliness and my duty towards her. I could not stand him . . . until I too got to know him better and personally witnessed Spilly's newfound happiness. I saw his genuine love surrounding her, his caring for her well-being, so learned to fight my jealousy and finally showed him my own respect and growing affection. Our 'tête caillou' (stonehead) nickname for a Walloon (inhabitant of the South part of Belgium) came to spend his annual holidays with Spilly in England after we had moved into our house and as a professional painter, he insisted on regularly painting our outside woodwork when necessary. He did not speak one word of English but accompanied Ronny to his local where he was introduced to Ron's drinking companions and friends and duly accepted. Not as popular as Spilly, though, as with her translation of her typical Antwerpian expressions and proverbs, she soon conquered the hearts of everyone she met.

Happiness has a way of coming to an abrupt halt at times!

About ten years after they first became a couple, Armand fell ill. Cancer of the liver was diagnosed. After his operation, when the end was near, I came to assist Spilly. In spite of all the care and love we lavished on him he died at the age of 67 and Spilly once more was alone. Her sorrow was heartbreaking as I am convinced, deep in my heart, that her life with Armand had been more peaceful than with Spil, as much as she loved the latter . . . Never before in my life, nor since, have I experienced so much compassion as when the

Sabena bus took me to Brussels and she again was left behind after Armand's demise. How could fate be so cruel? I was torn apart between two loves and had to ignore the one of the umbilical cord!

Chapter Twelve

Helping Nature

The records of British weather mention Winter 1962/3 as one of the most severe of this century. During that Siberian weather cattle farmers suffered most, especially those domiciled on the Moors and the hilly parts of Wales, Scotland and North England. With the stormy winds and squalls from the Atlantic Ocean and the cold currents from the Urals, howling like banshees over the British Isles, the snow fell in such droves that hundreds of sheep, trying to find shelter against one another, were buried alive. As if this was not enough misery, lambing started earlier than expected.

One weekend a cry for assistance, via the BBC, went out to recruit volunteers for help to rescue cattle still alive. From all over the place animal lovers called their families to arms, with whatever appropriate transport available, and proceeded one early Sunday morning into action. We too went, to Wales, a two-hour long drive. Dressed as Eskimos, me complete with Ronny's thick pull-over, my raincoat, two pairs of thick tights normally worn to Yoga class and a pair of ski pants, we vamoosed. We had stocked a spade and fork, brandy, sandwiches and Thermos flasks with hot coffee and soup and were armed with the determination to cock a snoot at the British climate.

Arriving at one farm, we already found a regiment of volunteers from all walks of life, ready for the onslaught, in age groups varying from 12 to about 70! We were divided into small groups, led by a farmer and were soon on our way to the higher parts where it was suspected sheep might still be alive. Where high snow heaps were mounted in crackling frost, we noticed small holes here and there and it was in those places that we were able to dig out some of the sheep still alive. Don't tell us sheep's eyes are sleepily dumb. We saw gratitude in all those pairs of blinkers. The men laughed at our unremitting efforts with the spade and with our childish molly-coddling each time we excitedly neared yet another liberation. Never in my life was I so pleased to be a human being and never afterwards were we able to do a better and more useful deed than that bitterly cold Sunday in Wales . . . It puzzled me how the animals could still be alive as some had been pressed together immobilised for over a week. The snow without doubt supplied the necessary water but they had not taken nourishment. Some were so weak we added our carefully preserved brandy to the warm milk. Those still able to stagger were driven to the farms where hastily fashioned refuges allowed them to partake in food and drink. Those in a worse state where helped into trucks or lorries and some caring people even hoisted a sheep into their car boots . . . a funny sight if it had not been so tragic.

And for the first time in my life I was witness to the wonder of Nature: the miracle of birth. As soon as the ewes, weak from cold, entered the warmth of the barn they started to lamb. After having watched the farmer assisting the ewe, we got the gist and the ladies present were able to help. The slimy little bodies were swiftly, but carefully, removed from the ewe. For a moment, I would hold my breath when no sign of life was detected and the little heads would just slump sideways but the farmer, efficient as any vet, would hold the head in one hand, lightly shake the body, give it a few taps on its hindquarters and place the lamb on its four legs. The ewe licked it over its entire body. The new-born would totter up like a drunk, lightly supported by the farmer until it found its feet and we proceeded with the full drying action.

In the meantime, the farmer's wife had prepared a vast number of feeding bottles with warm milk and in the twinkling of an eye the quiet barn was transformed into a nursery full of activity, running 'to and fro', excited but subdued chatter and soft clucking noises of the sucking lambs. We ate our sandwiches in the same barn, drank our hot coffee and even shared our soup with the sheep. We could hardly move, stiff as we were with the unexpected exercise. Ronny's war wounds to his leg caused him hell but our Sunday had passed - a day of rest? I do not think one single inhabitant of the valley had remained seated by his fireplace. We left our telephone number with the farmer so that, should the occasion arise again, he could count on our assistance. The lambs were finally baptised with the most comical names such as: 'Chiver, Borealis, Beep and Greedy Guts'. We were promised we could come and see our ' godchildren' as often as desired. After having insisted not to receive any lamb chops come next Spring from our 'miracle kids' we left the Welsh farm. Lamb chops were significantly absent from our table for a long time to come . . .

Chapter Thirteen

Covering A Royal Visit

As my name figures on the list of journalists filed at the Belgian Embassy in London, I was advised early 1963 of the forthcoming visit of the Belgian Royal Pair to the British Court. My press pack and card were ready and the Editor of De Nieuwe Gazet requested me to cover the event. Rooms were reserved for the visiting journalists in one of the London hotels and a telex-machine duly installed in one of the halls for our free use. The visit took place from 14th till 16th May inclusive and the Belgian Royals would return to Belgium during the morning of the 17th.

A l'occasion de la visite de
Leurs Majestés le Roi et la Reine des Belges
l'Ambassadeur de Belgique a l'honneur d'inviter

madame Anne Evans

à la réception qui aura lieu à l'Ambassade
le mercredi 15 mai 1963 à 17 heures

R.S.V.P.
36, Belgrave Square
London S.W.1.

Jaquette ou tenue de ville sombre

Invitation card to a reception for the visit of the
Belgian Royal Family to England.

Never before nor since have I worked so extensively as during those days! It would be nearer 2am when, upon finalising my articles, I would fall into bed and at 6am was already prepared to telex them to Antwerp. I was the only journalist representing De Nieuwe Gazet although other papers had designated at least two reporters plus some photographers and we formed a mini-army furtive as a beehive. Thanks to my cheeky but polite daring, I was able to sometimes look behind the scenes. In any event it had been decided the emphasis was to be on 'off the cuff' remarks rather than generalising the Royal visits to the various places. Also, the female readers were most interested in the apparel of the Royals and as a vast number of men are colour blind this reporting especially befell little me.

During the dinner the City of London had offered the Belgian Royals at the Guildhall, no reporters were allowed. Before this ceremony took place, while the guests presumably had been seated already at their tables, I had an animated chat with one of the Security Policemen. After having pleaded to allow me entrance so that I could boast profusely of the pomp and circumstance of this piece of London in my widely distributed newspaper, he relented, born Cockney as he was, and so I virtually gatecrashed, via a back door, mounting the stairs to the balcony. The famous dining hall indeed revealed the panoply of history with its memorabilia on the rich panelling, the luxury of beautifully laid tables awash with antique solid silver tableware and crystal. The blinding flash of jewels and colourful outfits of the female guests vying with the dinner jackets and uniforms of the gentlemen covered in a profusion of medals.

When the Belgian Royals entered, a slow handclapping greeted them as a sign of respect. As soon as they were seated, however, and as promised to the Security Guard, I reluctantly left . . . The following day some Belgian nationals had been

235

invited at the Embassy to be presented to King Baudoin and Queen Fabiola. The guests formed two ranks. The King exchanged a few words with those in the one, the Queen took the other. I happened to stand at the end of the Queen's line. All of a sudden I had an impulse. She had by then been talking to people in English, French and Flemish for the last two days.

Here I must digress for a while. Prior to our Spanish holiday in 1958, I had started to learn Spanish from a book 'Teach Yourself Spanish'. Ronny had remarked that English was spoken in Spain and I parried with a typical Flemish comment: 'Yes, maybe, but I do like to hear what they say behind our back . . . ' Later, in Spain, during our first sojourn in a still untouched virginal Lloret de Mar, with undisturbed beautiful views of picturesque valleys and dales, still bereft of its present concrete jungle, we still found a natural mentality. A foreigner having taken the trouble to learn their language was virtually revered and the many mistakes I originally made during conversations in the hotel, shops or Bodegas, caused considerable joy and laughter and cemented an entente cordiale. Back home I enlisted for Spanish at the College of Further Education here in Solihull and, prior to the Royal visit, was getting more familiar with the language.

So, when Queen Fabiola in turn was introduced to me, I told her in Spanish, with my heart in my throat, that it was the happiest day of my life in England. She seemed most pleasantly surprised judging by her sunny smile and after a brief conversation thanked me for my thoughtfulness. A little later, posing at the exit, allowing the photographers to take a few more shots before leaving, she turned her head and nodded briefly to me. I'm afraid I cried . . . I was exhausted after the visit and received not only much praise from the Newspaper Management but also a substantial honorarium although my satisfaction was with the fact of having performed a task honestly and honourably.

It had been my dream, since my early teens, to one day own a real and fashionable fur coat - not rabbit, sheepskin or musquash. Ronny was flabbergasted when shortly afterwards I came home with a beautiful, natural grey American broadtail coat, made to measure by a well known furrier. (Although nowadays I would refrain from purchasing garments made of precious wildlife.) *'Did it fall off a lorry?'* he asked. *'No, darling, it was purchased with the 'pocket money' you always said you did not mind my earning with my 'little jobs' . . . '* I replied tongue in cheek.

Central heating became more popular around the 1960s and Ronny too succumbed to this innovation, to my gratitude, and we decided on its installation as well as further modernising of our home by having the dining room and lounge made into a through-lounge. Unfortunately our beautiful hearth fell victim and the resulting gaping hole was bricked in. One of the doors was bricked in and created into an alcove with thick glass shelves for our growing collection of nick-nacks and I stumbled upon the idea of leaving a low part of the wall between the two original rooms partly standing, finishing its end like a column. This prevented draught from the now single door while the top of the column acted as support for a Grecian-style lamp. New fitted carpet was soon to follow. During the cold Winter months I was in heaven! Released forever from the dirty coal mess. Could even walk naked from bath to bedroom without catching pneumonia!

✻

As shipping merchandise evolved to containers instead of loose stowage in holds, it had been necessary for Ronny to find a depot as a central storage yard for the crates of export goods emanating from manufacturers in the Midlands and the

North. Some would be shipped via Hull, others via London or Felixstowe. He found the necessary accommodation in an industrial estate near Wolverhampton, about 40 minutes drive from Solihull. As business escalated he often left home at 7.15am in order to deal with his correspondence prior to the arrival of his secretary. As I insisted on preparing his breakfast (fresh coffee and toast as he had never been able to come to terms with a full English breakfast) I was faced with a very long day especially as, leaving the office by 6pm he would visit his club for relaxation to avoid the rat race before returning home. It had always amused me to learn that a meeting of business acquaintances or friends at regular times was called 'a school' . . . didn't see the need for teaching anybody a thing about the golden liquid passing through the gullet! What's more they have golden rules. Anyone suffering from 'short arms and low-placed pockets' . . . in other words not standing one's round, is definitely ignored, cold-shouldered. A further idiosyncrasy of British pub life!

During the inauguration of this Depot, for two consecutive years, holidays fell by the wayside! One of Ronny's friends was employed by a leading Birmingham travel agent and told him they had been unexpectedly let down by one of their interpreter/couriers. After much pleading on my part, Ronny gave me permission to join the firm in taking over for this one, albeit long period.

Chapter Fourteen

Part-Time Courier

I had to accompany a bus driver complete with bus naturally, acting simultaneously as navigator, destination Naples, there to meet a group of people, converted to Catholicism and arriving by ship from Sri Lanka. The driver soon proved to be a fairly obstinate Irishman with a preference for wine to water and, although the journey out was far from heavenly at times, driving for hours on end in murderous Summer heat, and many mountainous parts of Switzerland and Italy, (his diminutive navigator sometimes misread the map!) the voyage back was sheer purgatory! It often proved the unbridgeable difference between East and West! As a convinced anti-racist it proved traumatic for me. We had left England in time and, in spite of hold-ups and wrong turnings, arrived in Naples a full day too early. We drove onto Pompeii and took advantage of a brief sunbathing session in the garden of a family hotel.

On the arrival day of our group, we drove back to Naples and parked the bus near the centre. When our group disembarked we were confronted with a colourful parade of ladies in beautiful, silk Saris, men in contrast, in sombre coats with a sort of officer's collar, slimfitting at the waist, and narrow trousers to the knee, then wide to the waist. Some also wore a kind of 'nappy' between the legs in the same fabric. Others had endeavoured to look slightly European by wearing a lounge-suit. They were extremely friendly and chattered like cackling hens in their jargon or in an accent of almost singing English. I thought their manner of greeting most romantic with the hands folded in front of their chest as in prayer, head bent. Their snow-white teeth shone like beacons in their tanned faces and they were most polite.

What soon became noticeable though was the obvious class distinction emphasised, for instance, by the almost humbling attitude when shopowner would talk to doctor. Even if the former was owner of a chain of stores and financially better off than the doctor. The latter belonged to the academically professional class and that sufficed. The majority of young girls and women were extremely beautiful with shiny black tresses and the only thing that spoiled the picture, as far as the married ladies were concerned, was their endemic big stomachs, in accordance with their religion, the personification of female fertility. Strange, in our midst most women are only too happy to regain a flat tummy after childbirth!

On the way to our bus we passed through a narrow alleyway. Suddenly I noticed a small animal head peeping hesitatingly from a broken wall and, animal lover as I am, thinking it was a kitten, bent down to caress it, only to jump back in horror when its full length revealed the long tail of a rat! The largest and ugliest I ever saw . . .

The leader of the group was a short man of nervous mien whose helpless and sycophantic efforts to assist the group - from the frying pan into the fire as it were - stretched my nerves to breaking point. The antagonism between us was instantaneous. Whichever city we entered during our 'pilgrimage', before I could request the driver to stop the bus in order to obtain directions to our scheduled hotel from passer-by or policeman, he invariably succeeded in breathing the words 'better to ask' in my neck, in his sing-song whining English. After four days I threatened to leave him behind if he continued with this repeat performance . . . it did not exactly encourage the entente cordiale . . .

I had realised from the beginning that my group of converts had no inkling whatsoever of time keeping. Wherever we visited, regular as clockwork, they would return at the rendezvous much later than stipulated. They ambled along just as they were used to in their own hot climate and could not be made to understand that it was essential arriving at their hotel in time for checking in (with the added time consuming task of looking for luggage, distribution of keys) and the arranged mealtime. It resulted in repetitious and annoying rows with the driver as he was forced into greater speed than was often safe, cringing excuses on my part to the hotel management, simultaneously avoiding the nasty looks of restaurant personnel as they were compelled to work later than anticipated, not to mention the group's irritation at my repeated insistence for hurrying along.

I rarely touched my pillow before 2am and was in competition with the sunrise. I was not only expected to translate miscellaneous facts and requests. The parents expected me to act as a governess for their young daughters which soon became a time-consuming activity especially in Italy where bottom-pinching is looked upon by the male population as a sort of national sport. Ergo, the young Italians, employed in hotels, did not seem to take 'no' for an answer and developed into a real pest in their intrusive attitude to the young ladies. I had already cottoned on to this during our first evening meal! After having settled the hotel bill with the management and having made the necessary arrangements for an early breakfast prior to our departure the following morning, I went from room to room where the young ladies were accommodated in pairs. I reiterated my specific recommendation not to open their door for anyone except their parents or myself. When at last I stumbled, dead with sleep, to my own room, I had to force myself into my ritual bath before falling into bed. Shortly afterwards I heard a knocking at the door. When I opened it I stood eye to eye with a smiling waiter, the one who earlier on had served our table. During the meal he had regularly enquired if 'all was in order' and I had smilingly, as is my nature, acknowledged this was indeed so. For reasons known to himself alone, this 'Signor' had interpreted it as an invitation to bed as he stood there smirking, with a bottle of Chianti in his hand, ready to enter. Not only did I loathe Chianti - red wine always worked like a red rag to a bull for me - but I categorically refused him in my mixture of French and Spanish explaining he had barked at the wrong door. After a prolonged discussion I concluded he had not the least intention of accepting my refusal. I threatened to shout for help. 'Then I'll say you lied and have invited me', he said, leering like a tomcat on heat. There was but one solution, again good advice from Spilly since my earliest years. With all my strength I brought my knee up between his legs and as he doubled up in agony, I pushed him outside, closing and locking the door at the same time.

When I left my room the following morning for breakfast I noticed cigarette ends near the door as witnesses to my would-be lover's patience. I was profoundly grateful for a well-disciplined bladder and did not have to get out during the night, the bathroom being along the corridor. On entering the dining room, I almost collided with that same waiter. He had the nerve to pull an ugly face at me which I reciprocated with the same phlegmatism and even blew him a raspberry . . .

During the tour we visited the principal cathedrals and churches of Rome, Milan, Florence, Padua and Lisières. Our next destination was Austria, then Switzerland with a visit and climb to the Kleine Scheidegg, one of its popular mountains. Unfortunately, while still in Rome, I found out that the group leader had omitted to obtain visas for the group to travel through Austria as coloured people were allowed entry only when in possession of this temporary document. I was obliged to take all the passports to the Austrian Consulate, had to indulge in a verbal battle with what was no doubt a female 'kapo' from a concentration camp about to close her office when I arrived. As it was still only 3pm, I thought this was too early . . . she did not. Mentally exhausted as I was by then, tears were very near when I saw the bus leave with the compassionately waving group, as the heavy satchel almost made me sag through the knees. I stubbornly refused to leave the consulate though until the visas had been stamped on the passports and, after having threatened to call the British Consul, the Austrian amazon realised she had lost the fight and complied with my insistence. I caught a taxi to the station and was just in time to board the next train to Florence where we would spend the night prior to our Austrian adventure. Once in my compartment I let the tears flow, longing for my man's safe and loving arms. A British couple soon entered and cheered me up with the compassionate sharing of their picnic lunch.

My protégés welcomed me with open arms and subsequently showed their preference for me over their group leader which was not a difficult task . . . When we reached the assembly point for climbing the Kleine Scheidegg, the Swiss guide refused to take us higher than half-way as the swiftly descending mist totally obliterated the panoramic view. This did not prevent the men showing their resentment, and the driver, already aglow from the hot toddies, and shivering little me, had to resort to real diplomacy in order to prevent them climbing without the guide . . . It would have been quite a sight: all the females in saris covered by multiple cardigans and pullovers, the male heads covered with towels and all the warm clothing they had been able to find, inclusive of ladies garments. They looked like impoverished emigrants . . .

To my pleasant surprise I found that, in every shop to which I accompanied the group for their purchases, in each land, the courier automatically was handed a percentage of the sale. This enabled me to keep my own pocket money and still return home with nice presents for Spilly, Ronny and a few friends. In Rome the group would normally acquire religious souvenirs but in Milan luxury leather goods were much in demand, while Florence was especially popular for its beautiful glassware. Soon the bus moaned under its extra weight and, although not exactly built pre-Ark of Noah, it left a lot to be desired mechanically speaking.

After we left Switzerland, the travellers were even obliged to sit on certain musical instruments and toys they had purchased there, which, when sitting down, brought forth some strange sounds and caused many red cheeks.

During our last evening in Boulogne - we had even visited the tomb of Bernadette - I felt as though I was able to 'take the veil' myself after these seemingly endless Church visits. My youngest wards insisted on dressing me in a sari before taking our last meal together on the Continent. Slightly embarrassed at first I entered, complete with dangling earrings, to loud and enthusiastic clapping and had to secretly admit I felt most majestic in this regal outfit.

I telephoned Ronny from the French port with ETA London. Exhausted as I was with my 'battle of energetic West versus ambling East', I still ran like some demented soul from the bus when, arriving in London, I spotted Ronny in our car in front of the entrance to the hotel, ultimate destination of this long voyage. I left it to the driver to have the group registered and this allowed him to pocket completely the inevitable tip and threw myself in the arms of my darling man, clasping him as though the end of the world was near. How much easier it proved the year after when I accompanied a group of British tourists, with the same bus and driver, to Nice to spend a week on the Riviera. Surely the British were the easiest travellers, never complaining, appreciative of the least assistance. Some, however, with the typical Northern white skin, were downright stupid where sunbathing was concerned. My regular insistence during the trip not to stay in the sun too long and to preferably use sunbathing oil or cream, was totally ignored by some. The first night in Nice I was woken during the early hours by the wife of one of our group. Her husband had fallen asleep during the afternoon in the hot sun and was now sitting upright in bed, in terrible pain, large blisters hanging grotesquely like mini-balloons from chest and back. I hastily summoned a taxi and upon arrival at the hospital nearby the French nurse threw her arms in the air exclaiming vexedly: *'These crazy English!!'* Which I translated, in order not to throw oil on the fire, as *'That poor Englishman!'* Each blister had to be emptied with the aid of a syringe, the man was then enveloped like a mummy and had to visit the hospital twice more before returning from a holiday distinguished by listless hours in the shade and painful misery when dressing.

Chapter Fifteen

Farewell Titch

In some of Spilly's letters, it was hinted that Titch, our mongrel dog, was ailing. Although he had reached the ripe old age of 16, it came as a shock for whenever I conjured up visions of home (to return to Antwerp in my thoughts was 'going home' as blood was still thicker than water at that time) my doggie always figured as part of our household. Then came a letter, the contents of which were barely discernible with dried ink spots caused by Spilly's tears. Our dearest pal, her faithful companion, had peacefully been put to sleep in Spilly's arms by the vet. I just could not believe that I would never again be welcomed by those faithful doggie eyes, that excited wagging of the tail and jumping up in my arms, that howl of happiness on meeting after each absence but most of all I could but think of Spilly. Her loss was greater than mine as it was Titch who, during the first lonely years after my marriage, lavished his friendship on her and gave new reason to her daily existence. To her it was like losing a child. I swore never again to adopt an animal so that I would never again feel the hurt of losing it....

Chapter Sixteen

Holiday Myths

With the Firm's Container Depot operating smoothly, Ronny and I were able to resume our annual holidays. In accordance with the rules, Managerial Staff were not supposed to be absent for more than two consecutive weeks which nevertheless allowed us annually to chase warmer climes. We holidayed in successive resorts of the Mediterranean, the Greek Islands, the Balearics, etc and, although Ronny had a penchant for the Riviera (he called it the only really civilised place) we also fell in love with Malta where we discovered indisputably the cleanest water of the Mediterranean. It was there, in an unbelievably romantic bay of Comino, the smallest of the three isles forming Malta, that I learnt to water ski, a sport so satisfying and pleasantly stimulating that one returns ashore tingling all over. Before I succeeded, however, Ronny offered two full film reels on my often comical efforts and later, when we showed these to friends, the spoken commentary said it all *'Anneke base over apex looking for lost skis'* . . . but I never gave up. One sunny morning I completely ignored all the advice I had been given by the Maltese Pro and simply listened to my instinct. 'Now or never', I thought, 'Push against the water pressure with your heels and pull yourself up simultaneously, arms straight' and yes, off I soared! When afterwards, triumphantly accosting the Pro, hoping for his approval, his dry remark made us all roar with laughter: *'Yes, you did well, but next time could you just get out of that lavatorial position and keep straight up?'* The following sessions went smoothly as I gained confidence, across the wash in zigzag and forgot the cramp of muscles in thighs and arms. During ensuing vacations in Juan-les-Pins, mono-ski came on the programme but as not all the holiday resorts we afterwards frequented offered this facility, coupled with the fact that I had a fairly painful fall during one session, when I feared I had wrenched my leg out of its socket, my enthusiasm for the mono-ski diminished.

Always interested in foreign languages I applied a certain method in order to learn Greek for our subsequent holidays in the Greek Islands as I could make neither head nor tail out of their alphabet in the 'Teach Yourself Greek' booklet. Ronny would make friends with bar personnel practically immediately upon arrival in whatever resort, honouring their domain with a twice daily and long-lasting visit. He was more than generous with tips, so much so he was often practically 'salaamed' upon entering. I took advantage of these established ententes and, during the evening aperitif would ask the barman to translate certain sentences to facilitate polite conversation. Writing these down phonetically, I would learn them by heart before going to sleep. This stabilised a friendly sphere between the ethnic population and the tourist with the result not only of a better service in shops but we even received an invitation to a wedding in Corfu, during which I pleasantly exhausted myself with the Greek dances.

We were never lucky on that island, weatherwise that is. Not during our first stay at the end of September nor our last at the end of May. They said it had been the earliest Autumn and latest Spring each time . . . we took this with a pinch of salt. Our first stay encompassed a miserable full fortnight of incessant rain! We had been allocated a bungalow-type chalet set in the grounds of a luxury hotel in Gouvia. After a week of heavy rain half the hotel rooms were uninhabitable. Electricity failed in some parts and the shops in Corfu town ran out of lightweight plastic raincoats. The bungalows had been built on different levels and in the evening, enjoying a warming glass of brandy in the bar of the hotel, when looking through the window, we were confronted by a sight straight out of a horror film. As the guests made their way to the restaurant from their bungalows, covered in their dark plastic raincoats reminiscent of drab shrouds, they resembled corpses arising from the grave. The long evening dresses of the ladies were held up to their waists, the legs, dripping water, grotesquely lit in the light of the flares strategically placed on the paths. The noise of the rain on our roof tiles sounded like the horses' hooves of an attacking horde. To keep warm we kept taking hot baths in the hotel complex where water had not already seeped through the ceiling. We were convinced the brown colour with which we returned home was rust instead of tan!

Yet we gave Corfu another chance the following Spring. Ronny had arranged for a ski instructor with a speedboat to give me ten further sessions and had paid in advance. It was a beautiful, large bay at Gouvia but again the weather was against us. Reluctantly I plodded, clad only in bikini and formless plastic raincoat, through the splashing rain. My 'flip-flop' sandals soaked up the mud with each step and I looked as glamorous as a leaking bag of demerara. Seated at the end of the pier, covered in an aura of grey cloud, water-skis dangling from my benumbed feet, the beach totally deserted, I awaited the speedboat as she carefully chug-chugged her way through the turbulent sea water to reach me in the calmer bay. It took more than ten minutes on the skis before my thighs stopped shivering like jelly, after which the stinging spray, swept against me at a 30mph speed, bombarded me until I glowed with warmth and I felt as one with sea and nature.

What in essence clinched the matter of so-called Winter holidays abroad, however, was a Christmas visit to Mallorca. We are wiser now and realised long ago only Africa, Florida and parts of South America, the Canary Islands and the islands of the Pacific, offer a continuous warm climate. In our innocence we had expected Mallorca to be a vast improvement on Corfu . . . not on your Gazpacho! We decided to celebrate the Christmas holidays on that island, a touch of the Flamencos for me, wine, women and . . . wishful thinking for the cock of my roost. The alfresco barbecue, as much a 'must' during a Spanish holiday as mussels in Antwerp, is an abrading example. Such adventure is indubitably a cure for any romantic notions lurking in one's soul with regard to the sunny South. In our case it was cold and . . . at times showers would descend in juicy bursts. Our barbecue took place in the barn of a rebuilt Spanish hacienda. Trestle tables and hard chairs placed so near together that it soon became clear why there was not one door mentioning 'Señors' or 'Señoras'. A Houdini could not have escaped from the ensnaring legs be them human or wood.

The wind blowing through the open roof neared hurricane force, ricocheted from the walls and attacked us from all sides. The candles, strategically placed on the tables remained miraculously aglow which undoubtedly proved that a secret ingredient is added to Spanish candle wax! While our shivering fingers groped in the semi darkness for the chicken drumstick, burnt by charcoal, and searched for a piece of suckling-pig that had obviously ceased suckling a few moons prior to its demise, we desperately fought to keep our knocking knees from interfering with the romantic plucking noises emanating from an Andalucian guitar, evidently strayed from the mainland. Then came the highlight of the evening. A more than chubby maiden appeared. She looked as Spanish as a Viking and, accompanied by a runt of a little man, functioning as a photographer but whose foot work seemed more familiar with the boxing ring than the camera, made a bee-line for her first victim. The idea was to allow the 'amigos turistas' to drink wine from those typical Spanish wine bottles with long spouts, without touching this, so that the wine flowed into the mouth from a distance of approximately 30cm.

At that precise moment your skill would be captured for eternity on celluloid . . .

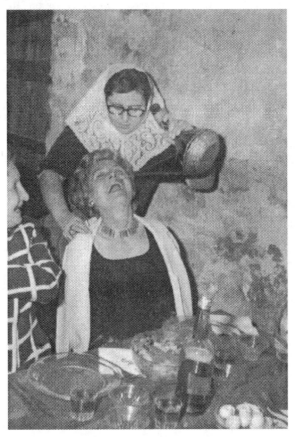

**During our holiday in Mallorca,
victim of the local wine-tasting ceremony.**

Our maiden took hold of my head in a vice-like grip which conjured visions of a sledgehammer in the hand of a wrestler, held the carafe above my head like the Sword of Damocles, and shouted, more like a hysterical fishwife than a Flamenco singer, 'Ole', and before the flash momentarily lit our flabbergasted faces, she already moved to the next mass production. Luckily the orchestra-of-three soon afterwards played a knees-up, so that our mood returned and we slightly defrosted.

Back in the hotel, the young Brits amongst us, not yet filled to overspill with red and white wine, or green-faced by mixing these brews with Spanish Champagne and brandy, fought off the looming colds with hot toddies. I took the midnight dip in the warm pool and afterwards dreamt of my Little Grey Home in the West, of chestnuts roasted by the open hearth, the innocent voices of children singing Christmas carols at the door and so out of tune I could have kissed them one by one. In one word: of Christmas à l'Anglais, heavy stomach isolating Christmas pud and all!

The Chef at our Hotel nevertheless surpassed himself with a variety of haute cuisine lunches and dinners. Not once in the full fortnight did he repeat a menu and we returned home pounds heavier! The most amusing happening of this holiday was Spilly's adventure. She had come along at my insistence and had flown in from Brussels. One morning during breakfast, the day of departure closing in, I enquired when she would be returning home. *'Tomorrow, I believe'* she said. *'Let's see your ticket'* Ronny asked. To our consternation we found her departure was due that same morning. We ran helter-skelter to her room like demented souls, packed her belongings, boarded a taxi and arrived at the airport heart in throat. *'Where is the plane for Brussels?'* we asked an official. Laconically he pointed to the air and, indeed, we could just discern the jet cloud of the Sabena Boeing . . . After enquiring, she was able to return by a later plane but via Paris and thence to Brussels. We rang Antwerp practically all evening, nailbitingly worried, but no reply. At last, about one o'clock in the morning, she answered the phone. *'Mother, are*

you alright? What happened? Where have you been?', I cried.
*'Oh, in Paris, child, I went for a walk on the Champs Elysees,
have made a few purchases and boarded a later plane!'*
Ronny laughed himself silly . . .

A year later she came with us to Ibiza. One of my best
English friends, Dulcie, whom we had met years before in
Malta, accompanied us as well. The hotel management offered
a special dance evening with orchestra provided. At a table
near ours a group of British pensioners of about Spilly's age
had arrived. When the dance band started, we, the two
younger women, hopefully awaited an invitation to dance
from some male; Ronny being in deep conversation with a
business acquaintance he had by chance encountered.
Suddenly a slight tap on my shoulder and Spilly sailed past us
having been invited by one of the pensioners. They danced an
old-fashioned tango. The following dance was a waltz. Spilly
again got up, asked by another gentleman and . . . they danced
an old-fashioned waltz. This was followed by a two-step and,
yes, you guessed it, Spilly was again on the dance floor and as
they were waiting for the next tune, the orchestra started up
with a modern disco number. My eyes became organ stops!
There was my mother in the centre of the dance floor with yet
another dancing partner and jiving as though she had never
done anything else in her life! We two? We remained seated
until Ronny, near the end of the evening, took pity on us.
*'Mum, I'll never bring you along again, you jolly well steal
our beaux'*, I laughed but was very happy to know she had
had a marvellous evening after all the ups and downs of the
latter years.

Chapter Seventeen

The Butcher Experiment

Since my initial introduction to the British butcher an intense love-hate relationship accrued reaching its zenith in 1967. Since the first days of our acquaintance it slowly but surely became clear that it was definitely not the customer who ruled as king on his premises! Since time immemorial he had acquired the privilege of establishing his own rules where meat cuts were concerned. I am more than pleased to state this is no longer the case. But, like everything else in Britain, change, divergence from the familiar, progresses very slowly. The Brit, as travelling consumer, has become more demanding and the butchers have been obliged to embody a vast change in the culinary evolution due to simple and healthy competition.

During my early years as a housewife, upon my choosing a pork roast, John Bull butcher would phlegmatically hack a chunk of meat from the leg. Not only was the bone left in but the skin left on, presumably to prove its authenticity . . . To be truthful a pork roast with its skin pre-oiled and duly salted is a delicacy when, after cooking, it becomes crackling. (Feel obliged to tell a joke in this respect. When collecting my weekly, meagre meat ration one day during my first year in Sheffield, my butcher, true to tradition, enquired if he should leave the skin on. I enthusiastically nodded and said, *'Of course, my husband is very partial to his bit of crackling!'* The butcher looked me up and down and replied, *'Yes, I can see why!'* At home I regaled Ronny with this to me rather puzzling retort. He laughingly explained the double-meaning of this predominantly Northern expression. I did not have to wait long to pull the butcher's leg in return. The week after I ordered a chicken. *'Do you want it dressed, love?'* *'But of course, I can't walk home with a naked bird!'* We both roared.)

Pork chops were a disaster, so small they seemed the produce of suckling pigs but still surrounded by a thick layer of fat. Totally spoilt as I was with the finicky modus operandi of the Belgian butcher, pulling my nose up here did not help one iota. John Bull butcher was adamant. Even the prize beef roast, baptised with the name of Sir Loin, consisted of a roll of meat, entwined by thick string. Very necessary, as the inside was filled with pieces of gristle, fat and bits of the tougher parts of the carcass. Charcuterie (now known as Delicatessen Meats) were virtually unknown and prepared dishes? Never heard of them.

After rationing came to its conclusion, I was able to pick and choose various butchers for different cuts of meat, according to their best offerings. I could not resist praising the Belgian butcher wherever I went. During an Agricultural Show in London which I covered for my paper, I met and argued with the editor of a British Meat Journal and he thought my remarks sufficiently interesting, requesting I put it all in writing in the form of an article for his Journal. It would appear this was syndicated to others involved in meat purveyance and I subsequently received challenges from diverse areas to substantiate my claims. After having written to a well-known slaughterhouse in Antwerp in order to obtain the name of an appropriate contact, I communicated with the Chairman of the Butchers Association and his secretary replied offering their colleagues from Albion a free week of tuition and demonstrations. Necessary advertising in the British Meat Journal resulted in requests from all parts of the country for this unusual project and we soon completed a list of 25 British butchers to travel to the City of the Scheldt, there to occupy school benches, especially after the campaign had previously been mentioned on Regional TV with a short appearancè on my part.

When at last I had arranged for their accommodation in a nice hotel in the very centre of Antwerp, with easy access by tram in all directions, we set off not without apprehension where I was concerned. We were received almost like Royalty at the teaching Centre, situated in Borgerhout, an immediate suburb of Antwerp. And there, during a full working week, they followed the various procedures for cutting fore and hindquarters of beef and half a pig. They were taught about different kinds of sausages, liver preparations and culinary Charcuterie. The last day the pupils and masters of the school had arranged for a buffet-like display of their art in prepared meat products and a discussion on Belgian methods of butchering. Everything was free of charge to the British participants inclusive of their snack lunches and drinks. Furthermore, they were graciously received in some of the adjoining butcher shops, observed the butchers at work and serving, and saw many delicatessen products and preparations they had missed at the school due to lack of time.

For me, it was not only acting as interpreter - a task somewhat daunting as till then I did not know 'one end of a cow from her udder' but in addition as a chaperone. The group, being accommodated in a hotel near a shopping centre were determined to return home with miscellaneous presents so they tagged me along everywhere they went! When we finally landed back onto British soil the door of the British butcher shop, true enough, stood ajar for major changes and slightly more variety but it was only after the following experiment in 1973 that 'things livened up in the brewery' as the saying goes. Indeed, the second group numbered 47 participants and these were received with just as much enthusiasm by the same Antwerpian corps of professionals.

One of the teachers had even foregone one week of his holidays in order to comply.

This time Charcuterie and prepared meals were even more specialised as they had got nowhere as yet in Great Britain on these subjects. Nor were British consumers conversant with refined pastry-covered meats and the group learned a lot regarding 'prepared dishes' on their own premises. Again their midday snacks were free, often rolls or sandwiches filled with the Charcuterie products they had prepared the day before, and gallons of tea and coffee. To the surprised pupils, the Belgian method of cutting meat approached delicate vivisection and they considered the end product a work of art. However, I nearly swallowed my tongue when one of the demonstrating teachers laconically declared: '*If the British butcher can succeed in serving his meat as in the past, he had better carry on, as the Belgian has made a rod for his own back!*' . . .

As the sausages in Albion those days were made up of only 65% meat, in some cases even less, and cereals were added, the sausage production of the Belgians, sans cereals but all meat, met with great approval. One of the British butchers, very much interested in what he was taught, not only applied it all immediately upon his return, but was engaged by Midlands BBC TV to demonstrate on 'Pebble Mill at One' each week most of what he had learnt in Antwerp.

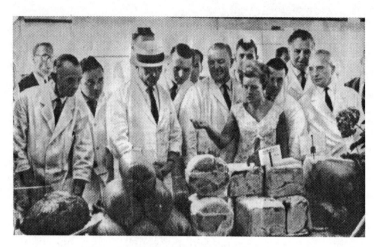

**Showing the visiting British butchers
some of the prepared delicatessen meats at a leading butchers
shop in Antwerp.**

**Translating for the butchers and hoping I know one end of the
cow from the udder!**

Chapter Eighteen

My First Mini

As far as I am concerned, the ultimate mechanical wonder was undoubtedly the Mini, feather in the cap of the automobile designer Issigonis, later to be honoured by Her Majesty. Initially it was referred to as 'the car for the woman' but soon proved extremely popular with the younger generation and even the nobility (in general more inclined towards prestige cars of national as well as foreign manufacture). Even some members of the Royal Family were regularly observed in such a jalopy.

Ronny was able to procure a secondhand Mini for me, not 8 months old, as the previous owner had not been able to honour the monthly payments. I had driven Ronny's car many a time with a temporary licence and L plates. Now that I had my own car I could take private driving lessons, for a female learner-driver in her husband's car is like cat and dog in a rabbit's warren! Soon I applied for my test which I think is one of the strictest, feared by both sexes, a nerve-racking experience which makes one feel like a wreck, in my case like a wrung out dishcloth . . . Prior to this though I enlisted with a Driving School. My instructor was exceptionally friendly with the patience of Job, necessary in his profession. When I watched the hilarious 'kangaroo' start of some learner which he superbly calmed down into a proper start, I could not help but think of Ronny who would have jumped out and left . . . After the third lesson, contrary to Ronny's mutterings that, in a car, I was the personification of the 'dumb blonde', he assured me I was a 'born driver' not because I drove so well I hasten to state, but because, behind that wheel, I always felt at home and indefatigable and he had sensed it. It was just as if in that little car I was ensconced in a cocoon, in my own domain. Since early teenage, I had cherished a dream;

foremost a happy married life, a comfortable home and, one day, my own car. This dream had now come true and, boy, did I feel rich and thankful!

After the ten customary lessons, the Test Centre set a date and I presented myself, accompanied by my instructor, feeling like a condemned walking to the place of execution. A typical English rain, soft, abundant and truly continuous, would keep us company all the way. The examiner seemed like a member of the inquisition and for a moment my brain stopped functioning in panic. Would he turn out to be the insentient creature with an automaton volition of his own all learner drivers accused examiners to be, or intent only on sending a competent driver on the road? Unobserved I picked up the front of my blouse, put my nose between skin and silk. 'Keep beating, pal' I beseeched my ticker.

Being Friday, midday, it was exceedingly busy on the roads, as a vast number of people, with a view to an early weekend, were already homeward bound, as well as many delivery vans and milk floats for whom Friday was bill settling day. I pressed my teeth together so that they would not chatter. The examiner explained one of the 'highlights' of the test, namely at one point he would knock his rolled-up newspaper against the dashboard in the assumption that a child unexpectedly ran out in front of the car . . . and I would have to stop at once to avoid collision. We are all conversant with the three-point turn, hill-start, reversing around a corner and through narrow aperture, the different traffic signs. There followed a long drive through the Stratford Road. At a certain moment, just as I had given the signal to overtake a slow milk float, the driver suddenly veered to the right, forcing me to detract my signal, and having given the opposite signal, I got back in the line of traffic. It was an instinctive manoeuvre confidently executed. A little later, in a side street, the rolled-up newspaper spattered against the dashboard. My left arm flew out in front for the protection of the examiner (seat belts had not yet become compulsory) and I simultaneously stamped on the brake with such force that I expected the car to prance like a stallion. Without my protective arm, I am convinced the man would have gone straight through the windscreen! 'Well, the child is still alive!' I said phlegmatically. While he continuously swallowed and his colour changed from blood red to grey putty, he opined: *'Nothing wrong with YOUR reflexes!'* He took my verbal exam in a falsetto voice . . . When I had answered successfully all his questions (I inwardly thanked the regular hours when Ronny asked impromptu test questions at the most unexpected moments) and surprised these were audible above my heartbeats, in the meantime heightened by several decibels, the event of the milk float was mentioned. *'You were in difficulties with that float, were you not?'*, he said. *'Not at all'*, I remonstrated. *'The driver was at fault and I placed myself back into the traffic line after first and correctly signalling, having looked into the mirror to ensure there was sufficient room for this manoeuvre'. 'Don't you think you endangered the following drivers?' 'Certainly not, as they were obviously experienced drivers and had sufficient time to observe my manoeuvre'.*

'Why do you wish to pass the test?' (This presumably was asked all candidates to establish if the reason was business or pleasure). *'Well, Sir, I am Belgian by birth and the standard of driving in that country is inferior in comparison with ours here. I would like to drive as safely as the best disciplined British driver'.* Sourpuss momentarily smiled. *'Yes, I know, I have lived in Belgium for a while'*, he said. You could have knocked me over with a feather! *'Well, Madame, I have to tell you . . .'* My courage sank into my shoes. Is he going to fail me? . . . *'that you have passed your test!'* I threw my arms around a flabbergasted man and gave him a smacking kiss on

the cheek. It was a quarter to one, lunchtime, and at two o'clock I found myself, alone and totally in control of my jalopy, in the centre of Birmingham, with its extended one-way system. Talk about jumping in at the deep end!

The incident with the milk float brings to mind the British milkman, a creature completely disappeared from the Belgian scene after WW2 but still much in evidence in our spheres. Like every other household we, too, had our regular purveyor of dairy produce. In addition to bottled milk he supplied us with eggs, sometimes potatoes or fruit drinks, occasionally even flour. Friday or Saturday was settling accounts day.

Ronny would sit by the window on a Saturday morning reading his paper and, especially in winter, when Jack Frost reigned supreme, he would call our milkman inside to partake of a warming dram of whisky. Ronny's idea of 'a tot' was at least 'three fingers' and his were of the sturdy kind. By the time it glided past the milkman's epiglottis (on a, by then, supposedly empty stomach) his walk towards his float was far from straight. He would rev up and speed around the block like Stirling Moss, loudly clanging the bottles in their crates. One day I was just about to drive off when I noticed our milkman at the end of the street. I whistled on two fingers, something Spil had taught me years ago, and when he looked my way I simulated milking a cow and held two fingers up. Laughing, he shouted *'OK, two bottles'*. Some time after the same situation occurred but this time I half bent down, winged my arms up and down like a chicken and stiffly pushed both hands with fingers spread skywards. Laughing loudly, the milkman shook his head and when I returned a dozen eggs stood neatly on the doorstep. The next Saturday, during the by now habitual whisky-session, when relating both incidents, he casually remarked to Ronny *'I dread to think how she would have demonstrated had she wanted spuds!'*

When my father-in-law passed away in 1968 and his widow followed him the year after, Ronny, having come into a small inheritance and true to his generous nature, spent most of it on a brand new white Mini for me. In spite of our familial connections having been on a friendly basis, they had never visited us in Solihull, a mentality and attitude so alien to me as I was blessed with the acknowledged Antwerp hospitality syndrome and had invited them numerous times. Perhaps father-in-law developed a dislike of driving since his eyesight had worsened and the steady increase of new traffic signs and boards, new motorways constructed plus more and more cars on the road made him nervous. Also he loathed trains.

Once a month Ronny would visit them combining his stay with meetings at the Firm's headquarters. However, he would stay at a nearby hotel, more for his parents' convenience. We would visit them together about once every three months.

I accepted this rather distancing of theirs and we remained in regular contact by telephone and letters and our mutual respect nor our love for one another ever suffered by it.

That same year Birmingham had undergone its modern metamorphosis and was virtually rebuilt, with a centre of one-way streets, slightly puzzling to the visitor but most interesting in my case as I discovered streets and terrains hitherto unknown. It was in effect during that same time span of the 60s that the car became the 'Steely Knight' of the road. Not only were many green belts offered on the altar of road modernisation. Everywhere express roads soon choked under the burden of increased traffic that would undulate like snakes through a tangled jungle of steel and concrete. Here and there, where houseowners had refused to offer their domain to the bulldozers, even now and throughout the whole of the country, at the edge of motorways, gracious houses in varying architectural style, still stand, huddled together in small groups like frightened relics of an age gone by. The network of under and over motorways which forms the nucleus of traffic going to and coming from North, East, South and West Birmingham was promptly called 'Spaghetti Junction' as viewed from the air it resembled a plate of this pasta.

Chapter Nineteen

End Of A Brave Jew

In the meantime our very good friend Zucker had fallen ill and the doctor's irrevocable diagnosis was incurable mental illness. His traumatic experiences and hardships in the Buchenwald concentration camp had ultimately taken their toll and had undoubtedly attributed to his plight. As his condition exacerbated he was taken to Geel, a village known for its specialised hospital. His Romanian girlfriend had left him in the meantime to return to her own country. We were convinced that her hysterical and nervous character had largely contributed to Zucker's madness. Indeed, each doctor's prescription for the inmates returned from the hell of the concentration camps was in the first place - calm; which in itself was totally absent from the Romanian's nature. Whenever I returned to Antwerp I would accompany Spilly on her visit to Zucker. It may seem strange that we never addressed him by his Christian name, as a matter of fact I never knew it, but to us he was our good friend Zucker . . . as simple as that.

I would return from such visits, sick at heart and crying like a baby. My compassionate nature could hardly cope when I entered the ward where he seemed to be incarcerated in a hell of his own, staring at the ceiling or continually touching the biceps of both arms, repeating the same word over and over: 'tapou, tapou'. I am writing this phonetically: was it a Jewish expression, a Hebrew word? We never discovered but presumed that it referred to his muscles as though he wanted to convince us that he was still a strong man . . . As soon as we opened the door he would look up and although he was not aware of his surroundings, as we and the medical personnel suspected, and never recognised anyone, he would nevertheless stretch his arms out at me and somewhere, in that lost labyrinth of his memories, the connection between myself and his sons must have created a temporary clarity. Sobbing, in his arms, I felt his tears too on my cheeks until suddenly I would be pushed aside gently and almost tenderly, and the 'tapou, tapou' was his signal for my touching his biceps and showing delighted acknowledgement.

We brought him delicacies, understandably never served at the hospital. They all disappeared in an orgy of dribbled chewing. Gefüllte Fisch, purchased from a Jewish shop, was mixed with salted beef and followed by a chicken drumstick with gherkin, a piece of tart and fruit. It all greedily disappeared. He would jealously watch his neighbour in the next bed and would not even allow him a grape . . . and he who was so generous in days of old! Spilly secretly handed some fruit to the patient. His death came as a welcome release and to us a blessed end to a disconsolate period. He was a brave Jew, a good Belgian, a victim of the inhuman, unforgettable and never to be repeated holocaust.

Chapter Twenty

BBC Pebble Mill Advisory Council

My life never seemed to be set to automatic pilot and one thing followed another with anything but monotonous rhythm! In the British media the pros and cons for joining the European Economic Community - as it was then known - were emphatically debated. As I had appeared a few times on Midlands TV in a minor capacity, for instance after the study visit of the British butchers to Antwerp, and various discussions regarding the advantages on acquiring membership status, also a musical contribution for the Commercial TV station (which became abortive after it was made abundantly clear there was a certain price to be paid if I wanted to make a success of it and I was not prepared to follow that path!) I presume that my name was put forward to the Directorship of the BBC in London. To my immeasurable surprise I received, on the 21st March 1972 to be precise, a letter from the Council of Governors of the BBC inviting me to become a member of their Advisory Council for Midlands TV for a period of four years as was customary. It had been decided to create eight new regional advisory councils in connection with transmissions outside the Metropolis. In accordance with the BBC's charter, their task would consist of advising the Corporation regarding the 'management and contents of programmes emanating from the BBC in respect of those areas to which the Council were appointed'.

It was to be an honorary post. Meetings took place in January, May and September each year. An extra one was called every July in order to meet the programming personnel, such as the producers, directors, newscasters, etc and to debate ideas, praise or criticise. Dear me! From my earliest teens I virtually grew up to maturity with the BBC in the background, whether it was musically or didactic in the form of news and discussions, and I felt as though I had been invited to the Council of God . . . Did not the entire world listen to the BBC? It was the daily and freely invited guest in the majority of British homes via both audio and visual means. During those seemingly endless war years we, on the Continent, under the boot of the occupying forces, daily pumped courage from her either good or bad news and the melodies sent through the ether we used to sing along, in secret, dreaming of future romance and freedom after the war. For this Corporation kept the hope alive in our otherwise so deprived hearts!

My letter of acceptance slid into the postal box before you could pronounce: British Broadcasting Corporation. The Council which I joined consisted of a cross-section of personalia such as a shopkeeper, a manufacturer, a female professor at Aston University, an editor of a provincial newspaper, a child-psychiatrist of Indian origin with his practice in Birmingham, a headmaster, the wife of a farmer, a councillor, a bank manager, a football manager, a mechanical engineer, a leader of a consumer group, a trade union official, a theatre impresario, a taxi driver and myself as 'housewife', all representative of public life, interests and culture in the province. The BBC personnel consisted of the regional director, newscasting managers, their assistants and programme controllers, chief editor and advisers, with regular visits from personnel involved in one service or another at the London management end.

My first meeting found me somewhat at a loss, flurried even with some of the TV-vocabulary and clichés which were unfamiliar in everyday conversation but I was never too proud to let my ignorance be known, resorting to my Antwerpian humour in free translation. After general sympathetic laughter all was patiently explained. The majority of personnel as well as some members of the Council boasted an academic education. All of a sudden I was confronted by a completely new English language, rich in synonyms, intriguing and enchanting to me and I soon felt converted to its terminology.

Ronny afterwards often pulled my leg about words or expressions he said 'I flogged to death' in my eagerness to remember them. From the onset, though, I realised we were not just meeting as 'a gesture' or to spend a pleasant·day including a super buffet meal! The emphasis was on research and intense viewing for all programmes emanating from the Pebble Mill studios and opt-outs, as well as national productions, came under the loupe. Our discussions and criticisms or praise were duly mentioned in the Minutes and it came as a revelation to me when I realised how strictly the BBC maintained her neutrality. Where criticisms were constructive the programme makers promptly responded. Ronny even presented me with a second TV set to be placed in the kitchen so that, during preparation of our evening meal, I would not miss one programme on which I had to report at a later date.

I threw myself with heart and soul into my task and was soon requested to write comments on children's programmes; this was followed by a second one in connection with the new networked midday magazine 'Pebble Mill at One', a programme of varying subjects and interest about which I most enthusiastically reported. It enhanced our lunch hours daily for fifteen years under the same title and until only recently was still in existence as 'Pebble Mill'. A further report concerned the comparative regional newscasts of BBC as against the by then well-established Commercial TV.

One of my proposals has been maintained to this day. It was my suggestion that the BBC needed something to avoid viewers deserting the 6pm news for the commercial one. I put it that in creating a more interesting children's programme, preferably between 5.30 and 6pm, once the children's attention was focused on this BBC output, the parents would normally continue to view the ensuing news bulletin. So said . . . so done . . .

During subsequent meetings my and other members comments on most productions from the Midlands were noted and acted upon and although the attitude of the producing staff was pragmatic they were most courteous; not one chauvinistic leaning discernible! I never missed a programme and began to fear this experiment would leave me with square eyes, especially as after my four years 'duty' I received a letter from Sir Michael Swann, the then Chairman of the Board of Directors of the BBC, offering me an extension of my services for two more years which, according to the Regional Director for Midlands TV was exceptional.

During these six years I partook in 24 meetings, never missed one and we even arranged our holidays so that they would not clash with any of these. This in itself proved to be a record. During our ultimate meeting I fought my tears, as personnel, as well as council members, had in the meantime become friends. My valedictory address was stencilled and distributed among the Pebble Mill personnel and council members. My personal eulogy in respect of the BBC I refuse to withdraw, although, since the mid-eighties and where total neutrality is concerned I can now only resort to a pallid panegyric. As far as I am concerned it is but a stale crumb of consolation that already, nearing the end of my service with the BBC Advisory Council, the minutes of our meetings reveal my criticism of some production leaders in their leaning towards the far left! Now we often witness a prejudice in favour of the anti-establishment and the culprits are undoubtedly some the programme makers of the last decennia, an attitude which, according to my Belgian family and friends, is very much in unison with the BRT, the Belgian equivalent of the BBC. (Since the late '90s, however, I'm pleased to say this is no longer the case!)

CHAIRMAN

SIR MICHAEL SWANN

BROADCASTING HOUSE

LONDON W1A 1AA

01·580 4468

11th February 1976

Dear Mrs. Evans,

As you know, your period of service on the Midlands Advisory Council is due to end on 31st April 1976. I am happy to be able to write on behalf of the BBC's Board of Governors offering you an extension of the service of approximately two years, with a retirement date of 31st July 1978.

Your valuable and always entertaining contributions to the Council's discussions have been much appreciated, and my hope is that you will be able to accept this extension of service so that we may continue to benefit from your interest in our programmes.

Yours sincerely,

Michael Swann.

Mrs. Anneke Evans,
"Quellin",
56, Cheltondale Road,
Solihull,
Warwickshire.

**Letter from the Chairman of the BBC,
Sir Michael Swann.**

Chapter Twenty One

As Time Goes By . . .

Our married life evolved, as with most couples, into a more or less set routine during which we strengthened our friendships, had our ups and downs, insignificant rows lasting a minimum of time (the making up was marvellous though!) and never about key issues, and saw the seasons relentlessly follow each other.

One evening, in 1972, Ronny returned home with the emperor of backaches. He could hardly crawl out of his car and stumbled, racked with pain, upstairs. After having served him with his evening meal in bed, I contacted our GP who was unfortunately on a refresher course at the time. His locum diagnosed sciatica and, apart from painkillers, prescribed the use of a wooden board under his mattress. After a fortnight in bed, still suffering, when each short visit to the lavatory crawling on hands and knees like an animal, must have been a Calvary for him, the pains refused to alleviate. I again rang our GP who, this time, answered the phone. Upon his request, I drove Ronny to his surgery and after a short discussion and examination, he rang his friend Mr Sneath, a leading back specialist. He had an extremely modern X-ray machine in his surgery in Edgbaston. As soon as he had studied Ronny's X-rays, the sentence fell: sciatica? No way! Two of his discs had partially disintegrated and Ronny was given a choice; he either wore metal corsets for the rest of his life or underwent surgery, preferably immediately. Ronny did not hesitate one single moment: operation please.

We had been told about this famous, still comparatively young surgeon. Indeed, his profession was also his hobby and he regularly visited the USA to give lectures at various hospitals, at their request, regarding his speciality subject and experiences. Ronny hardly had the time to instruct his second in command at the office as, in the meantime, his responsibilities had accrued. However, nobody is indispensable!

Through the Firm we were members of a private health insurance and he was soon installed in a single room with TV and bathroom in a special clinic of the Nuffield Trust in Edgbaston. For a few days he underwent some intensive tests and, after a negative report on cancer - what I had feared most of all in view of his heavy smoking with 60 'stink-sticks' on his daily tally - or other blood deviations, the operation took place. I had been warned it would take about two hours. I walked up and down like a caged animal near our telephone in the hall. I dared no longer ring Spilly as on tearfully reporting about his suffering during these last two weeks, she too was completely upset for the sun shone out of her son-in-law's posteria!

At last the phone rang. It was the Matron to warn me that the surgeon had detected two more discs, directly above the initial ones, which also showed, albeit in lesser degrees, signs of disintegrating. Rather than leave his patient to be confronted with the same excruciating pains in years to come resulting yet again in the inevitable operation, he decided to carry on with the repair. While there seemed to be an inclination amongst some spine specialists during that period to replace disintegrating discs with plastic ones, Ronny's specialist was not in favour and swore that the natural growth active in a healthy human body would renew these discs within a two year span. Although warned it could still take a further two hours till the conclusion of the operation, one hour later Matron's phone call reassured me that it had been completely successful. I could breathe again . . . after all, Ronny was already 60 years old. I did not visit him that day as I presumed he would not be entirely aware of things, still half under the anaesthetic as he must have been, and the Matron

273

was grateful for my decision. Nothing, after all, is as irritating to nursing personnel as tearful relatives, unnecessarily worried and constantly in the way . . .

Even the following morning he was not entirely on his qui vive mainly due to soporific painkillers. When in the afternoon tea was served Ronny suddenly had an attack of diarrhoea. Momentarily alarmed, the young nurse and I were able to place him on the commode. While she supported him afterwards I washed and tended him like a baby. He never knew about it.

Mr Sneath, in the meantime, had become a national and international celebrity in his field, not only as a spinal specialist but especially in treating children suffering from bonemarrow cancer. When we left the nursing home I was warned that Ronny should avoid picking up or carrying heavy articles during the next two years. Were they kidding? The heaviest object my man ever picked up was his foot when fastening his shoelaces! However, afterwards he never suffered from any back pain, always walked straight as a candle, when on holiday could walk for miles and stood for hours on end . . . at a bar!

*

I was only 40 when I started with the menopause and my monthly periods disappeared for ever. Thanks to our GP, Dr Craig, blessed with advanced opinions and adaptation of modern medical evolution, I was to visit a Hormone Replacement Therapy clinic at Showell Green Lane, Birmingham. After the necessary tests I was put on HRT which put an end to uncomfortable hot flushes, and as we were in the early 60s I must have been one of the very first to benefit from this fine invention. A vast number of doctors were still anti-HRT but Dr Craig saw no reason why the woman today should suffer as their grandmothers did provided tests were taken on a regular basis. Some years afterwards the medical profession came to the conclusion that a mixture of oestrogen and progesterone was the ideal replacement for the monthly cycles lacking in the older woman. It was imperative that the progesterone pill was to be manufactured with ingredients from natural sources. I carried on taking the pills for over 20 years, the last 10 of which I was prescribed the oestrogen Premarin of 0,625 mgr and a contraceptive one, Micronor, but of such low percentage that it would not represent a completely safe contraceptive to a young woman. This last combination was in effect the result of years of research and avoided the burdensome bleeding hitherto caused by the combination pill.

I felt very healthy, more energetic than ever, no hot flushes nor bleeding and safe in the knowledge that sufficient calcium was thus produced for the continuous strength of my bone structure. During consequent visits to the Clinic my blood and urine were tested, blood pressure taken, as well as regular smears not just from the uterus but from the womb lining. The latter, as experience had shown, because cancer cells could form after prolonged intake of oestrogen on its own. As I had never been pregnant, however, the entrance to my womb was extremely small and I had to be put under an anaesthetic for this test. It meant an overnight stay in hospital for about three times over the years until a local anaesthetic was applied at later occasions which meant but a minimum of discomfort. As I developed hardening in my breasts I underwent three mammograms over a period of three years with satisfying results. The last diagnosis was: benign calcifying of glands. I smile now when I think of how I loathed my two 'soldiers buttons' of breasts when a young teenager and look down on what Ronny once described as 'his magnificent two handfuls' . . . Still, everything comes to a conclusion. In confrontation with my present doctor, Dr Kotecha, and the female specialist at the HRT clinic, kind Dr Stuart, it was decided to take me off HRT. In their opinion the pills had produced sufficient calcium to keep my bone structure stabilised and the Medical Profession ultimately lacked experience of taking HRT over an extensive period such as 20 years . . . Although I never suffered side effects after the cessation of my HRT treatment, I must admit I again mildly suffer from hot flushes.

We celebrated our 25th Wedding Anniversary in 1973 with a dinner dance offered to our friends, Ronny's business acquaintances and his mates of the regular 'school' at their club. I had requested them not to bring presents as we were by then blessed with sufficient nick-nacks, and I have a fierce dislike of a home so full of bits and bobs that it resembles a secondhand shop! In spite of this we were presented with a set of silver wine glasses to which they all contributed. Spilly was not off the dance floor one single moment!

As a personal present, I gave Ronny a stereo set in a beautiful cabinet for his favourite LPs and he bought me a short mink coat to which an anecdote follows. (Some months afterwards in Antwerp, cosily chatting with my friend Yvonne she told me she had acquired a beautiful mink coat. *A very dark one'* she assured me *'as I call those light coloured ones prostitute coats seeing they are mostly worn by those ladies'* 'Yes, Ronny bought me a short mink coat as well', I said casually. 'Which colour?' asked Yvonne. *'One of those usually worn by the ladies of easy virtue'* I retorted, after which we both burst out laughing.)

After our party we had to virtually stow Ronny into the car and he promptly fell asleep on the passenger seat. I was livid as I had repeatedly advised him during the evening to take less of the drinks but as the band had kept us busy on the dance floor, being a task of thirsty nature, Ronny saw to it that his throat kept well oiled. I drove the car into the garage and Spilly unsuccessfully tried to wake Ronny. He slept the sleep of the contented innocent and I did not even try to wake him, took Spilly by the arm out of the garage, and closed the door. *'You can't leave him there all night, it is bitterly cold and he'll catch something'* she pleaded. *'We are going to bed and, as you taught me from an early age, he who does not listen will have to feel'* I said, fully expecting him to come to bed shortly afterwards. I had ignored Bacchus' tricks . . . Ronny slept the whole night in the car and, as I too had fallen asleep, Spilly crept downstairs with a blanket and covered him like a baby. A very stiff-boned husband crept into our bed around 6am and snuggled up to his better half as though nothing had happened . . . I never could resist his loving.

Chapter Twenty Two

The Umbilical Cord Severed

January 1974 and a telephone call from Spilly gripped me by the throat. About 11 years prior she had been operated on for prolapse and although she had an inborn horror of operations, she nevertheless joked, upon advising me, *'My lining has sagged, I've got to go under the scalpel'.* Afterwards she was told to remain stretched out and as still as possible for a few days. When she thought it safe and she had slipped rather low down on the mattress, not wishing to disturb a nurse for such a small manoeuvre, she pulled herself up by a contraption secured above the bed. She felt something wet and when the visiting surgeon examined her was told that the prolapse had recurred and nothing more could be done as this operation could only take place once. Her GP decided to insert a ring. Normally this would not be allowed to remain for longer than 10 years, with regular cleansing and disinfecting by the doctor. I also insisted that she should regularly be subject to smears and these always showed a satisfying negative result.

Years passed . . . During one of the routine visits for disinfecting, etc the doctor casually asked how long she had carried the ring. Spilly saw consternation on his face when he heard 12 years had passed . . . He immediately removed it and after the necessary medical care sent her homewards having reassured her minimal bleeding would occur but for a day or so.

Two days later Spilly was still bleeding and anxiously telephoned her doctor who advised her to see him at once. After thorough examination, he informed her in an almost business-like manner she would have to undergo cobalt treatment in the Middelheim Hospital, one of Antwerp's main medical centres. From his sombre expression Spilly, not born yesterday, deducted it was serious and cobalt? Didn't this come into cancer treatment? After our telephone conversation, I decided to travel the following day to Antwerp, lead heavy in my shoes.

Upon arrival, I phoned her doctor who received me that same afternoon. It appeared that there was a presence of cancer cells in the cervix but by virtue of the early detection there was an almost certain chance for a complete cure on the understanding cobalt was applied. By telling her a white lie, I hoped to reassure her that she only had a small wound and that the cobalt treatment was just precautionary. The tragic fact - which haunts me to this day - is that she was aware of what the real trouble was and only kept it to herself to spare my feelings, and I continued fibbing to instil false courage in her. Although I was intending to remain with her throughout her treatment, the doctor assured me it was unnecessary as she would be fetched and returned by special ambulance service and she would sustain no harmful results apart from a tendency to vomit after a certain period. I did accompany her a few times but she herself insisted I returned to England so that 'I would not neglect my husband' . . .

We remained in daily contact by phone and it appeared that she even avoided the vomiting part. Indeed, having a stomach that could withstand the tumultuous North Sea weather better than any dyed-in-the-wool tar, to her cobalt was but 'small beer'. After the prescribed treatments she was transferred to the St Elizabeth Hospital where she had to remain stretched out in bed with radium in the uterus, without her being able to resort to the calls of nature, so as to assure that the cancer cells were totally destroyed. I again travelled to Antwerp to be with her. After this treatment, she underwent a few more cobalt sessions and again two days with the radium inserts as before. The second radium cure had not been as successful as this strong stuff had caused burn damage in the colon. By then she was quite weak. When visiting her specialist, she told him that she thought this time she was 'a bird for the cat', an Antwerpian saying, meaning one is finished. To which the man replied: 'Another 8 months'. Naturally Spilly came to the conclusion that she only had 8 more months to live.

Spilly and I just prior to her last visit to England

My heart broke when I saw her sitting, almost hidden in her armchair, white as a sheet, continuously running to the lavatory and as weak as a kitten as she hardly ate. Every time she relieved herself, she lost bloody phlegm and her strength ebbed away like snow before the sun as she was deprived of sleep as well. After having received her medical notes from the specialist her own GP prescribed a medicine to be inserted twice daily into her back passage which necessitated her staying in bed. The disinfecting liquid would remain both day and night in her body, and a sanitary towel absorbed the small quantity of escaping liquid. The Nuns from the nearby Home for the Aged came twice a day for this task until I asked them to teach me. After regular feeding, she began to look better and I chanced taking her with me to England. Ronny awaited us at Elmdon Airport and looked most alarmed and worried and treated her like a brittle piece of porcelain.

Our own GP placed her on his list and assured me that the cancer of the cervix had been completely cured according to the specialist in Antwerp. The burn caused by the radium in the colon was a sadder affair! According to the cancer specialist we subsequently visited in Birmingham, the treatment for cancer of the cervix would have been conducted in England in an identical fashion except that, in view of her slight build, the second radium cure would never have been applied. It would appear the colon had 'shrunk' in its centre due to the burn caused by the radium and it was this wound that caused the bleeding phlegm. On the specialist's advice we continued with the same disinfecting medicine to be inserted, a speciality manufactured by the Glaxo Combine, my baby-milk producers (!) and as Spilly had automatically become a member of the National Health, was free of charge. I never had any complaints with this Service. Nowadays people talk about lengthy waiting lists. Although the medical profession has advanced with gigantic steps, here, as indeed everywhere in the civilised world, people are cured from illnesses to which, half a century ago, they would have succumbed and older people as a result stay alive longer. Most operations, serious though they may be are successful. People remain alive longer than ever before, sporadically liable only to illness coupled with a 'worn mechanism'.

After a few weeks Spilly was strong enough to leave her bed during the day. When she arrived in England we had noticed that her left leg was slightly dragging although she could not tell us why as she was in no pain. One evening she lightly tapped me on the shoulder requesting we should watch her. I was amazed to see her walk in a normal manner, up and down the living room, no sign of a lame leg! Her Calvary - and mine - had only just begun, however. With the shrinking of her colon, I had to regularly control her food. To find the right balance proved to be a nightmare. Either she was constipated and most uncomfortable or, at the least deviation of the diet, it worked like a purgative and she was unable to control her bowels. I found myself washing and dressing her with clean clothes almost twice daily, sometimes scrubbing 'accidents' from and disinfecting carpets, and as I was afraid to hurt her and categorically refused to wear rubber gloves, my hands soon became rough. The smell of these 'accidents' was indescribable and I constantly retched. I apologised for this and asked her to completely ignore it as, above all, I wanted to help her. *'Yes, child'* she replied, *'You always were a retcher at the least provocation. But, I have sponged your baby bottom numerous times in the past, it is your turn now!!'* I checked her weight weekly. One day I realised she was putting on weight. *'Mother, do you realise that almost 9 months have passed since you came to live with us?'* *'Yes, so?'* *'Well, didn't you say the doctor in Antwerp had only given you 8 months to live? I always promised that I would cure you!'* I laughed. We had dispensed with the daily medicine as she did not seem to suffer anymore in that respect.

We decided to take a holiday in Malta and as Spilly hankered after Antwerp we parted for a fortnight. Although I was worried, she assured me she felt marvellous and we booked a hotel room in the centre of her city. During the ensuing fortnight I longed for the return voyage and kept ringing her at the hotel, finding her rarely there as she lived it up every day with all her friends. Back home, she told me what a marvellous time she had experienced with her friends of the White Brigade Fidelio and ex-neighbours and, although a 'small accident' had occurred a few times, she had been able to neatly eradicate all traces . . . I was so happy for her as I recalled with sorrow the sad day when, after having sold the contents of her flat and her prized possessions and clothes shipped by container to England, she said her ultimate goodbye to her life: over 70 years in the same city, her beloved Antwerp. All her long-standing neighbours waved her off . . . another blow in her life, the path of which was already strewn with more downs than ups!

In the meantime Ronny's container Depot expanded more and more as the list of manufacturers exporting to the Continent grew. Spilly and I would take our evening meal before Ronny's return from work and I would keep his warm in the oven between two plates. Sometimes I would find him asleep in the kitchen next to his plate. One evening, when unexpectedly entering the kitchen where he was untying his laces to change shoes for slippers, I saw him nodding his head from side to side and heard him emitting noises as though in pain. Alarmed, I asked what was the matter. *'Little woman, I don't think that my constitution can stand it much longer, I am totally exhausted!'*

Frightened, I recalled a similar episode when, at the introduction of containerisation in Shipping, he worked such long hours and so hard that he was on the verge of a nervous breakdown. Our young GP had placed him at once on special medication to slow down his brain and forbade him all work for at least six weeks. His assistants had to take over at the command of his worried Chairman. Whether we liked it or not, we found ourselves boarding one of their ships, destination Copenhagen, forcing Ronny to rest. Our first choice, Triest, had been cancelled due to an unexpected strike in that Port. It was February and I get seasick yet again when I think of that stormy passage through Kattegat and Sund! Does he find himself yet again at the brink of a nervous breakdown, I asked myself.

'The document recently addressed to all Branches encouraging the older staff to apply for early retirement, does this not include you?' I asked as after all he was 63 by then. *'Indeed, but we will suffer financially' 'And what will be the difference with respect to our income?' 'At least £2 per week' 'And you would kill yourself for two miserable pounds? It's never worth it! As Shakespeare wrote in The Merchant of Venice, they have had their pound of flesh long ago with your 43 years service! Besides there are no pockets in a shroud!'*

The following day Ronny duly completed the special form. Afterwards he received many telephone calls from Management in London and his HQ as well as puzzled colleagues. They tempted him with a substantial salary increase, ironical to us as, if he was worth so much more, why had the offer not come long ago? . . . Ronny persevered, and enjoyed a happy and satisfying retirement lasting ten years and we were never forced to eat one slice of bread less, as the saying goes.

Although he always enjoyed a drink, yet not at all born three drinks below par, during our 36 years of marriage I only witnessed my husband really drunk as a newt four times. One occasion ran parallel with his retirement when he celebrated with a party of all parties with friends and club pals. (In contrast to my own father, Ronny, when happily drunk, was a sentimentalist, loving me to the point of irritation and quarrelling was an absent factor. For that reason I never objected when he had the proverbial one too many although I feared that, if he should fall, he might damage his spine, still his proverbial Achilles Heel). When he returned home in the late afternoon, just one look sufficed; I could read him like a book. *'You're drunk, Ronny; no, really befuddled'* I reproached him. *'No, little woman, thash not twue, I'm shobel as a Jugg'* he replied simultaneously removing his shoes. We had had our kitchen extended and modernised, new glossy lino laid. Before he could reach his slippers he placed himself with his back to one of the kitchen cabinets. Still assuring us of his sober condition, he softly slid to the ground, like a slowed down film, as his socks slid over the lino until with a slight bump he sat on the floor. He eyed us, bewildered, Spilly howled with laughter and I worriedly hastened to him, but his fall had been too slow and deliberate to cause any damage.

Then my irritation took over. I left him lying on the ground and forbade Spilly to assist him. It would have been cruel if it had not been so comical for, due to war wounds to his leg he could not sit on his knees, kept sliding down on the lino until at last he succeeded in getting hold of the cabinet edge and heaved himself up. *'It's easier climbing Everest, and you don't love me anymore!'* he shouted, stamping upstairs, hurt in his macho-image. A while later I brought him a ewer of water and placed it on his night table. A strong fist grabbed hold of me. *'Do you still love me?'* *'Man, I adore you!'* Curtain . . .

*

Arthur, my cousin and widower of one of my favourite cousins Irene, suggested we should join him and his son and daughter-in-law for a holiday in Juan-les-Pins during September 1975. We reserved an apartment each in a building fronting the beach where he and Irene had lodged several years running. After Ronny's retirement we had sold my Mini and acquired a Ford Escort Ghia, easily driven by both of us which was paramount in view of the difference in our size. Ford had recently introduced this particular model to Great Britain and had distributed it throughout the country in a very small quantity. It was manufactured in Germany, a completely new concept. The roof was constructed of dark coloured vinyl, the body of a Winter white. I rather insistently suggested we should run it in by driving through France to Juan and with me as chauffeur, as the thought of a long distance trek made Ronny's lip drop to his navel! After he retired he disliked driving.

Landing in Boulogne, I felt slightly nervous with traffic conducted on the right hand side. Soon though I became accustomed to it probably due to my inherent instinct of a former life in Belgium. We leisurely drove through the country of Marianne and took a snack each lunchtime, stopping for the night at a conveniently situated hotel en route to one little town or another noted on our map. We tried to avoid the Auto Route as we wanted to take our time and view something of the lush countryside. Spilly was comfortably installed on the passenger seat, although sometimes troubled with her ailment, when we had to stop at wayside cafés. The family would meet and stay the night at a hotel, in the past frequented by Arthur, and about one hour's drive from Nice and would leave in convoy the following morning. We arrived on a dark evening and found the hotel . . . closed. No sign of life until, after my loud banging on the front door, somebody appeared and explained the business was temporarily closed for modernising. I explained our predicament and they kindly phoned a motel some kilometres further on reserving four rooms. A note was pinned to the door addressed to Arthur and we said good-bye to this friendly and helpful Frenchman. And indeed, our family found us there a few hours later.

The following morning I followed Arthur onto the autostrade to Juan-les-Pins. He had been a driver of some vehicle or another practically all his life and his conduct on the road was impeccable. While driving I gave all the necessary signals as I was taught in England. When leaving the car upon arrival at Juan, Arthur said; *'Well, kid, you drive well and careful!'* A real compliment, for whenever I was a passenger in his car in the past and we saw stupidity on the road, he would say derisively: *'It's another female wretch!'*

Our car was much admired en route as other drivers subsequently owning the same model experienced and as manufacture in Britain commenced shortly after, perhaps we were partly responsible for bringing this new model to the attention of many.

It was obvious to me during this holiday that Spilly's appetite diminished almost day by day. She blamed grilled meats which were served in practically all the restaurants and which she disliked. She would also join us at the beach very late in the morning and I suspected she was suffering from her constipation/diarrhoea trouble although she did not want me to stay with her. This 'to allow me to enjoy a well-earned rest'. Mother darling, how did I earn this unselfish love??

We thoroughly enjoyed our holiday and the return voyage went smoothly as, after having stayed overnight in a motel not far from Paris, I accosted a 'routier' - the professional French heavy vehicle drivers - who showed me clearly on my map which route to take and insisted that I remain in one specific lane upon approaching Paris. With his assistance, I was able to take the right periphery road avoiding ending up in the very centre of this metropolis, the trap of so many drivers.

From the moment we landed in Dover, our return trip became a calamity for both Spilly and myself. Ronny had taken over the driving but as it was a very dark evening with signposting not always clear, he lost his way several times in the unfamiliar English landscape. Hours passed and we could not stop anywhere suitable. In the meantime, Spilly's diarrhoea had started and when at last we could stop at a pub, cleaning her up in the Ladies became a major operation. The next days at home her condition turned for the worse at alarming speed; she hardly ate and whatever she took went straight through her body. All day long it was a case of washing her and issuing clean clothes. Her tanned face became yellowish and this spread throughout her body, even her scalp. Our GP arranged for her to see the cancer specialist again and, after thorough examination and X-rays it was found a malignant swelling, a carcinoma, blocked the small tube leading to the gall preventing the process of digestion. He recommended a rare operation involving the insertion of a plastic replacement tube. I was at my wits' end. Spilly was petrified of surgery. The specialist explained to me that, for the majority of operations connected with carcinomas, opening a body often increases the growth. Without surgery, she would remain bedridden to the end, unable to keep any food or drink inside, subject to an uninterrupted flow of faeces, like a helpless baby.

She had just reached 80 and her condition prevented us from celebrating this milestone in her life . . . What could I say to her, how could I decide? Eventually I put my cards on the table and gave her the specialist's verdict. *'You suffered enough discomfort and trouble, child, I agree to the operation'*, and then a bewildered little voice I will always remember: *'Why do I have to suffer from such filth, I've always been a true Christian, helped others wherever I could, never hurt a fly, and so intent in the first place on personal hygiene!'* Perhaps God exists only for thieves and murderers and drunkards, I thought, as they seem to sail through life like a knife through butter!

In Birmingham there was but one surgeon with the necessary skill for this particular operation. We visited him privately but the actual op came under the NHS free of charge. Afterwards I was deliriously happy on learning that it had been a success and, full of optimism, I visited her daily until her discharge. She was thin as a rake. Ronny carried her in his arms from the ward to the invalid chair and wheeled her to the car. Once home he carried her upstairs to her room where I undressed her and, soon after, with the warmth of her electric blanket engulfing her, she fell in a deep sleep. A strong beef tea and a one-egg omelette with mushroom were the first home-cooked foods she was able to take since our return from Juan. Her former appetite never returned though. Nevertheless her food was normally digested to the relief of both of us. Our excitement was of short duration. A few days later, during the routine visit, our GP warned me that the carcinoma was growing at an alarming rate. It had settled on the pancreas. Spilly spent the next few afternoons with us in our living room but complained about terrible back pain shortly after.

I had just made arrangements with Arthur to take her to Antwerp. where he kept his guest room available for us as I hoped she would die there, in peace, in her beloved city, surrounded perhaps by her friends. My prayer was not answered. When we urgently summoned the doctor he prescribed a liquid drug to deaden the pain which was increasing due to the pressure of the growth against the spinal nerves. I had to administer this one tablespoonful every 4 hours. Night and day I stayed with her, dozing now and then at night, on thickly folded winter blankets on the carpet near her bed, covered by the eiderdown. I had little or no experience in respect of proper nursing. Nobody had taught me the procedure to change a patient. Each time this was necessary, I would pick her two feet up by the ankles as kindly as I could, carefully brought her legs up as I had witnessed mothers do with a baby, washed her with a flannel rinsed in warm, soapy water, dried and powdered her, everything with one hand, and placed the clean, specially supplied undercover with plastic backing, under her.

When on occasion she would open her eyes and see me sitting there, she would say: *'Child, are you still there, do go to bed'* . . . I'd pretend to have just got up and as I was in a dressing gown, she believed me.

If there are 'walking angels' in England, they must indubitably be the District Nurses! Their dedication is legendary, their services free of charge even if they are called at night. Two such nurses visited us daily and they taught me how to put her on her side to change her. Sometimes they came three times in one day easing my burden considerably. One night I was longing for a few hours sleep. I had just given her 'the cocktail' as she called it and as the next dose was due four hours later, I crept to my bed and tried to sleep. Tossing and turning, fitful sleep refused to come, and all at once I heard a heavy thud emanating from Spilly's room. I rushed in and found her lying between the night table and built-in wardrobe, in the foetus position. Light as a feather as she was, I carried her to her commode near her bed, hastily covering her with her dressing gown. As I opened the bed the biting ammonia smell of her urine nearly felled me and demented as I felt pulled the linen off, put clean sheets from the wardrobe onto the bed and placed her back onto the clean 'nappy'. She shivered with cold, but drugged as she was, she did not open her eyes. I presume she had dreamt of being in her old flat in Antwerp and wanted to go to the door leading to the lavatory there. The wall prevented this and unable to withstand this collision she must have slipped to the ground.

A few mornings thereafter her death-struggle started and she fell into a coma. One of my friends had come to visit, thinking she could help and while I made her a pot of tea, at 5.15 on Sunday 11th April 1976, my darling mother blew out her last breath, alone, cruel irony, after all the days and nights of faithful care and vigilance! At last the umbilical cord was severed . . .

At her request cremation took place and I begged the Funeral Director for her ashes which he supplied in a nice, plastic urn. Once in the past I casually asked her if, in case of her demise in the UK, she would agree to my taking her ashes for scattering at Schoonselhof, our Antwerp Cemetery, where Spil, Armand and all her departed friends were resting and which she so often had visited when she resided in that city. *'Oh, child, if only that were possible!'* she had cried, eyes filled with tears. *'Mother, to me everything is possible and if you so desire, I'll see to it'* I promised. *'How on earth are you going to manage that?'* *'Well, I'll claim your ashes from the Funeral Director and even if I have to personally carry these in a travelling bag, a promise is a promise, I'll do it'*. I shall never forget her expression. It was as though the sun lit upon her eyes and with a *'Is it promised?'* and my affirmative nod, we embraced in earnest pact.

The urn with Spilly's ashes passes the flags and members of the White Brigade, en route to the scattering ground.

Indeed, I carried the ashes of my Mother in my personal luggage. On arrival in Antwerp, a Funeral Director, a member of the White Brigade group of Spil, took immediate possession and put the contents of the English urn into one of his own. At the appropriate date, the family, ex-neighbours

291

and friends and especially Colonel Louette, the unforgettable eponymous 'Fidelio' of the White Brigade, gathered at the mortuary reception building. The standard bearers with the flags of this Resistance Movement formed the archway of honour and the procession accompanied Spilly to her last resting place, the Garden of Rest. A soft April breeze caressed the surrounding fir trees and I swear some of her ashes blew over the grass towards the part of the 'Heropark' where Spil too rests in peace. Ronny clutched me in a strong embrace as if to pump into me his own strength . . .

As is customary, we offered a reception for those present at the service in the restaurant of a Swimming Complex owned by one of the survivors of Buchenwald concentration camp, also a member of the White Brigade. Looking at the gathering of friends, it came as a great consolation to me knowing Spilly was so much loved and respected. 'They don't make 'em like her anymore, little Spilly' one sincerely commented. To be sure, my heart is at peace knowing I was given a chance to repay her in a small way for her unselfish mother-love and devotion, little enough under the circumstances, and even now I feel this pain and this 'mea-culpa' that, from my earlier years, I should have been less selfish, less pre-occupied with self and caused her less heartache. But then . . . such is life . . . as people always try to convince me. And I shall be forever grateful she was never forced to spend her last days in a home for the Aged. I have visited many such institutions during my lifetime, here and abroad, and more often than not I was confronted by frail old people looking at me with eyes older than time. I saw benches in small gardens or on minimal patios occupied by old ones, staring blankly at nothing, the human residue of lost relations, often repudiated by their offspring who could not stand their presence any longer, refusing to concern themselves with their ailments, senility and complaints. Old people, victims of a sophisticated society that succeeded in extending their life-span but could not stand their existence . . .

After Spilly's death I endeavoured not to show my sorrow when Ronny was present as he could never stand the sight of women's tears, it seemed to wrench his heart to pieces. Once, as was his routine, he left for a lunch session at this Club. Half-way there he realised he had forgotten his wallet, returned, drove up the drive, dashed through the garage to the kitchen back door. He heard me howl like a wounded animal, calling repetitiously: *'Mâke, Mâke, Mâke!'* the Flemish equivalent of Little Mother. Disconcerted he took me in his arms and rocking me softly like a child tried to console me until my sobbing ceased. We decided there and then that I should undertake an outside interest to overcome my traumatic memories, still so fresh in my mind.

Chapter Twenty Three

National Exhibition Centre

About a year previously the National Exhibition Centre had been built. They had advertised for interpreters for the International Exhibitions and Fairs to be held at various dates. There were no difficulties with French and Flemish as my basic languages, but I found it necessary to brush up on German and Spanish, the first language not having been spoken since the war and the second but sporadic during holidays.

After having visited a local Agency I was soon engaged for the International Plastics Exhibition, one of the largest events in respect of the plastics industry. My language qualifications were most important, also past experience in business and interpreting at various factories for the Chamber of Commerce in the past. Soon after the Fair I applied to join a different Agency, whose girls I had met and liked. After an interview at the Director's home, where we established an instant rapport, she placed my name on her list and soon afterwards I was engaged for my first employment with her. Not long afterwards she received enquiries about 'that nippy little Belgian' and I consequently started another exhibition at the Organiser's office which this time entailed interpreting and organising work during the build-up, the opening days proper and the breakdown of International Fairs.

Overseas exhibitors send their stand-building personnel well in advance. These, although specialists in their field, are used to working with their hands and have never found the necessity to learn a foreign language, a fact which already floors the general consensus that *all* foreigners speak English! They are greatly relieved to find someone assisting them in their own tongue. Plugs, switches and other electric necessities brought with them, are often unsuitable for British norms or installations at the NEC. Plans sometimes have faults in design or are contrary to the rules of the complex. Forms for stand telephones, to be requested prior to building a Stand, have been known to go missing or have never been sent. In short, all irritations coupled to stand building, land in the lap of organising personnel, not to mention personal calls from or to overseas firms and the numerous messages to be sent over the tannoy system in the Halls, all in the appropriate languages. It required total attention and stamina but it encouraged the flow of adrenalin in my veins and I absorbed it all like a lost soul tortured by thirst stumbling on an oasis!

The majority of organising personnel are generally chosen, not only for their ability but predominantly for their patience and sense of humour. As the proverb goes: 'One has not to be crazy to work here but . . . it does help!' Assisting and co-operating with the Organisers and their personnel became most satisfying where I am concerned and was reciprocated as many have become friends over the past years. Perhaps my occasional translation of a typical and juicy Antwerpian saying or proverb basically contributed to much hilarity; we would bend over backwards as the saying goes to help one another. Soon everybody knew me as 'Anneke'. Ronny had given me that name many years before simply because this diminutive of my name intrigued him and so this was how I became known to all friends and NEC acquaintances.

Bearing in mind International Exhibitions occur but intermittently, some take place every two or even three years, it took some time before I was fully conversant with the various services and/or persons to contact for all necessary requirements in the successful building of a Stand and subsequent running of any Exhibition. As I write this, I have worked with organisers over a period of 20 years!

∗

It was not until 1979 that all alterations and extensions to our house were satisfactorily completed; we had our 'ideal home' at last. My days were pleasantly filled from early morning to evening as I insisted on executing my daily household chores, look after the garden with the multi-duties this represented, and the continuation of my outside interests. Towards the end of April Ronny caught a serious case of bronchitis, against which his earlier smoke-damaged lungs had little resistance in spite of the fact he had given up smoking for almost 20 years! Looking after him, as usual, was my priority and upon his recovery even played the role of barmaid as his numerous friends and acquaintances daily visited him. At one stage the bedroom looked like the bar at his local; for the better part of the evening I would be running up and down the stairs like a yo-yo serving drinks and titbits. During the day it meant administering medicines, serving food on a tray with his favourite dishes in order to induce a normal appetite, hot drinks, cold drinks, shopping, frequent washing and ironing of his personal linen and bedclothes as he was bedridden for such a long time. Came May, there was the garden to be dug over, weeding, planting of the shrubs for summer, etc.

One Sunday evening found me still in my jeans, on top of a ladder in the front garden pruning the Japanese flowering cherry trees. Suddenly Ronny's 'sergeant major' voice roared over me. He had come down in his dressing gown and stood by the wrought iron gate to the rear garden. *'Isn't it time you stopped this?'* he shouted, looking daggers at me and giving me a most reproachful look, undoubtedly pointed at himself rather than me due to his obvious inability to tackle any menial job himself at the time, after his feverish attacks left him much weakened. I realise this now in retrospect but at that moment, after weeks of nursing and extra duties, it must have been the straw that broke the camel's back as I erupted in what I call 'my Flemish fury'. I jumped from the ladder, folded it and, marching through the now heaped, cut branches, which I left for the grass-cutting gardener to collect the following morning, stormed to the garage. I practically threw the ladder against the garage wall instead of hanging it neatly on the bracket as was my wont. In clean, English syntaxes, interspersed with a few non-ladylike curses, the knowledge of which hitherto had only been esoteric, I repeated my daily duties to him in a clear conceptual frame and pointed out in a most convincing manner that the three rules paramount to the success of our marriage, ie: charlady in the morning, lady of the 'Manor' at noon and lady-of-easy-virtue at night, were difficult to uphold when clad from Monday am to Sunday pm in jeans, executing tasks a navvy would be reluctant to undertake! *'And tomorrow I'm going to search for an apartment without a garden!'* I further retorted leaving a surprised and by then silent husband behind as such outbursts were something of a rarity in our marriage.

Indeed, the following morning, coming down to breakfast, he found me dressed to go out, a tidy kitchen, the floor of which would normally at that time be strewn with assorted linen and clothing with the washing machine softly beating in uninterrupted cycle. Before my astonished husband realised the position (we had made up the previous evening as tiffs only lasted from 12am until high noon) I sat in our car and drove straight to an area in Solihull where a few apartment buildings had been erected around the 70s. Whenever we would pass these Ronny often remarked on the beautiful surroundings and preference, in case we should ever have to move to a flat.

Chapter Twenty Four

'Custer's Last Stand'?

Again it proved that life is often stranger than fiction.

I parked the car at the first building and rang the bell of a ground floor dwelling. An elderly lady opened the door. I assured her that I was not selling, nor a Jehovah's witness . . . but did she know of a flat for sale in the neighbourhood? She most pleasantly invited me in, in spite of my apologetic remonstrations that I had no intention of troubling her, with a 'How else would you know whether a similar place would be satisfactory to your expectations? In any case you are no stranger as I happened to have been one of your neighbours when my husband was still alive'. What a small world!

From the moment I stepped over her threshold I felt thoroughly at home and in no time, in my imagination, our furniture was deposited in its place and alterations were made to the structure. In addition she handed me a list of all expenses incurred in the ownership of these specific apartments. It so happened one was vacant on the top floor of the next building, which pleased me as, being easily awoken during even deep sleep, I did not fancy the noise of habitation above. In effect there were only two stories to each building and, to our delight, we later found the flats were practically soundproof.

Back home, I casually remarked to Ronny: *'I have found something which will please you'* and rang the owner for a viewing appointment. Until then Ronny had still not believed I was serious about moving. From the moment we entered the premises everything seemed to fall into place. Both front and rear offered a marvellous view. The edifice was surrounded by lawns with a rich variety of trees, evergreen firs and bushes and even old fruit trees, including a rare, very old mulberry tree, which later supplied me with gorgeous berries in the season allowing me to make exceptionally tasty jelly. To my utter chagrin the tree fell victim to a vicious winter in 1990-91 infamous for stormy gales accompanied by heavy snowfalls.

As seems to be a prerogative in Britain, besides the selling price, a sum of £1000 was expected for carpets and curtains. However, after having convinced the vendor that his apartment was to be 'Custer's Last Stand' for us, and I wished to apply my own colour schemes, bearing in mind we had cash in hand, we became owners at the originally offered price. True enough our house had not yet been sold at that moment but was fully paid off with the Building Society. We decided to sell without the intervention of an Estate Agent and, upon advice of our Solicitor, placed an advert in the local paper known for its weekly house sales advertising. Normally this was distributed every Saturday morning and . . . by midday, our house was sold!

Afterwards I was often asked why I so abruptly decided to move from a house I had taken so much trouble in perfecting with alterations and decorating. I am convinced that Spilly's death was the dominating incentive, the only way in which I could lay her ghost! Ronny's outburst that Sunday evening had just been the ultimate push . . .

My mainspring for home-building once more became oiled upon receipt of the keys and we planned the transformation of our abode with vigour, virtually completely modernising it. As these buildings were bereft of chimneys, we created a false hearth, a 'trompe d'oeil' in Adam style, most effective, especially as the auxiliary electric fire with coal-effect enhanced the welcoming look when aglow during cold evenings. With enthusiasm I papered the kitchen, ours and the guest bedrooms, the lavatory and the entrance hall, in between engagements at the NEC, made curtains and bedspreads with the aid of the electric sewing machine Spilly had bought me a few years prior to her moving to our house, an indispensable little mate. The creative work filled me with an extreme satisfaction; I felt thoroughly happy for the first time since Spilly's death. From the very moment we moved in, in spite of the hellish noise of constant hammering, sawing, knocking and drilling poor Ronny had to suffer during the alterations, as I was often working away from home, we were both ecstatically happy! Indeed, during a visit of one of his friends on Christmas Day 6 years later, I heard Ronny declare that we should have moved to this place at least ten years earlier as he 'felt as snug as a bug in a rug' . . . 'The only way by which they can move me from this place is in a box', he commented.

*

We had decided, after Spilly's death, to regularly visit Antwerp, choosing August, to reassure my links with my city of birth were not entirely broken. We chose a very old hotel, practically under the magnificent Cathedral of Our Lady in the ancient part, where majestic houses, dating from the early 17th century had been restored, their façades partly re-gilded. Each one had been the seat of a Guild of yesteryear. Luckily, demolition of old houses of antique architecture had been halted in time before that part of the city had become a concrete jungle of modern junk. Now, perambulating the diversity of old and new in the Port of Antwerp is a pleasant, even didacting experience! The hotel where we lodged was full of character with old, creaking staircases curling up to the attics past sloping landings and rickety stairs and bereft of outward trappings. As August was often boiling hot, we would keep the windows open all night. Poor Ronny! He would wake up in the morning like Lazarus, covered in mosquito bites (sweet blood, you know). His verdict: Antwerp mozzies are in fact flying piranhas!

Chapter Twenty Five

America

In 1981 visiting America became the rage. And talking of coincidence: I advised my employer at the Agency about the date of our holidays. *'Funny'*, she replied, *'I too will be on holiday during that period'* *'Yes, but I think we are going slightly further afield'* I joked. *'And where would that be?'* *'America'* I sighed almost breathless. A short hush . . . and then: *'Well, we too. Where and which airline?'* *'To California with Pan-Am'* *'We too'* came the somewhat excited reply and *'which departure?'* *'Half past four in the afternoon'* I was by then practically shouting with glee. I thought I would explode with excitement when she said: 'We too' once again . . . We howled with laughter and decided to meet at Heathrow.

Judy, who after all those years had become a friend as well as an employer, would be staying with her new husband in Beverly Hills and as Los Angeles was on the itinerary during our tour, we made an appointment to meet at the restaurant of our hotel with panoramic views onto the Japanese Garden and hills beyond. Our voyage was an overwhelming success from day one. The flight more than comfortable. San Francisco promptly became our favourite city and we unexpectedly found the American people courteous and friendly, sharply in contrast to the boozy GIs publicly peeing in the clean streets during the first months of the liberation of Antwerp!

The famous tram, not always with room inside for passengers when many are forced to literally hang onto its sides by fingers and toes, took us to Fisherman's Wharf which had not taken its famous name in vain; gigantic, pink crabs and clams rested side by side with wriggling lobsters still alive, and although I did not judge the popular 'clam-chowder' to be of the same taste as a fine crab-bisque, we found solace, as fish-aficionados, in the variety of unfamiliar kinds displayed on the slabs. In the prominent restaurant of the late Joe di Maggio, Marilyn Monroe's second and still famous husband, we at first looked puzzled at menus numbering the courses whose names were as unknown to us as the craters on Mars . . . Next to our table I noticed a lady enjoying a lobster tail. I pointed it out to the waitress. *'That's a di Maggio Special'*, she replied. So said, so ordered. In due course, a platter was placed in front of me, loaded to the brim with a steak as large as a man's hand, about 4cm thick, as well as a lobster tail with half of the crustacean still anchored to it. *'Have you made a mistake?' I ordered just a lobster tail'* I feebly ventured to ask. *'No, a di Maggio Special is a steak plus a lobster tail my dear' 'I can't eat all that!'* I stammered. *'I'll bring you a doggie-bag'*.

This seems to be the norm in the USA, but Ronny somewhat abruptly retorted: 'We are tourists and have not got a dog' . . . Well, an Englishman worth his weight in gold could not possibly walk out with his food leavings. Dumbfounded, I looked at the waitress. My eyes must have registered the precious dollar-value of that thick steak, not that we were on an economy trip. After all, we did not possess an ever-open Sesame at home . . . Ronny excused himself momentarily as by then the over generous aperitifs made a heavy demand on his bladder. No sooner had his posteria left the chair when our waitress jumped into the adjoining kitchen, reappeared with a plastic bag, forked my steak from my plate into it and pushed it unceremoniously into my handbag. On his return Ronny proceeded with his scallops, a miniature portion in comparison with mine and, as I had left half of my gigantic baked potato, must have presumed my steak was hidden behind it.

The following day we visited yet another famous place, the Muir Woods with their world famous, ancient trees, the Sequoia Sempervirens to give them their Latin name. Never in my wildest imagination had I expected such majesty of nature! On the return trip we called on Sausalito, an artists village with many galleries, coffee shops in varied style and boutiques of exaggeratedly priced goods aimed at the gullible tourist. By 4pm we arrived at the hotel. Ronny, thirsty as ever, made a bee-line for the bar. I expressed preference for returning to our room and resting, prior to a busily scheduled evening. After deliberating with my conscience, I rang for room service and pretended to be suffering from an overburdened stomach. Could I order a pot of coffee, a few slices of bread and butter and some gherkins? The vinegary acid would stabilise my stomach . . . Shortly afterwards a waiter arrived with a tray laden with my 'goodies'. I dared not look at him as all colour seemed to have risen from my bottom to my cheeks. Fact is he had not taken any more notice of my unusual request than from the hundreds of others he must have received in the course of his career . . . I took the plastic bag from the drawer in which I had hidden it, under my underwear, the previous night. That impromptu meal was one of the most enjoyable during my sojourn in the good old USA. I confessed it all to Ronny after our return home, but contrary to my expectations, he laughingly said: *'You cunning little thing!'* The route we had taken alongside the Californian Coast was unforgettable, meeting the Chipmunks, comical to the point of hysterics, born clowns as they are, but to my extreme disappointment, we never ran into Clint Eastwood at Carmel!

Las Vegas was an undreamt of revelation, magnificent in her vulgarity, vulgar in her magnificence, where we witnessed one of the most impressive beautiful shows with costumes succeeding one after the other in a dream of a living colour palette, and made of breathtaking silks and materials; scene changes rising from under the ground seemingly accomplished in the batting of an eye! Caesar's Palace was the jewel in the crown with its pseudo-Roman statues of naked young men placed at regular intervals on each side of the long drive to the entrance, the gambling hall with its hundreds of machines and 'one-armed bandits', its sailing ship reminiscent of the pirate eras and simultaneously equipped as a nightclub, its boutiques and restaurants for every taste. Being slightly nauseous by then with the over generous food portions, we decided to order a sandwich with Virginia Ham in the Quick Snack restaurant. The chef, at his meat slicing machine, was having a chat while slicing the ham. We presumed there was a keen demand for this type of sandwich . . . until we saw him fill ours with all the slices, at least 200 gr per person! Biting into it was a sheer impossibility, our mouth simply did not open that far so we had to tackle it with a knife and fork. The American capacity for eating is phenomenal, more than likely the reason why so many could figure as an advert for Michelin tyres.

Our flight over the Grand Canyon, in a plane for four passengers, with a pilot boasting a few thousand flying hours to his credit or to be precise on his Pilot's Licence, (many of those gained during the Korean war) and who steered his craft in normal weather like a well-tamed horse or, when it started to rain, simply flew between or above it, was exciting and I somehow felt safer than in a large Jumbo Jet. Beneath us the Colorado river curled along like a green ribbon; the lava-torrent, rapids, the extinct volcano, were unbelievably majestic and the Havasupai Indian village at the base of the Canyon with its adjoining blue lake where the ethnic Indians used to bathe in pre-colonial times, inspired in both of us the hankering to thresh out America's history once home again. It was only upon landing that we realised the pilot's face was as rock-like as his canyon and furrowed as its map.

Returning to Caesar's Palace, we decided on one of their special ices. Our request for a small portion was politely dismissed but as the customer still is very much king in that part of the globe, were advised to order but one dish. Two plates were duly placed in front of us. The Banana Split consisted of three ice-cream balls. The middle one as large as a baby's head, adjoining two about a third smaller. On each side of the glass dish a full-size banana, the size of a zeppelin, rested in its golden glory. The three balls were covered with what looked like a ladle of berry jelly topped by at least half a pint of cream on which 150 gr of broken nuts was sprinkled . . . We valiantly tackled and finished the smaller ice cream balls with a banana, and some of the additions. By the time we had consumed all this the 'baby-head' sized one had melted and dripped in slow motion over the sides of the dish. We were stumbling to the exit more than elegantly satisfied, mercifully no doggie bag was offered on this occasion although we overheard the waitress's retort upon leaving: 'The English have a stomach like a mouse!'

Los Angeles, negatively speaking, was more of a disappointment except for the hand-prints captured for eternity in the cement in front of the Chinese Theatre of those famous film stars of yesteryear whose names formed part of our youth, and of those still enjoyed to-date. The beautiful Beverly Hills homes, castles really, of the stars were so varied in style I thought we were in wonderland. And naturally I had to pose on the site of the Hollywood Bowl, arms stretched, mouth open but not a sound to be heard . . . The streets in the vicinity of our popular hotel, belonging to a chain extending its tentacles over the entire world, were extremely dirty and the vagabonds, drug addicts or drunken flotsam of humanity stood on every street corner or were lying on the ground. It was in the centre mainly that we witnessed wealth parallel to the scenes of the old black/white films of the past. Boutiques and leading French fashion designers competed with Gucci and Vuitton leathershops.

Our visit to the Universal Studios ran smoothly with its productions beforehand programmed. In a miniature train we drove past an artificial sea out of which the plastic 'Jaws' arose and momentarily gave me the heebie-jeebies in its frightening reality. The inevitable cowboys indulged in their staged 'saloon fight' with Colts drawn at the flick of a wrist to the amusement of young and old. We also visited a 'ghost town', a fiesta village and the set of one of the 'roaring twenties' films when the Charleston was at its peak. In short, the places where dreams become reality and entire streets but consisted of façades with total void at the rear. 'Tinseltown' has not stolen its name!

The trip to a museum with panoramic view at San Diego almost marred our holiday as both Ronny and myself felt extremely emotional when the special bus took us very slowly and seemingly endlessly past rows and rows, as far as the eye could see, of white, identical gravestones. San Diego houses the headquarters of the American Navy. Under those thousands of gravestones rested the flower of American manhood, killed in action during the war fighting the Japanese while liberating the islands in the Pacific, and in Korea and Vietnam. It was unbelievable, a continuous sea of white stone, during a run of 25 minutes. Ronny was exceptionally quiet, I could hardly keep from sobbing aloud and I silently whispered a subdued *'thank you'*.

Tijuana, just across the Mexican border, was indescribably dirty and noisy with cheap shops where tourists are fleeced for inferior goods and it was out of compassion mainly for the Mexican vendors at small stalls that Ronny bought me two of their handmade sandals. Their fruit market, however, was a sight to behold and we ate ourselves silly with the juiciest apricots and peaches.

Disneyland! I was a child again. Our courier and I spent the entire day in it escapist surrounds and, apart from the carousel, entered, sat on and viewed all that was offered. 'It can't be done in one day' I was assured. I proved the contrary. We ran like hares from one scene or spectacle to the next. In the theatre of the Children of all Nations we sang along with the automation dolls in their national costumes. In the submarine with water engulfing us we found ourselves in a Cousteau area, with unbelievable kaleidoscopes of colour of underwater life and all kinds of fish in their identical form. The reality of a copied isle in the Caribbean with animated plastic pirates and scenes of plundering, open imitation leather trunks spilling jewels, all in constant movement, was breathtaking. The trip aboard the Mississippi paddle steamer was unique and the plastic elephants, complete with flapping ears, crocodiles, lions and other wild animals along the banks of the river were so real that the cassette recording of the elephant's roar sent shivers down my spine.

I skipped like a 12 year old, excitedly chattering, pulling the courier along like an appendage. What impressed me in addition to this expansive wonderland and the crowds going about at leisure was the total absence of any litter! Youths (apparently students bent on extra pocket money)walked about non-stop with long, sharp sticks but the majority of visitors threw their wrappings neatly in the litter bins provided. The little sky-train had transported us to the Disneyland centre upon arrival and halted in front of a real Wild West Saloon. Before I could say: 'Lasso' Ronny was inside! Tired and thirsty ourselves we afterwards joined him. He stood at the longest bar I ever saw in any pub. The barman regaled us with one of his tricks. He stood at the farthest corner of the bar, poured Ronny's beer and with one movement of the flat of his hand sent the glass along the entire length of the smooth bar top to his customer at the other end. It came to a halt in front of his flabbergasted face, nonetheless momentarily tottering about, spattering a few drops of beer,

307

which would normally have been an exception. Laconically his colleague shouted: *'Eh, Mac, he wants to drink it, not wear it!'*

*

When we had first moved into our apartment I noticed that the lawns stretched right up to the walls of the buildings with no derivative colour in sight. As soon as our own home had been totally completed, I asked and got permission from the agents responsible for our maintenance to dig a flowerbed along the wall surface of the building. I planted stunning delphiniums, a rose tree, magenta flowered clematis, a hydrangea, a miniature rhododendron and, during the summer months a mixture of geraniums, busy lizzies and petunias in a rainbow of colours. On the patio, in front of the window of the downstairs flat, I placed three artificial Greek urns, filled in summer with geraniums and/or busy lizzies, petunias and hanging lobelia. In Spring groups of daffodils amongst purple aubrietia vividly coloured the brown soil while white and purple crocus peeped out of the newly growing lawn.

In the shrubbery in front of our building, I had a miniature Japanese weeping cherry tree planted by a gardener friend and surrounded it with green bushes and slow-growing fir trees, clumps of daffodils and ericas and set it in a frame of purple coloured aubrietia. It was not long before other flat owners followed suit and nowadays flowers and plants adorn the hitherto bleak brick walls of the five buildings in our area. We are lucky in Summer with a private garden where we can sunbathe in privacy and have tea with one or two of the flat dwellers so inclined, and within but 25 metres distance from our front door.

Between the lawn and the wooden fence surrounding this garden with its many fir trees and laurel bushes, nothing grew but hundreds of nettles, and after having likewise removed these prior to planting, I returned home covered like a Lazarus and itching like a flea-bitten dog. Evergreen creepers, leaning against the fence now compete with deep rose coloured mallows and low growing lavatera bushes, multicoloured lupins and hollyhocks and when the buddleias are in flower, all kinds of bees, moths and butterflies busily buzz and flutter around them. *'Back to gardening?'* ask friends surprised. *'Indeed, but this time by virtue of its size; I'm not its slave!'*

As time passed, employment at the NEC snowballed, to the amusement of Ronny when, in the morning, it was he who waved bye-bye to me; our roles had reversed. We would sit comfortably together at the end of a day, he with his whisky, I with my Dutch Warninks Advocaat, waiting for the BBC news and discussing the events of my working day. He would refer to this daily ritual as *'the best part of the day, with my aperitif enjoyed in the comfort of my little nest and my own little woman'* . . . *'In which order this praise?'* I would ask. *'You know darned well'* was his reply.

Chapter Twenty Six

My Dusk

Then, one fateful day, during one of the largest exhibitions annually to be held, I caught a serious flu which kept me in bed for three days. Afterwards, it was poor Ronny's turn. His attack lasted much longer and when he woke one morning with unbearably excruciating knee pain, I called our doctor. As Ronny had hardly eaten for almost a week and had perspired continuously with a high fever practically living on water only, we were alarmed at his weight loss. It was not the first time that Ronny had suffered from aching joints. The previous year his hand had caused him much pain and sleepless nights, and blood tests had been taken which nevertheless proved negative, even for gout, and as the pains ultimately disappeared we put it down to 'wear and tear'. In retrospect, I believe that even then a blood clot was in circulation in his body. This time the doctor prescribed special pills and ordered Ronny not to leave his bed under any circumstances as the knee had to rest three full days. Indeed, the pain disappeared after the stipulated period.

It was Saturday morning and he decided to shower and shave as he hated facial growth on himself and, ill or not, it was his priority. As I hastily replaced the bed linen, and opened the window to refresh the room, I heard him moan. He had already expressed concern about his weakness while shaving, during the days prior to the doctor's visit. *'Is it difficult again, darling?'* I called through the slightly ajar bathroom door. *'It's a beggar!'* came the reply immediately followed by a heavy thud and a slamming shut of the door. I hastily pushed with all my might to open it. Ronny was lying on the carpet, left side of mouth half pulled downwards, gasping for breath, his right arm partly resting on the side of the bath. I unsuccessfully tried to sit him upright, ran into the

310

guest room where I had just deposited a washed and aired, woollen blanket, draped this over him as he was still naked. I propped him up with a pillow to assist his breathing and, from the phone in the inner hall by the bathroom, telephoned the surgery for our GP, ran to the front door to open it and back to Ronny. As he was still fighting for breath, I propped him up against my half bent knees.

A full quarter of an hour passed and I feared the pain in my thighs would prevent me from holding him much longer. When the doctor arrived at last he took one look at his patient and rang for an ambulance. I had already suspected a slight stroke but felt the blood drain from my veins when I heard him say 'A massive stroke' - with a tragic resultant loss of speech as the right side was affected. I would never again hear my beloved's voice . . .

Two elderly ambulance men stumbled eventually downstairs, Ronny half lying, half sitting in a chair, his nakedness skimpily covered by one of the cotton hospital blankets, like a crocheted bedspread, and I, holding his long legs to prevent them knocking against the stairs. What an anachronism these days of modern medical care! At that moment my irritation verged upon sheer despondence.

As soon as he had been installed in the ambulance, I ran upstairs, filled a hold-all with pyjamas, dressing gown and toilet articles and drove to Solihull Hospital where a doctor had given him an injection to ease his breathing, and X-rays were taken. After consultation with other medical personnel, it was decided to transfer him to the then East Birmingham Hospital (since renamed Heartlands) with specialised care for stroke patients. I followed the ambulance; my heart beating like a steamhammer.

With Ronny installed in a bed in a men's ward, three doctors started to examine him after having drawn the curtain around his bed. A special contraption had, in the meantime,

311

been wheeled in and the siphon part was inserted through the mouth. A male nurse then proceeded to remove the mucus which, throughout the previous years, Ronny had regularly brought up during coughing, again the sad relic of his excessive smoking in the past. But then, half a century ago, not even the members of the medical profession realised the danger of nicotine poisoning. After a seeming infinity, the curtains opened and one of the specialists called me aside. The diagnosis was irrevocable: it was a massive stroke and the lung infection usually allied to it would prove fatal. I had to prepare myself for the worst.

In the meantime, as I approached the bed, I saw Ronny's head turned to the left as I suspected he only had part sight in the corner of his left eye. I moved within the perimeter of this sight, took his left hand in mine and felt his fingers automatically wrapped around mine as he so often used to do when laughingly he compared his large hand with my small one. He squeezed with all his might and I thought my finger bones would be crushed. He must have realised what had happened to him and knew I was there. I kissed his hands and kept repeating: *'I love you, how I love you!'*

Suddenly, he released my hand and pushed the fingers of his left hand in his mouth followed by a significant stroking of his cheeks and chin. I immediately understood. 'Your dentures have been removed to facilitate the removal by siphon of the mucus in your lungs and the barber will call today to shave you', I spoke with mouth against his left ear. The suddenness of the attack had prevented him from shaving himself.

I endeavoured to encourage him by talking about his return home and our second voyage to America planned for the following Summer. In the late afternoon, the sister persuaded me to go home as Ronny needed complete rest and my early visit in the morning was guaranteed. I climbed the stairs with feet like lead and rang some of our closest friends. My dear neighbours, alarmed by the ambulance's arrival and my hasty flight, had guessed Ronny had been taken ill and assured me of their assistance at all times. 'A nearby neighbour is better than a faraway friend' as the Flemish saying goes. Luckily I had the immediate assistance of Barbara, my friend. I could not eat a bite and tossed and turned in bed until about 3 in the morning. At half past five the phone rang. Anxiously I jumped out of bed, fearing the worst but it appeared that the siphoning had caused bleeding and although immediate danger had passed, my presence would be advisable. One could not imagine the speed by which I got ready and drove, as though pursued by the devil, through all the red lights, luckily too early for busy traffic. On tiptoe, I ran through the corridors of the hospital to avoid waking the patients.

Ronny looked peaceful and wearing clean pyjamas but still fighting for breath. A male nurse would regularly arrive with the contraption and its siphon, fighting a lost battle with mucus and slime as the lighter substance was removed but the thicker residue remained in his lungs. After he was moved to a private room, I was given permission to stay with him day and night. As I had not eaten since the previous day and had drunk little, one of the nurses brought me a strong cup of very sweet tea which seemed to revive me a little and some time after, I was virtually forced to partake of a hot meal. It was by then Sunday evening.

Friends regularly called the hospital ward enquiring about Ronny's condition. Most of them wanted to visit him. Being familiar with his loathing to be seen unshaven, in a pitiful state and ill, I refused permission and some amongst them took this as a personal affront. As I later explained: my beloved man, the reason for my existence, was about to pass into eternity without me and these last precious hours I did not wish to share with anybody!

Early Monday morning, he sank into a coma and, as he had a high fever due to the lung infection, an electric fan was placed near his headboard blowing cold air onto his head and shoulders to counteract the over-heating of his body. Blankly staring, numb in mind and body, I sat for hours, his hand in mine. My request to administer a drink was refused by the doctors as they feared he would suffocate . . . I was only too aware of his enormous daily intake of water after many whisky tots and this decision seemed incomprehensive in view of the fact that I had known patients with the same complaint still able to drink and eat . . . Mine is not to reason why though . . . His lips were covered in brown, dry spots and when I furtively pressed a rather wet tissue against them, he greedily sucked at it, which made me feel even more desperate. I still regret not having ignored doctor's orders in this respect but in our layman's eyes they seem a kind of all-knowing god . . .

At 1am Tuesday 5th March 1985, the male nurse reappeared with the siphon after having impatiently been called by me as Ronny's breathing became heavier and more forced. Upon opening the bed clothes, I saw that his legs had already turned that particular grey-white colour of death, his body had emptied itself. I wanted to cleanse him, but the nurse prevented this. *'That is our task, my dear'* he said kindly and steered me away. All of a sudden we heard a noise like a heavy hiccup. A thick substance erupted from each side of Ronny's mouth. *'What a blessing, he has got rid of that heavy mucus!'* I cried. The nurse hastily felt his neck artery, then his pulse. His assistant did likewise. *'I'm sorry, my dear, he is gone!'*

After cleansing him all medical staff quietly retired and left me alone with him; I pushed my fist in my mouth to avoid screaming out loud. Went up to him, kissed his hair, his eyes, now forever closed, his face, his broad shoulders I was always so proud to behold, his chest, his hands. My hot tears dripped in vain on his now indifferent features and if, as is written in the Christian doctrine, the soul is still present for a while, it must have been broken by my heart-rendering, inconsolable grief. The bottom had suddenly fallen out of my world, the sun disappeared from my life . . .

Like many couples, we discussed and declared our preference in case of eventual decease. Ronny, like myself, was in favour of cremation and referred to a Padre, the priest usually connected with the armed forces, to conduct the service. As a member of the Royal British Legion, he had befriended the local Padre, a man who, like Ronny, had known what it was to be under fire. In addition, he forbade the presence of women at his funeral because, kind of character and compassionate of nature, he could never see a woman cry and it was out of the kindness of his heart that he had arrived at this decision. When we discussed it I had been indignant. 'When the time comes, am I too to be excluded? I think that is cruel' I had cried. 'Darling, especially not you, and later when the time comes you will be grateful' and I had to give him my word of honour and accede to his insistence.

In the obituary column of the local newspapers, the message was clear: 'By special request, no ladies at the funeral'. A few journalists thought it necessary to question me on the subject. 'Was there something cryptic in my husband's life?' 'Was he a woman hater?' To my bewilderment, my explanation as well as a synopsis of his serving war years was consequently printed in all syndicated local and national newspapers. The late Jean Rook, Assistant Editor of the Daily Express, sent me one of the most consoling letters. She wrote in her article: 'Fondest Farewell: these mugged raped days when women are prey to everything that moves in the shadows of our dark society, I was touched by the last wish of Old Soldier Ronald Evans. He banned women from his funeral. Including his wife of 37 years who, during the ex-Green Howards captain's 'stag' send off, sat at home with women friends to comfort her. She explained that, whenever her 73-year old husband went to a comrade's final passing out ceremony, he always came back upset because he couldn't bear to see the women mourners cry. I trust Captain Evans sleeps bravely. There aren't many like him left'.

Ronny's remains (what a horrible expression) were brought from the hospital to the funeral parlour where his friends were able to pay their last respects. On the stipulated morning, the funeral car arrived at the entrance to our flat. The guests invited boarded the cars while I tottered downstairs to once more behold some object transporting my beloved away from me. The coffin was covered by the Union Jack. My wreath, a heart of red and white roses - the colours of Antwerp that he had loved so much - at his head and underneath this the simple but touching circle of red poppies, symbol of the British Legion since the end of WW1 in memory of the thousands who perished in the cornfields of Flanders. For a moment, I pressed my lips against the glass that separated me from the coffin and ran howling back upstairs. At the window, I watched the procession slowly leaving the street.

Much later, I heard from the Padre: upon entering the chapel at Robin Hood, the organist softly played 'On Wings of Song', the music that engulfed us so sweetly and emotionally during our wedding ceremony in the Antwerp Town Hall. The Chapel was crowded with veterans, many had to remain standing, the doors were ultimately left open so that those left outside could follow the service. All present, without exception, sang the hymn Abide with Me. The Padre had kindly taken a recording of the ceremony so that,

afterwards, I would still feel as though I had been present . . .
Only then did I realise what Ronny had meant and his wisdom
to refuse my presence at his funeral; the emotion would have
been so overwhelming that I would have collapsed.

And so I reach the end of my story.

Indubitably my Antwerpian blood and Flemish courage
urged me on in life. Although proud of my mother tongue, I
remained aloof of fanaticism. To the Belgians, I will always
say: 'I am Belgian born, my cradle stood in the Flemish part
of the country by chance, and I became very British by
marriage . . . I dearly love both countries!'

Many years have passed since Ronny's demise. Time has,
indeed, healed the wound but agonisingly slowly. Although I
do not believe in ghosts, I am certain Ronny never entirely left
me. Sometimes, I still feel his two arms around me and his
kiss on my neck, when I am washing up in the kitchen, as was
his habit. Not long after he died, one evening I sat on the sofa
looking down on some sewing. Suddenly I felt as though
something was brushing against my neck, another one of his
caresses, and instinctively I cried: 'Ronny, I know you're
there!' Even Spilly came to my assistance one day. During the
week after Ronny's funeral, I was at my lowest ebb. 'I'm
going to take an overdose, I have nobody or nothing to live for
anymore', I thought. All at once I heard my mother's voice as
clear as though she were in the room: 'Oh child, I suffered
such agony to bring you into this world!' My healthy reason
prevailed and, as she herself so often metaphorically had done
in the past I stood up, dusted myself off and resolutely started
anew.

1985 to 1986 proved to be exceptionally busy at the NEC.
International and National exhibitions followed each other
non-stop and my dear friend Judy, the Director of the Agency
I had joined so long ago, practically pushed me into every one
to get me away from my home full of memories, to be with

people, keeping the mind busy and off my loss. It helped me through that first fateful year . . . I still enjoy regular activities at this now famous Exhibition Centre. It keeps my 'grey matter' active, my (nervous?) energy keeps the legs going and thanks to hereditary genes from Spilly I have kept my figure.

I am more than grateful for the love and friendship of my still surviving relatives and friends in Antwerp and Solihull, a friendship which, according to a philosophical friend, is cemented by 'unsolicited and generous giving-of-myself'. In life one cannot expect to receive if one is unwilling to give... I would like to think he is right.

Out of my life's occurrences, be they traumatic, dramatic or humorous, I hope to have risen like a butterfly from its chrysalis, as a better human being, broadminded in my understanding of the other person's attitude. My ego was felled at an early age - although I managed to keep my self-respect - especially during the war when it became all too obvious that, on this world's stage, we but momentarily function like an ant in its wriggling nest and too much love of self lies at the basis of many psychological conflicts. Experience has proved that during the span of a lifetime, and never more so than during a war, there are those occasions when the moment of truth reveals itself not only in terms of insight into one's courage; those are the times when one realises that, as a human being, one is only of value to oneself or to the person who gave one life in the first place!

At this late Autumn of my life, before going to sleep at night, I often think of a line in the poem of one of my favourite Flemish poets, Alice Nahon, and hope that I too 'van dageraad tot avond geen enkel hart heb zeer gedaan' (I have not hurt one single heart from dawn to dusk!) be it inadvertently or not . . .

APPENDIX

I hope the reader will bear with me if I refer to a most important event, hopefully reassuring of the friendship between Belgium and Britain.

September the 4th 1994 - noted for the Commemoration of the 50th Anniversary of Antwerp's Liberation Day.

I have not known such deeply, pleasant emotion since that fateful day fifty years ago! An earthquake would not have prevented me from travelling to my native city to take part in the celebrations. By virtue of my father's activities in the Resistance during the war and as a member of the White Brigade Fidelio group still in existence, I was able to procure special tickets for all the ceremonies held on the 3rd and 4th respectively. The King and Queen of the Belgians, accompanied by our own Duke of York, were present at some of the festivities; crowds gathered in their thousands, cheered the veterans and applauded as they did on that wonderful day in 1944.

The veterans were wined and dined by the City of Antwerp and the then Burgomaster, Mr Bob Cools, read speeches that were pregnant with cheer and gratitude, in an accent seemingly fresh out of Oxford! The first ceremony on the 3rd involved the inauguration of a Square at the Jan Van Rijswijcklei, just outside Antwerp, where a Cromwell tank had stood since Liberation Day, into 'General Roberts Square'. This military man was responsible at the time for the entire operation involving the liberation of Antwerp and its Port. Wreaths to the fallen were laid by the King and Queen and the Duke of York, and General Roberts, now a frail octogenarian present at the ceremony, was enthusiastically applauded and visibly touched.

Afterwards the guests were transported by buses to the Meir, the main through road in Antwerp, to witness the Parade of British, American, Canadian, Polish and Belgian veterans including the Resistance, their military vehicles, accompanied by the Bands of the Grenadier Guards, the American Air Force and many more. We were further regaled by a magnificent flypast by the Battle of Britain Memorial Flight. I was fortunate enough to have been allocated a seat, with some of my White Brigade friends, on the VIP tribune about two rows behind the Royal Family, and cheered and cried and shouted as the veterans passed by, most of them still upright as ever, others slightly more doddery on the legs but everyone smiling and obviously emotional, affected by the cheering of the multitudinous crowd . . .

We were then invited to a series of speeches by the Burgomaster and some of the Allied Army dignitaries at the nearby recently refurbished Bourla Theatre. On the way out I found myself next to Mr Churchill, grandson of Sir Winston. I asked to shake his hand as I had done precisely that fifty years ago with his grandfather, the man who kept our hopes alive throughout those dark years of Nazi occupation.

Early evening found us at the Grote Markt witnessing a military tattoo with Grenadier Guards, the 5th Battalion The Light Infantry Band, the Antwerp Police and Gendarmes Bands, a Dutch Army Band, the American Airforce Band, and even a Russian one as the Burgomaster of St Petersburg (sister port to Antwerp) was present for the first time since the end of the war. We were all invited to sing along with those melodies we knew, and did the people sing! Very Lynn honoured us with her presence and was loudly, almost hysterically applauded for her inevitable White Cliffs of Dover song.

Due to the speeches at the Bourla Theatre having lasted longer than anticipated, we were running late. The superb fireworks scheduled as a prelude to the end of this ceremonial day started on time though, which meant that we, at the tattoo, missed it, apart from the noises emanating from the fireworks, reminiscent of the V-1 bombardment of Antwerp and her Port.

320

We should have viewed these fireworks from one of the pleasure boats on the Scheldt river, the 'Flandria', accompanied by a reception on board to which we were nevertheless afterwards invited. This had been provided free to the veteran guests by the management of the firm owning the boats.

It was 2am before my head touched my pillow and the following morning it seemed like dawn when I arose to get ready for the celebrations of the actual Liberation Day, the 4th of September. 9.30am found me at the edge of the Scheldt, quay 24, almost opposite where I was born, for the official unveiling of a plaque to the commemoration of the group called Antwerp X. This was dedicated to the members of an ack-ack gunning section responsible for shooting down 97.8% of all V-1s and V-2s aimed at the Port and without whose accuracy Antwerp would have been wiped off the map!

The next ceremony was dedicated to the Belgian members of the Resistance who gave their life in the liberation of the Port itself. At the conclusion of this event, all veterans had been invited to a lunch at the 'Belle Époque Hall' at the Antwerp Hilton at the Groenplaats. As I had made friends with some of the ladies present, ex-members of the ATS, we decided to sit together at one of the many, large, round tables provided, where we joined other male veterans. The meal was presented, once more, by the City of Antwerp authorities and the Burgomaster, who seemed present everywhere and read his interesting speeches with much vim and vigour at all times, presented some of the Allied Army hierarchy with commemorative presents, receiving some in return. Again, as the speeches took longer than we hoped, we missed the flypast of the Red Arrows over the City.

We afterwards proceeded by buses to the Schoonselhof, Antwerp's main cemetery for a service at the special ground where Britain's unforgettable sons were resting having given their lives for our liberation . . . On conclusion I asked the veterans present if any of them would like to accompany me just opposite to the 'Heropark' where the members of my father's Resistance group were laid to rest, who, at the time of the liberation of the Port and city, were languishing or had died in the inhuman concentration camps. Most of them came along and I told them not only my father's story but that of Colonel Louette, the never to be forgotten hero of Antwerp's own White Brigade.

Months prior to this I had written to the Burgomaster expressing my gratitude for the beautiful upkeep of the graves but at the same time my disgust at the state of the gravestones. I had received a gracious reply promising me new stones would be installed in time for the 50th Anniversary Celebrations. This had duly been undertaken. While I told my captive audience about all this, I was stroking the top of my father's gravestone and I realised many of the ladies present were crying. They all expressed pleasure in my efforts to tell a true story of which they would have been otherwise ignorant.

We returned to their hotel and I went home to have a bath and change for the highlight of the day: the Popular Ball at the Grote Markt. Unfortunately, shortly afterwards, the family with whom I stay returned, and as they had not seen me for two days were anxious to hear all about the ceremonies and my adventures. By the time I had finished my story it was 10pm and my zeal for any ball be it popular or not, just deflated. I was whacked!

Before concluding I must quote one of the old veterans: '*I am 82 - my days are growing short and when I am on my deathbed I will remember this day as one of the highlights of my life! Never, in my wildest dreams would I have expected the people of Antwerp to be so grateful and loving after fifty long years. It is incredible!*'

I have kept the Burgomaster's speeches as nobody else could have put so succinctly into words what all Antwerpians felt . . . Before my return home I was presented with a magnificent plate in pure pewter, in commemoration of the 50th Anniversary of the Allied landings. It depicts the regimental insignia of all the American, British and Canadian Units who landed that memorable day in Normandy, with the exact positions and code names of the beaches, even the names of the villages on which soil they first set foot; also the unfortunate American paratrooper, caught in his chute and dangling from the roof of the Church at St Mère Eglise; the advance of the troops and their armour, at the bottom of the plate a small plaque which mentioned:

D-DAY

6 juin, 6h. du matin

Jour J

1944   1994

50

everything beautifully sculptured. This plate has now been donated to the Royal British Legion of Solihull as a token of the gratitude from the people of Antwerp and in memory of my father and my husband.

Belgium might have become a swear word in the vocabulary of the anti-EC brigade but the country and especially Antwerp will always remain faithful to her liberators, a pragmatic bond that exists between our two countries.

Letter From Colonel Louette

Madame,

As I have been exceptionally busy during the last month of the past year, I was unable to send you a special word of thanks and high esteem with regard to the article: 'The attack on Odette Churchill' which appeared in our Antwerp newspaper De Nieuwe Gazet.

Unnecessary to tell you that all the friends - and espeically the undersigned - were very pleasantly surprised by the last two paragraphs of this article, in which you pay a touching tribute to the Resistance in general and to the National Commandant of the White Brigade (Fidelio), and especially, as you wrote, for the members of his Group.

May I, therefore, thank you most heartily for this touching expression of devotion and loyalty, especially as I had already decided to congratulate you, as soon as the occasion would arise, for your devotion not only to England, but also to Belgium and also because your reporting is always so gripping. I am not trying to flatter you but we, in Belgium, could still very much do with Anne Evans.

Furthermore, we are especially impressed to find in all your articles the symbol of your jovial and heroic parents and thus you do remind us of your dear, departed father, who played such an enormous part in everything without ever putting himself forward. How his nose would curl if he had been able to read the work of his daughter.

We fervently hope, in the future, to continue reading your newsy articles and would add, as our actual order of the day, that we must fight still for the defence of our youth, the children of our brothers-in-arms who, during their early years, and even now, had to miss so much.

I would like to take this opportunity to wish you and your husband the very best, hoping we may still count on you in the future as it must be said, not without bitterness - and yet very true - that, as the years pass by, the number of genuinely faithful friends is diminishing. With the result that more value is placed on the young that are left, nevertheless with the happy knowledge that most are such worthy successors.

With my repeated gratitude and expression of warm sympathy and sincere appreciation,

Sgd Louette Marcel

(Col G W Louette Marcel,

National Commandant of the White Brigade, alias Fidelio)

(The article in question dealt with one that appeared in the Sunday Dispatch regarding the war heroine Odette Churchill in which she was challenged by three members of her wartime espionage-group to prove one single action in which she heroically took part. She appeared on BBC's 'Late Special' TV programme and vindicated her past activities in a manner which oozed sincerity. In the meantime the three wouldbe accusers had telephoned from Paris to contradict their so-called remarks, repudiated them unconditionally and apologised for the outrage. In my article I reiterated the heroism of the captured Resistance fighters and recalled the inhuman torture at the hands of the Gestapo and praised Louette and his members of the White Brigade.)

With the plaque commemorating the D-Day landings at
Normandy when I presented it to the Royal British Legion
branch in Solihull. The plaque had been given to me by the
White Brigade Fidelio Resistance of Antwerp.

The rhododendron I planted in memory of Ronny, amongst the trees which he loved, in the garden of our flat.